IMAGES
of America

LOCKHART

On the Cover: Nancy Stripling is shown on top of a 1948 centennial parade float. Photographer Paul B. Conley of Luling, Texas, took this photograph. (Courtesy of the Caldwell County Historical Commission.)

IMAGES
of America

LOCKHART

Ronda Anton Reagan

ARCADIA
PUBLISHING

ISBN 978-0-7385-8519-2

Published by Arcadia Publishing
Charleston, South Carolina

Printed in the United States of America

Library of Congress Control Number: 2011931233

For all general information, please contact Arcadia Publishing:
Telephone 843-853-2070
Fax 843-853-0044
E-mail sales@arcadiapublishing.com
For customer service and orders:
Toll-Free 1-888-313-2665

Visit us on the Internet at www.arcadiapublishing.com

In memory of my ancestors and all the other settlers of Lockhart whose true grit helped shape this Lone Star State.

Contents

Acknowledgments

This book would not be possible without the many friends, neighbors and acquaintances who made significant contributions by sharing their treasured, old family photograph collections. A special thanks to my neighbor and friend, Joe Henry Bunch, who shared not only his photographs with me but also his wonderful memories and stories of growing up here; and to Harry Hilgers Jr., who also brought me many beautiful images and the stories that went with them. Joe and Harry both assisted me numerous times in verifying facts. Thank you to my friend and neighbor, Dianne Stevenson, who loaned her precious collection of 100-plus-year-old photographs that were gifted to her by her former neighbor Nora Lee Magee before her passing. I am especially indebted to my new friend Gerry Ohlendorf who shared her huge collection of historical photographs, many collected from other Lockhart residents for Caldwell County's sesquicentennial celebration.

And, a generous thank you to friend and neighbor Donaly Brice—local author, historian, and former chair of the Caldwell County Historical Commission—who graciously agreed to serve as my final proofreader and factual editor and provided me with much encouragement. Thanks also to Lauren Hummer, my Arcadia Publishing editor, who remained forever cheerful while guiding me from start to finish. Assisting me with genealogy information was my dear friend Caroline Thornburg, who helped research names, dates, and facts.

Others who made this book possible were Kathy McCormick, Floyd Wilhelm Jr., Ed Strayer, John Baker, Amelia Smith, Janet Christian, and Homer and Shirley Williams. Many images were borrowed from collections donated to the Caldwell County Historical Commission, the Caldwell County Genealogical and Historical Society, and the Eugene Clark Library, whose staff were delightfully helpful.

And finally, a very special thank you to my dear, sweet mother, Ona Lea McGee Anton, who shared with me a wealth of information including photographs, newspaper clippings, research material, genealogy, records, books, volumes of factual, and historic information as well as memories about growing up in Lockhart. If I needed something verified, I needed only to call her. Without her help and encouragement, this book would not be possible.

INTRODUCTION

Called the "Devil's Half-Acre of Texas," Lockhart had a reputation of lawlessness from its start. This book depicts Lockhart, Caldwell County, from before the county's creation in 1848, when life was hard, yet relatively simple, to just past the centennial celebration in 1948. Part prairie and part wooded with a main natural spring known as the Town Branch, this area was originally surveyed in 1831 by Byrd Lockhart, a surveyor for Stephen F. Austin. Austin later gave Byrd the townsite in return for work. Plum Creek also meanders through the county, and along it to the east of town, Isham J. Good and John A. Neill were the first settlers. In 1832, Ambrose Tinney, the author's maternal great-great-great-great-grandfather, received a Spanish land grant, signed by Green DeWitt, to settle a league of land to the east, where Tinney Creek is today.

The Texas State Legislature created the county in 1848 out of lands formerly known as DeWitt Colony, and now Gonzales County, when the town leaders petitioned the state to become a county and split off from Gonzales. They asked to be named Plum Creek County, but the legislature officially named the area Caldwell County for Matthew "Old Paint" Caldwell. Caldwell was a signer of the Texas Declaration of Independence, a Texas Ranger, and a striking Indian fighter who fought alongside Gen. Edward Burleson at the Battle of Plum Creek in 1840. This battle eliminated an entire tribe of the fierce Comanche, thus ending the raids and opening up the area for settlement. The Texas Legislature named the county seat Lockhart after Byrd Lockhart, and on February 10, 1852, it was incorporated. C.B. Porter was elected as the first mayor of Lockhart in 1853. Perhaps Lockhart's most famous resident was Susanna Dickinson (1814–1883), who survived the Battle of the Alamo with her 15-month-old baby, Angelina Dickinson. After defying Santa Anna's request to adopt the beautiful child, Santa Anna released her on the condition that she carry the news of the Alamo's capture to Gen. Sam Houston, thus giving her the name "Messenger of the Alamo." She eventually settled in Lockhart where she ran a boardinghouse and was well known as a great cook. In 1857, she married a German immigrant 20 years her junior and one of her frequent guests, Joseph William Hannig. Their home and his cabinet shop were torn down to build Lockhart's city hall. A Texas Historical Marker stands nearby to mark the site.

The backbone of any town is its people. Those that emigrated from Germany to Texas, leaving their homeland to sail for six weeks, often in terrible conditions, had a wanderlust for a better life. They arrived to learn a new language and experienced new foods and ways. They brought with them fine skills and an ingrained industriousness, a good work ethic. Their true grit helped shape this Lone Star State.

In 1898, the early businesses around the town square included six grocery stores, two barbershops, four saloons, six blacksmith shops, a livery and buggy shed, confectionery, hardware, bank, cobbler shop, jewelry store, drugstore, tin shop, dentist's office, restaurant, meat market, photograph gallery, and several churches and hotels.

By its centennial year in 1948, the population had grown to 5,018, according to the *Texas Almanac*.

Lockhart was officially named the "Barbecue Capital of Texas" by the 76th Texas Legislature House Resolution No. 1024 on May 26, 1999. The resolution states: "Whereas, of all the culinary arts mastered in the Lone Star State, none commands the type of respect and admiration that is accorded barbecue, and no community in Texas can best the city of Lockhart when it comes to an appreciation for the extraordinary alchemy of post oak and patience, and whereas . . . Lockhart's fortuitous location witnessed the confluence of Plains Indians, Hispanic Vaqueros and German immigrants, the technique, substance and skill of a variety of cultures combined to establish barbecue as a favorite food . . . And the City's role as a major center on the historic Chisholm Trail spurred the continued refinement of barbecue and today Lockhart is home to some of the State's most historic and best barbecue establishments: Black's owned by the same family since 1932, and Kreuz Market, which first fired its pits in 1900 [at its original location]; Chisholm Trail founded in 1978; [and, Smitty's in 1998, in what was the original Kreuz location], be it resolved, that . . . Lockhart is the Barbecue Capital of Texas."

The last remnant of the pioneering spirit that formed Caldwell County is the Andrew Lee and Rebecca Brock log cabin, built in 1850. In the 1970s, the Brocks' granddaughter Alma Cardwell Harrell gave the cabin to historic preservationists. It was moved to and restored in the city-owned Lions Park on State Highway 183. It was later gifted by bill of sale to the City of Lockhart in 1985 to be maintained as a museum. But due to lack of funding appropriations by the city to maintain it, it has fallen into disrepair and was threaten to be torn down in 2008.

At the time of this printing, there is a grassroots effort of the citizens working to restore this historical structure as both a museum and a teaching tool so that students, area residents, and visitors alike can enjoy and learn about the rich heritage embodied in this dwelling. Concerned citizens of Caldwell County, as appointed by the Caldwell County Historical Commission (CCHC), formed the Save the Brock Cabin Committee in late 2008. Today, the committee is a 501(c)(3) nonprofit Texas corporation known as the Friends of the Brock Cabin. It is the wish of this author to donate her portion of the royalties from the sale of this book to the future maintenance of this cabin so that visitors can learn about the history of Caldwell County's pioneering and founding fathers as they lived in the 1850s.

Lockhart's population as of the most recent 2010 census is approximately 13,700. It is a prime location just 29 miles southeast of the state capital of Austin, 27 miles to Bergstrom International Airport and 120 miles to the Gulf Coast. It is centrally located between three of the top-10 largest cities in the United States: San Antonio, Houston, and Dallas. Because of its central location near these major cities and its beauty, more than 30 movies have been filmed in and around Lockhart. And it will soon benefit from the newly constructed 91-mile toll road, State Highway 130, from Interstate 10 at Seguin to Interstate 35 to Georgetown, north of Austin.

One

The Early Settlers

Settlers came to Texas for many and varied reasons, but perhaps the single most important reason to encourage immigration was the vast amount of land, which was made available to them on easy terms. In the early years of Spanish Texas around 1820, the Spanish government promoted Anglo colonization, awarding land grants to foreigners to open Texas. Later, after the Mexican War of Independence, the Mexican government awarded impresarios, like Green DeWitt, five leagues of land provided that the impresarios picked colonists to settle the land and enforced Mexican law. Seeking greater fortunes, a better life, and opportunities, more than 400 families initially came to DeWitt Colony, located west of the Lavaca River and south of Old San Antonio Road. Later, DeWitt recruited 300 more families to lands between the Guadalupe and Colorado Rivers. Much of this would later become Gonzales County, and then in 1848, about 546 square miles of the land would be named Caldwell County with Lockhart being named the county seat. They were not all gunslingers as often depicted. But rather, they were able, aggressive, and friendly, practical, and self-sufficient. They came on horseback and in wagons at first. After the Indians were no longer a threat, the War Between the States had ended, and the railroad lines increased, the number of settlers grew rapidly as the news spread about all the land that was available in the West. During 1876, more than 400,000 people came to Texas. Lockhart was more than just one of the new towns in which they settled. Lockhart boasted fresh spring water, hills, and trees and was in a good location between Gonzales, Bastrop, and the state capitol, Austin. One wagon-train diary recorded what a beautiful place it was as pioneers approached it, and today, one can still see its many virtues. Life was simple in early Lockhart.

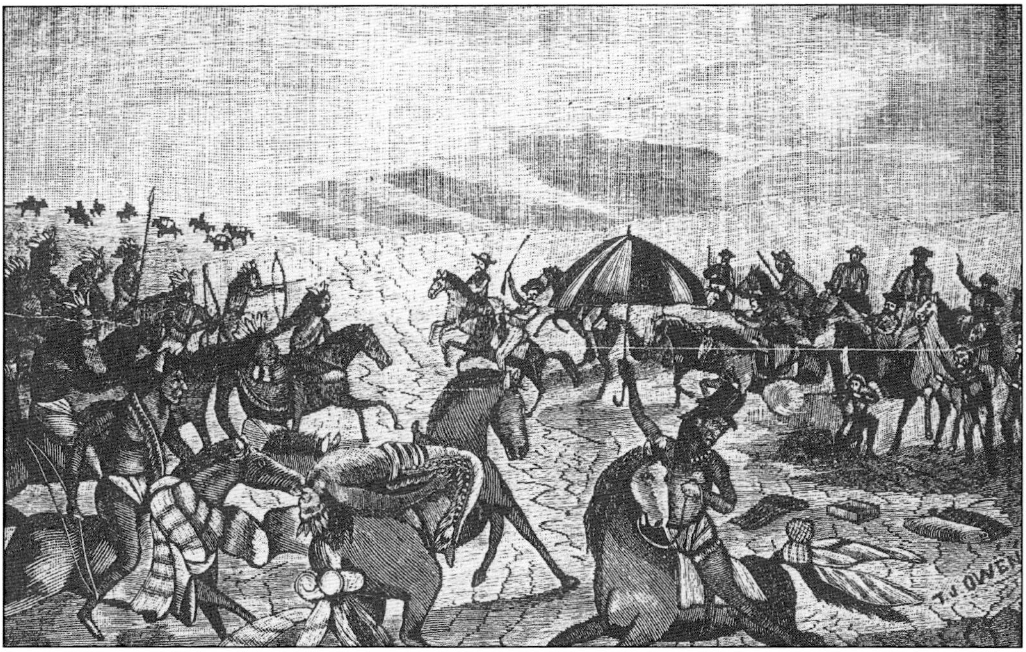

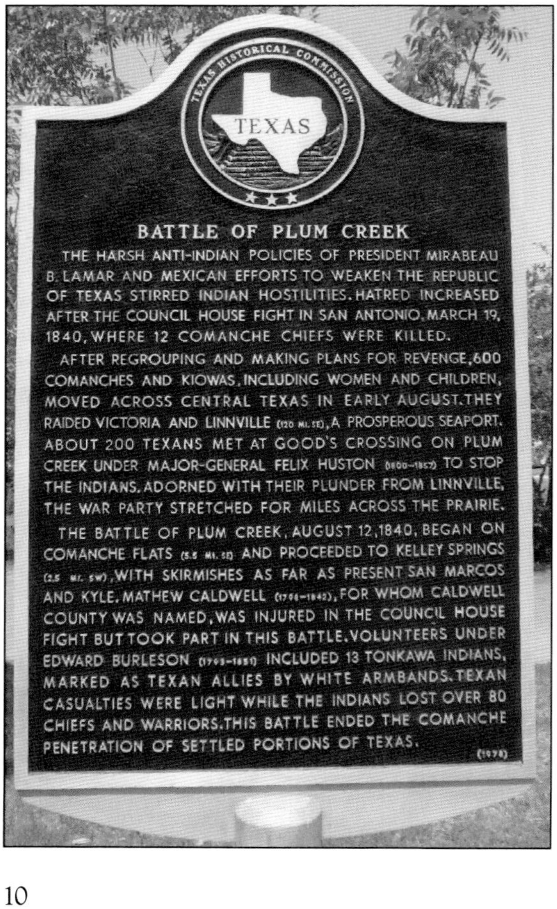

In 1840, after a summit in San Antonio where 12 Comanche chiefs were killed, more than 600 Comanche and Kiowa took revenge. They came down from the hill country along Plum Creek, traveled to Victoria, looting, ravaging, and burning the town, and stole several thousand horses. They headed toward the coast to Linnville, a prosperous seaport. There, they broke open cargo shipments of fine clothing from Europe. After burning the town, they rode off with silk top hats, topcoats on backwards, and red ribbons streaming from their horses. As they headed back along the same creek, the settlers planned an attack, and word was sent to Gen. Edward Burleson in Bastrop to help. The Battle of Plum Creek ensued, and on August 12, 1840, more than 80 chiefs and warriors lay dead. Texas casualties were few. Local settlers who fought in it included Col. Matthew "Old Paint" Cardwell, for whom the county would later be named in 1848, and Gen. Edward Burleson and Felix Huston. Huston brought with him the friendly Tonkawa Indians because they feared the Comanche as their enemy. (Above, illustration by J.W. Wilbarger; left, courtesy of Ronda A. Reagan.)

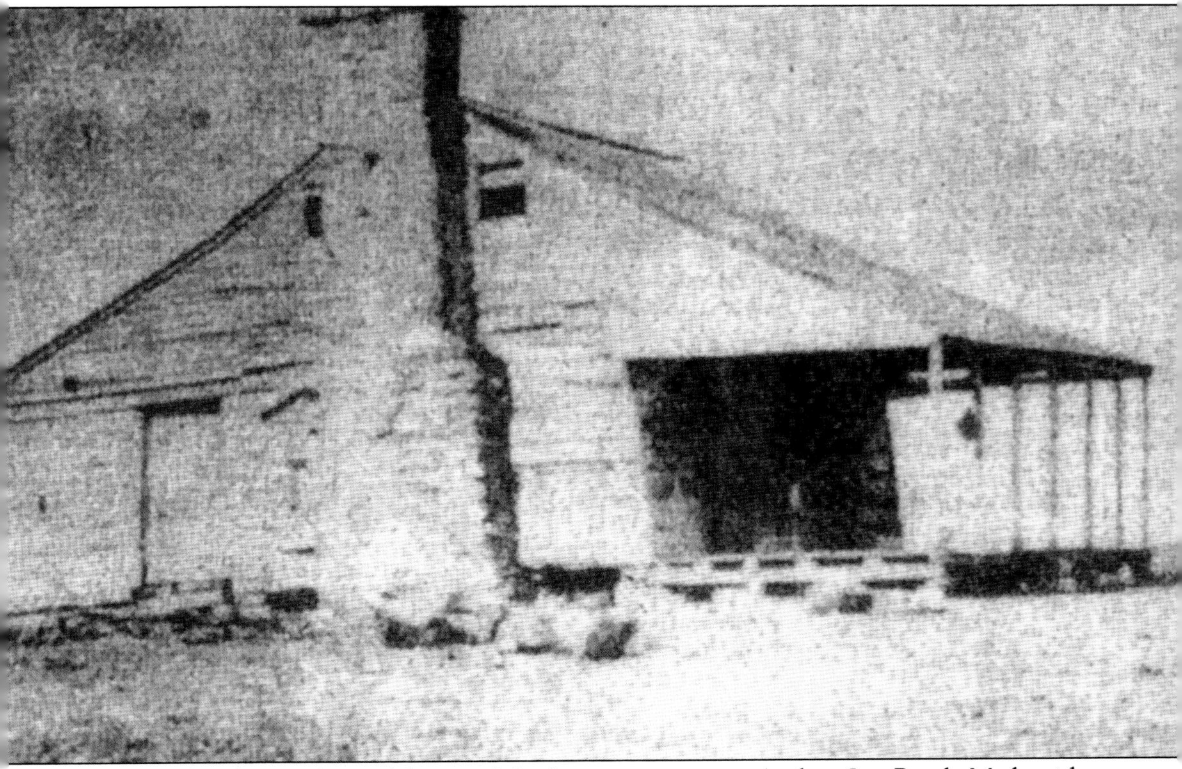

This is the first home of one of the town's leading entrepreneurs, Andrew Lee Brock. Made with his hands, it was like many in the area. It was a hand-hewn, two-room log cabin made from local trees, generally oak, native elm, cypress, ash, or hickory, harvested by the phase of the moon so not to rot. They used mud, clay, and sand from the Boggy Creek to chink between the logs and area stones to build a fireplace for heat as well as cooking. The cabin provided shelter from the north wind, rain, and the wild. The Brock cabin, now owned by the City of Lockhart, is the oldest wooden structure in Caldwell County. It was moved near the town square in the 1970s, and it currently stands in Lions Park. Over the years, it has suffered from neglect. There is hope that it will be saved, restored, and rehabilitated as a museum through fundraising efforts of the Friends of the Brock Cabin. (Courtesy of the Friends of the Brock Cabin.)

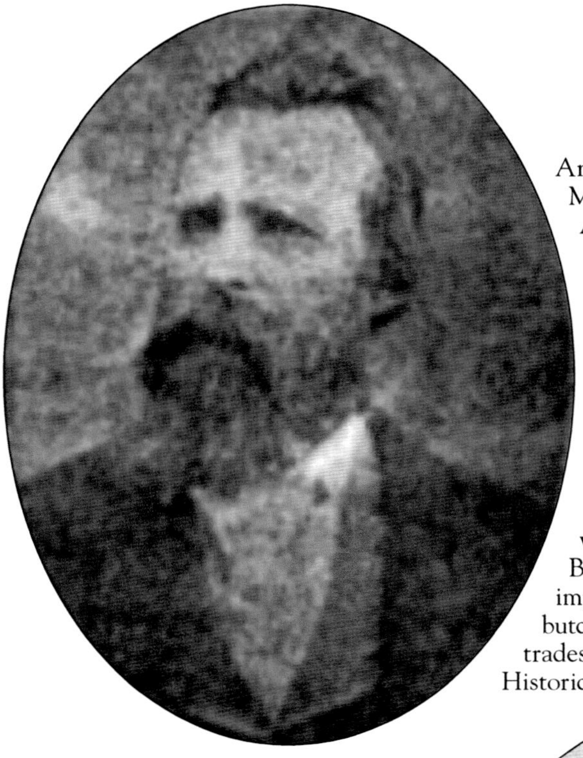

Andrew Lee Brock and Rebecca Wayland Montgomery Brock were early settlers. Andrew arrived in Caldwell County in 1848. Two years later, he married widow Rebecca Wayland Montgomery, who had arrived by wagon train. They had nine children. All but the youngest, Sally, were born in their original cabin, shown on the previous and following page. Early settlers like the Brocks were jacks-of-all-trades. Brock farmed, trailed cattle, trained racehorses, and soon became one of Lockhart's leading businessmen. Hard-working pioneering forefathers, like the Brocks, were home builders, hunters, farmers, importers, furniture makers, animal breeders, butchers, and family leaders, just to name a few trades. (Both, courtesy of the Caldwell County Historical Commission [CCHC].)

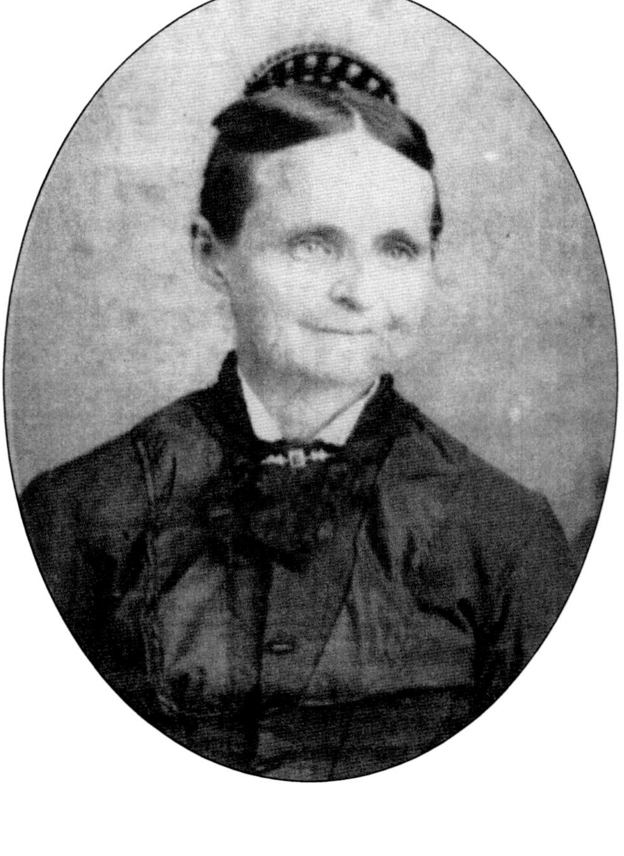

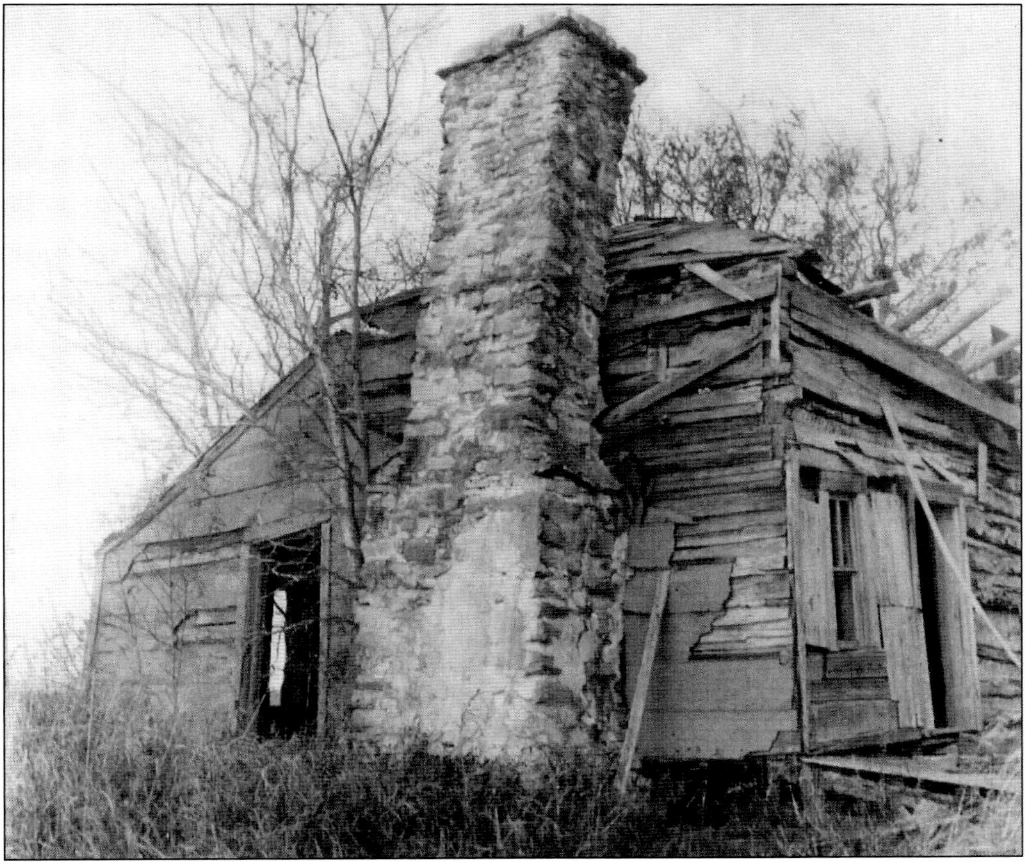

Pictured in the early 1970s, on its original site two miles west of the town center near Boggy Creek, is the Brock cabin. The Brocks built it on land given to them by her father. This cabin is a good example of the early architecture that was common in Central Texas. Visitors are greeted by a long gallery porch on the front. Inside are two rooms with a loft. At the rear of the house is a long shed room that may have originally been open space for their livestock. Brock descendants donated the cabin to a Lockhart preservation group, which relocated it in 1979 to Lions Park, as shown in the more recent photograph below. According to the Texas Historical Commission, it is eligible for the National Register of Historic Places. (Above, courtesy of Gerry and Conrad Ohlendorf; below, courtesy of Ronda A. Reagan.)

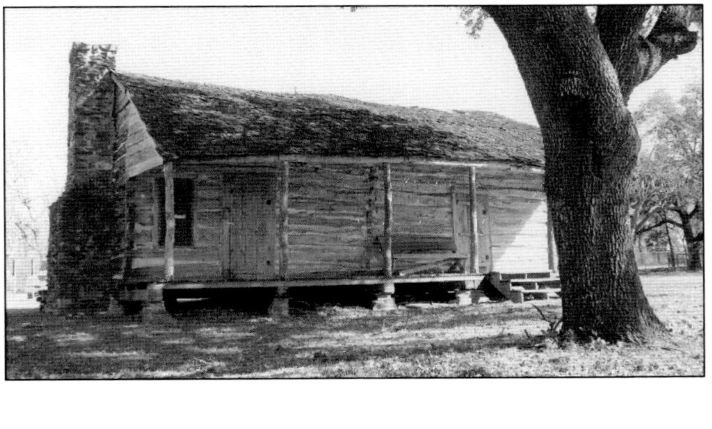

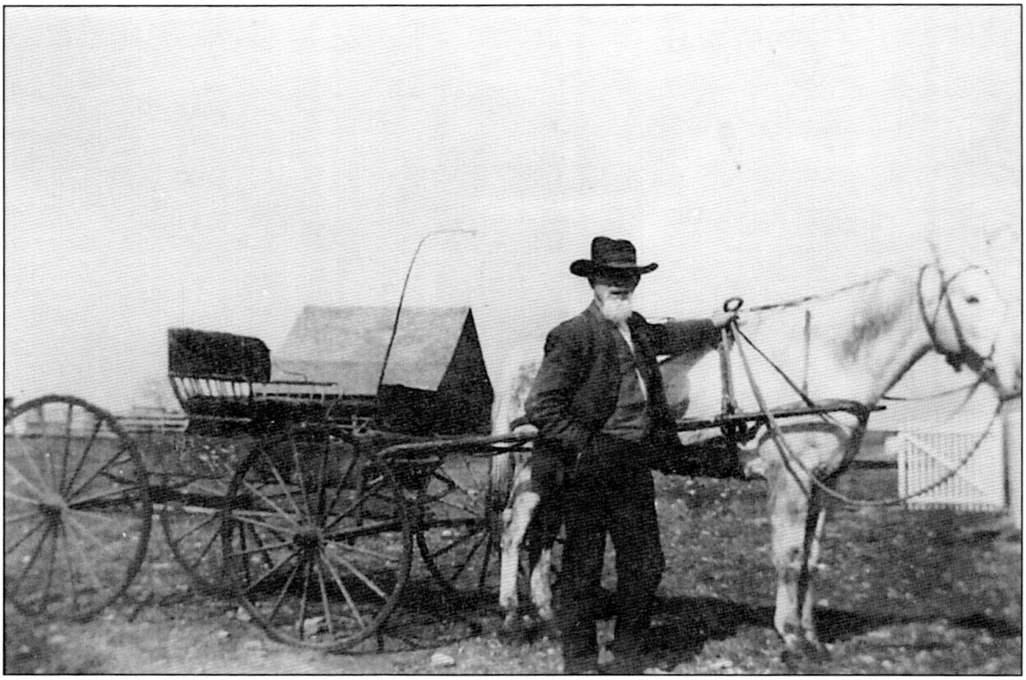

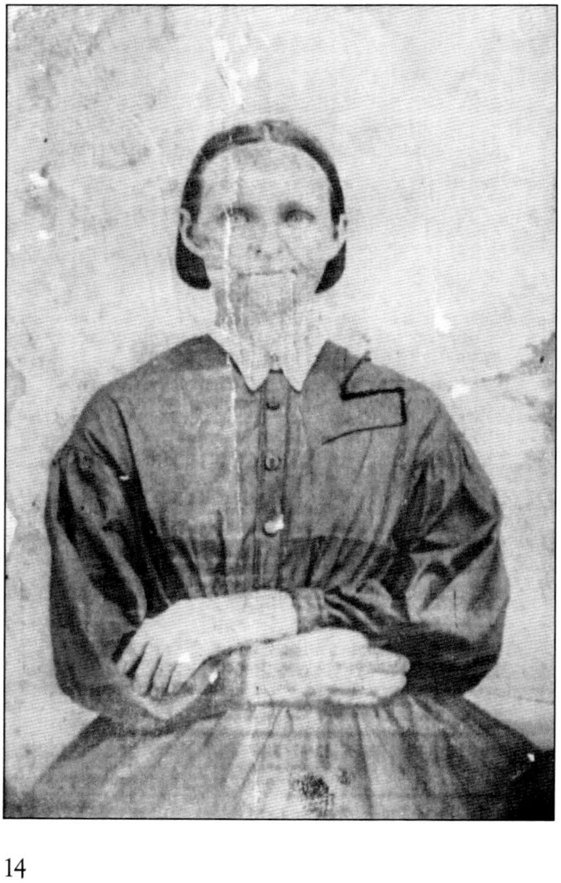

Another early family to settle in Lockhart was that of William Smith Bunch and wife, Martha Holcomb Bunch. They arrived in 1882 from Lafayette County, Mississippi. Their son Henry H. Bunch, who followed his parents and arrived here in 1889, is shown with his horse and buggy outside their home just west of town. Dressed in a suit and vest, he must have been getting ready to take his wife, Alva, to town. (Courtesy of Joe Henry Bunch.)

The widowed Rebecca Wayland Montgomery arrived by wagon train to Lockhart. She met and married Andrew Lee Brock in 1850, bringing a daughter to the union. While Andrew was away on business, Rebecca took care of the homestead and their nine children, six of whom lived to adulthood. She was well known for her green grape pie. She died in 1900 and is buried in the Lockhart City Cemetery. (Courtesy of the CCHC.)

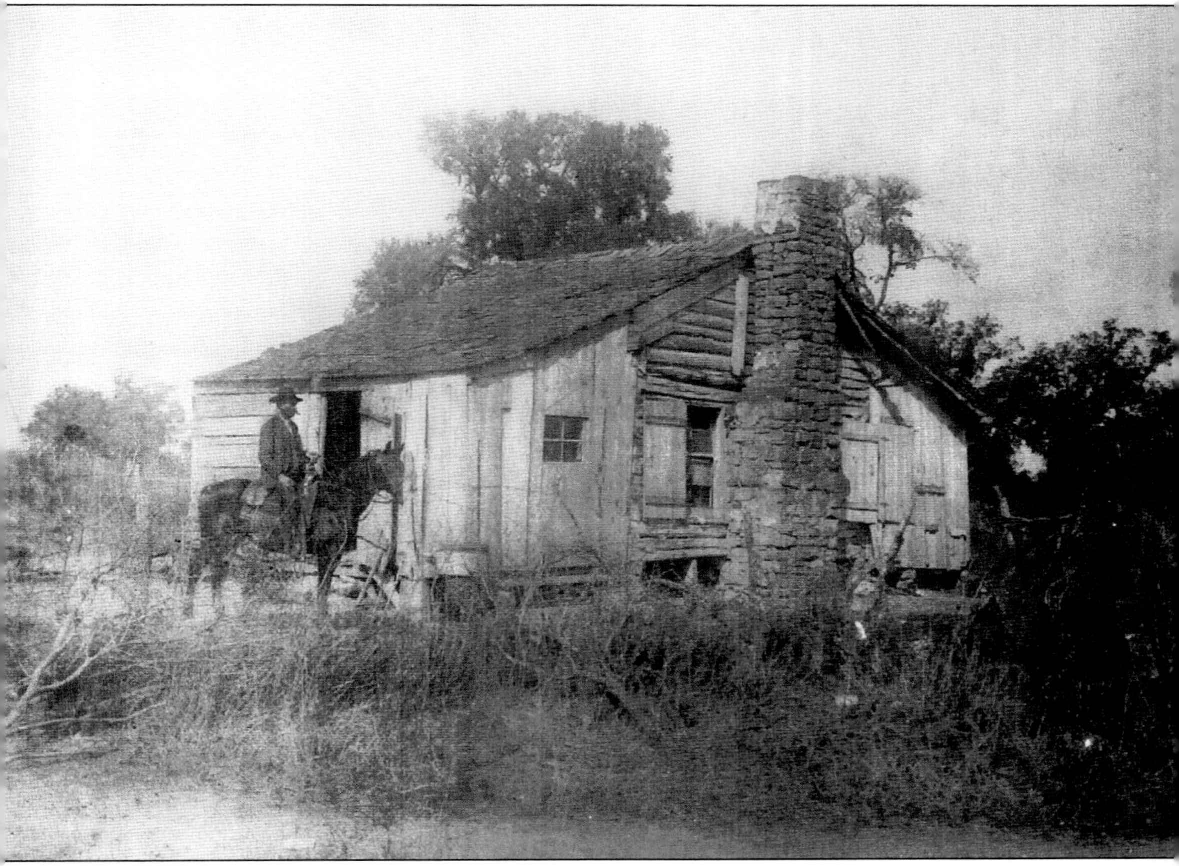

Another example of a frontier home is this c. 1851 log home, which belonged to settler William H. Jennings. Jennings is pictured mounted on his horse in front of his cabin. With strong arms, crosscut saws, and axes, these pioneering forebearers harvested the trees for such homes by the phase of the moon so that the sap was in the right position. Otherwise, the logs would rot in just a few months. Then they would "draw shave" the logs and notch them to stack together without nails, like modern-day Lego toys. Such a home could be built in just a few days. They were crude, but sturdy, kept the rain out, and could be warmed with a fireplace. Yet, their size and primitiveness deprived these early Texas settlers of modern comforts they might have had in their previous homes. Life on the frontier was inconvenient, harsh, and often exhausting. (Courtesy of the Eugene Clark Library.)

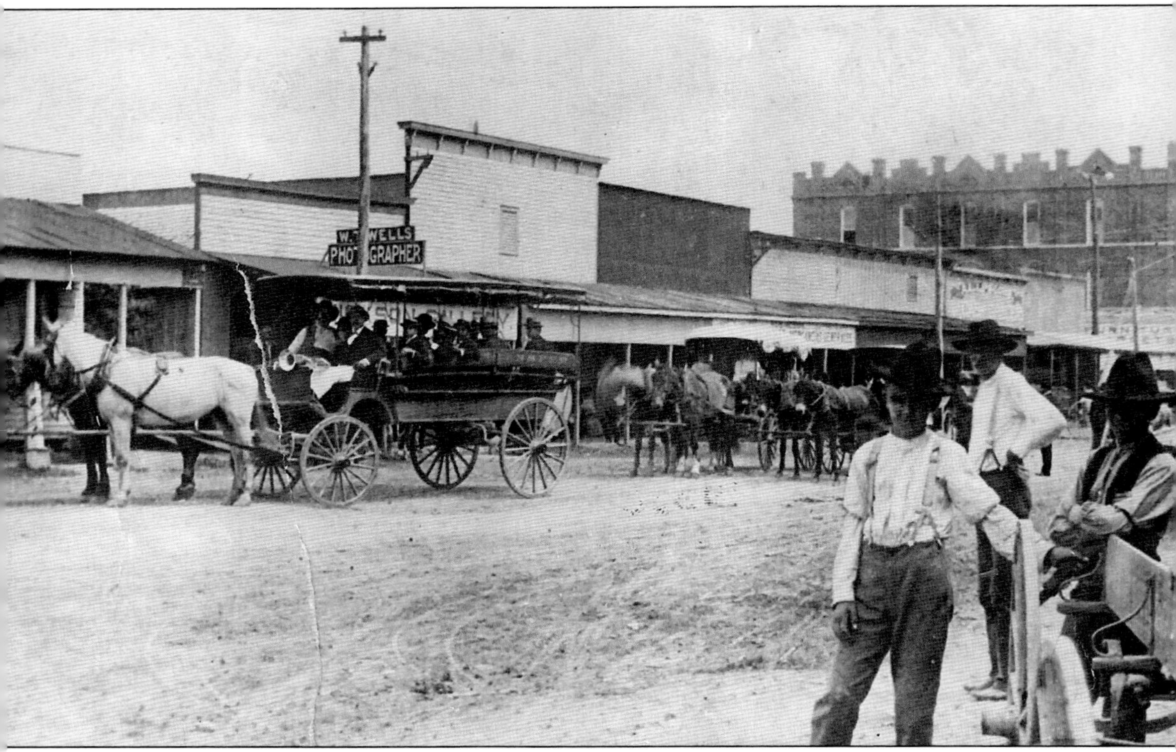

This is an early photograph of downtown Lockhart in 1898. The view is of the north side of San Antonio Street just one block off the square, looking northeast. The street, a dirt road, appears busy with several horse-drawn carriages, including a mule-drawn trolley carrying eight to 10 passengers to town. It was most likely coming from the train depot. The studio of photographer W.T. Wells is displayed just behind this wagon. Note the wagon on the far right with its large wooden wheels. Most of the single-story buildings burned in a fire or were torn down and replaced with brick ones. Visible on the back right at the corner of Main Street is the three-story Brock Building, constructed in 1898 by well-known settler Andrew Lee Brock. It has housed many businesses, including the Lockhart National Bank from 1902 to 1934, Swartz Dry Goods, a dirt-floor basement saloon, Lockhart Savings and Loan Association, the Chamber of Commerce, and Stephens Electric. Today, the Southwest Museum of Clocks and Watches operates from there. The local townspeople pictured here are unidentified. (Collection of Gerry and Conrad Ohlendorf, courtesy of Thelma Seeliger.)

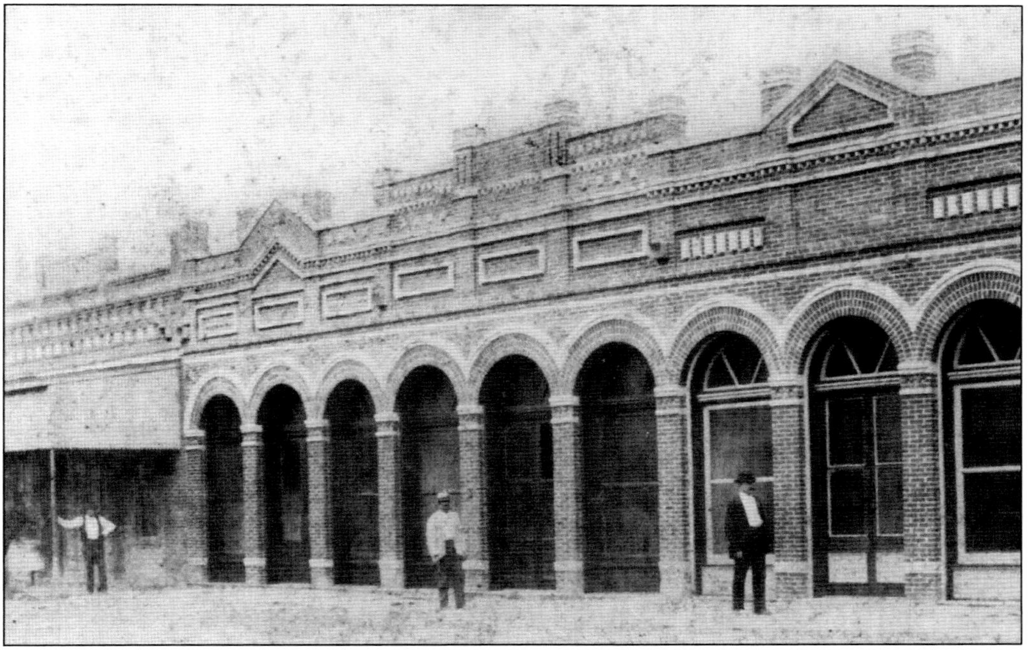

Andrew Lee Brock (right) is recognized for having financed the construction of 12 masonry buildings on the public square by 1901. In this picture, Brock strolls in front of several of the structures he built in 1896 that stand on today's North Main Street. Fields Stables operated out of the north end (not shown), while O. Seeliger, a carriage maker, occupied at least two of the connecting spaces. Arched openings in the connecting walls allowed the proprietor to roll the carriages between the rooms. In 1978, many of his buildings became part of the National Register of Historic Places. In his lifetime, Brock also built a gristmill and cotton gin and applied for and received a patent in 1898 for new and useful improvements to the disc cultivator, as depicted below. He lived until 1903 and is buried in the Lockhart City Cemetery. (Both, courtesy of the CCHC.)

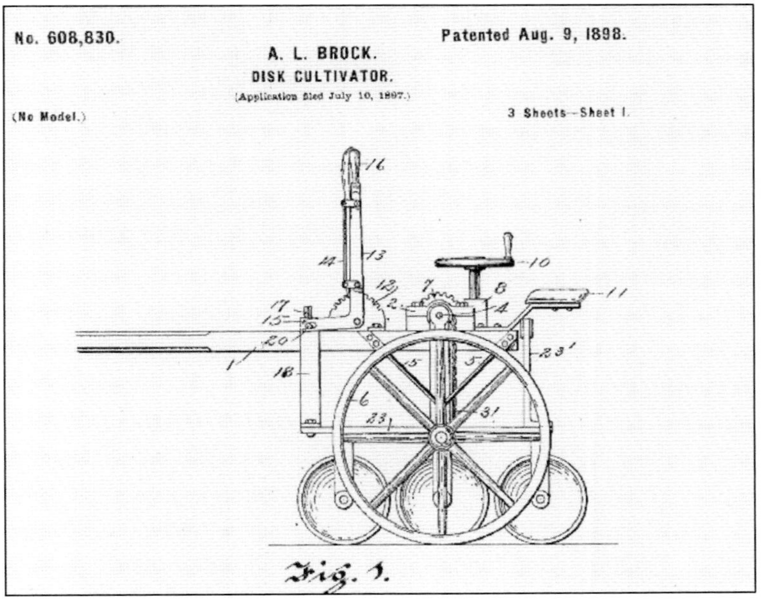

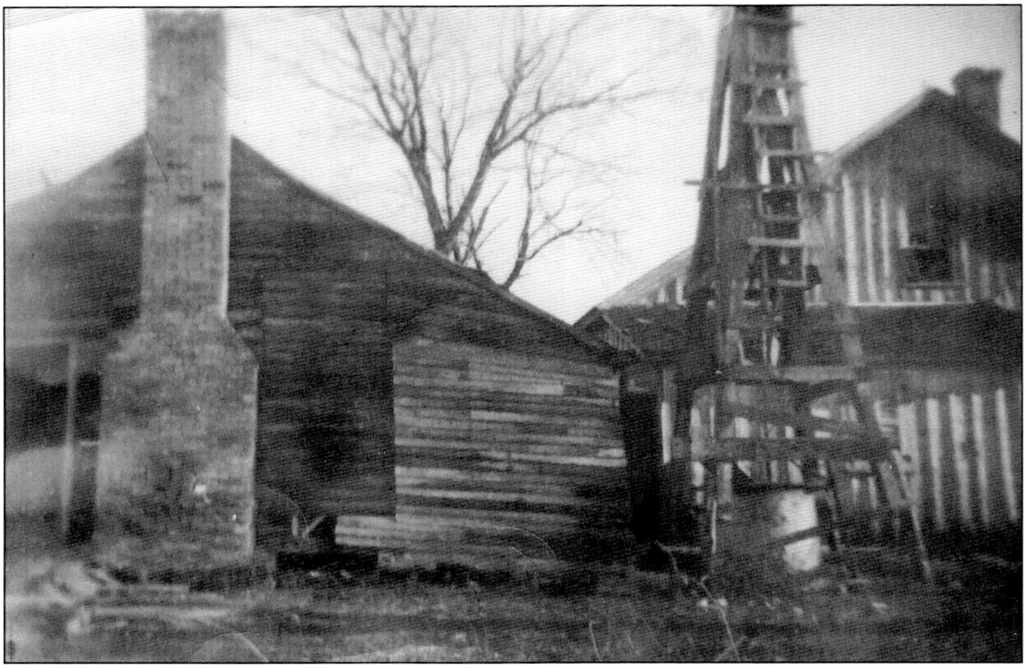

These are just two examples of early homes. The image above shows a wooded windmill with a newer home in the background. The photograph below shows a one-room cabin with sleeping loft and rear shed design. Original roofing would have been wooden shake shingles. At the time this was taken, a metal roof had been added. Once sawmills were built, log homes were often sheathed with other wood, which helped them to survive for many years. As owners moved to town, they continued to use their log cabins as storage buildings for feed or hay, often attaching corrals and building barns nearby. (Above, courtesy of Ronda A. Reagan; below, courtesy of the CCHC.)

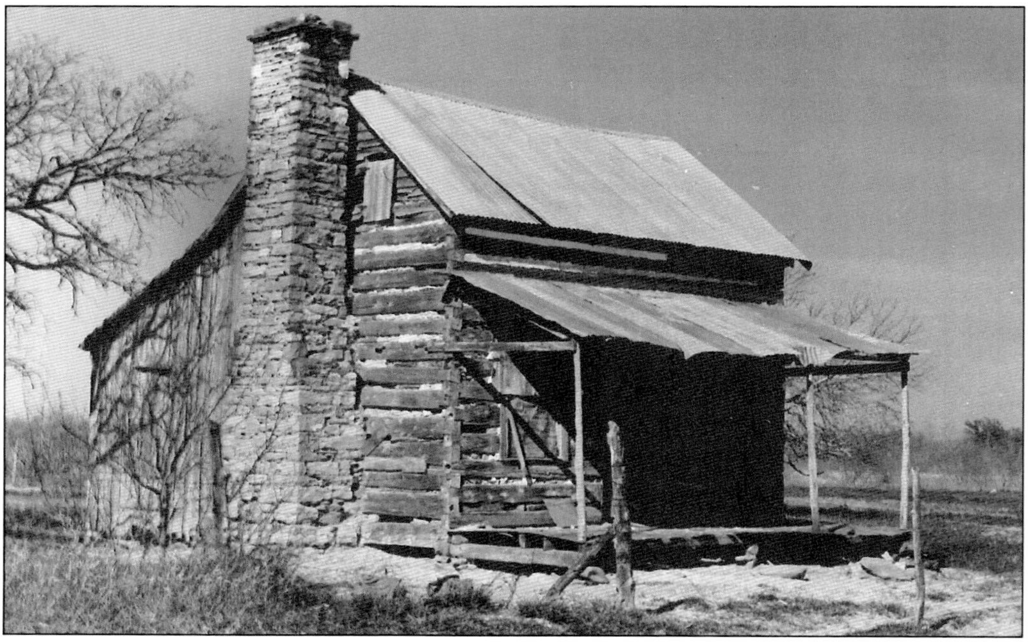

Two

Cattle, Cotton, and Transportation

Spaniards introduced the first cattle into the New World and to what is now Texas in the 16th century. By 1821, land grant settlers were bringing in various breeds of domestic cattle. These strains mixed with the Spanish long-horned cattle. It is estimated that by 1833, there were 75,000 cattle in the state. By 1846, about 383,000 head were assessed for taxes in Texas. And in 1855, the taxable cattle number had grown to 1,363,688. Five years later, by 1860, the herds had increased to 3,786,443, making Texas six times more populated with cattle than people. But there was no market for all the cattle because, during the War Between the States, the North controlled the Mississippi River and maintained a blockade in the Gulf, making it impossible for the Texans to supply beef to the Confederate Army and Northern markets. So, the idea of driving herds north to Kansas and Missouri from Lockhart became a reality for early Lockhart ranchers, and the Chisholm Trail led the way.

In addition to raising beef cattle for their own tables, Lockhart's early families were productive farmers and grew their own food. They toiled many hours from dawn to dusk, clearing their fields and planting and harvesting their crops. Farming required a strong back as well as a heavy plow, a harrow, a hoe, an ax, and a strong team. With 270 days of growing season and a decent mixture of soil composed of black dirt, clay, and sand, Lockhart soon became a leading grower of cotton and other crops. By 1845, cotton production in Texas approximated 30,000 bales per year, and Lockhart and Caldwell County ginned 8,562 bales in 1946, according to the *1947–1948 Texas Almanac*. Trail driving ended with the advancement of the railroad, so by 1900, cotton was king in Lockhart. Farming and growing crops would become one of Lockhart's leading commercial agribusinesses. Today, Texas is still the nation's leader in livestock production. With farming coming after ranching, cotton is leading the way as the number one crop and is followed by grain production.

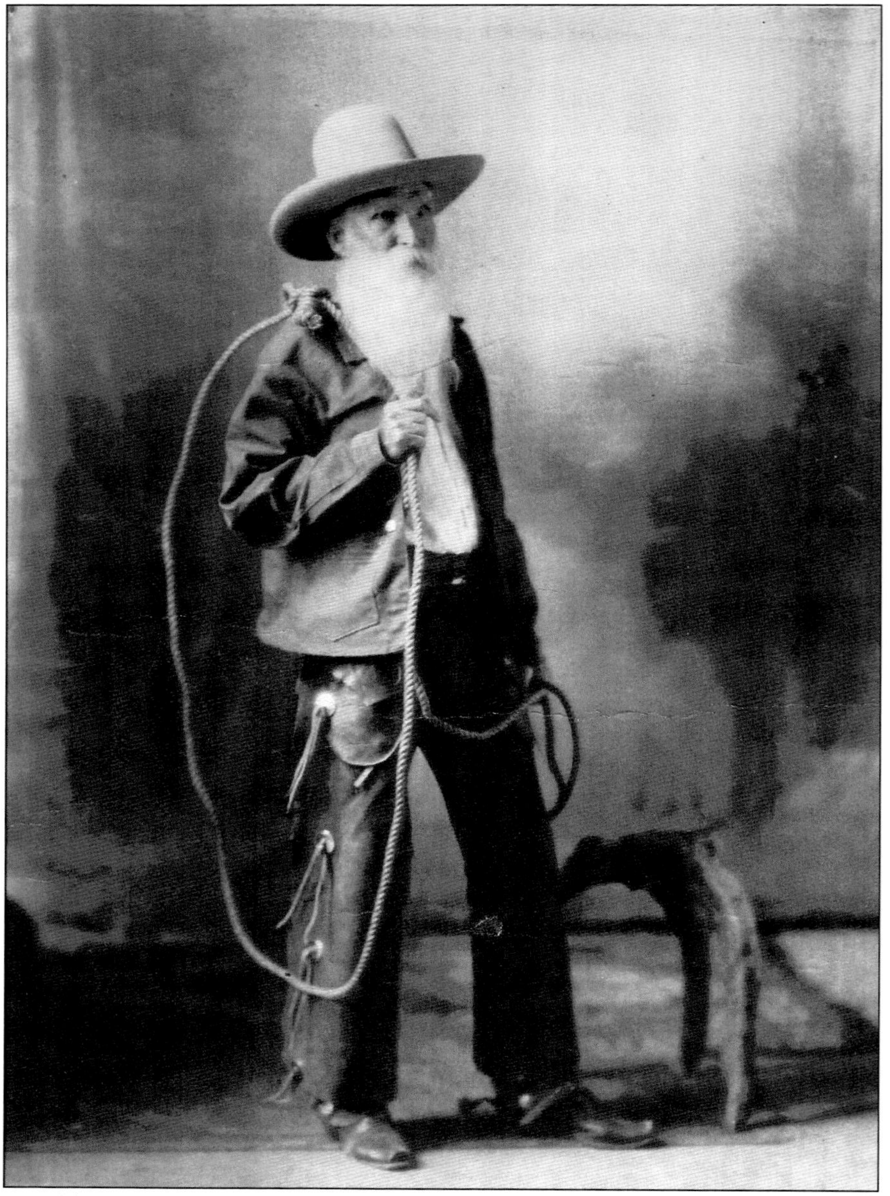

Perhaps Lockhart's most colorful cowboy was Sam Roberson Garner, who drove cattle up the Chisholm Trail from in 1869 to 1882. Born in Tennessee on June 28, 1847, he joined the Confederate army at the age of 16. He moved to Texas and built a home on Tinney Creek, located nine miles east of Lockhart, in 1873. The home still stands today and is in good condition. Garner married Mary Lucinda Halsell. They raised 11 children. In *The Trail Drivers of Texas*, when speaking of driving his first herd of 3,000 in Kansas, he said, "I fit, bled and died for that herd." Garner recalled that at night they would sit around the campfire and tell their stories. "Many is the time I have listened to the chant of the night songs as the boys went around the herd," stated Garner. He quit the trail but continued to stay "after the cow." He lived in Caldwell County for more than 63 years. He died in McMahan on September 9, 1924, at the age of 77 and is buried in the Jeffrey Cemetery. (Courtesy of the CCHC.)

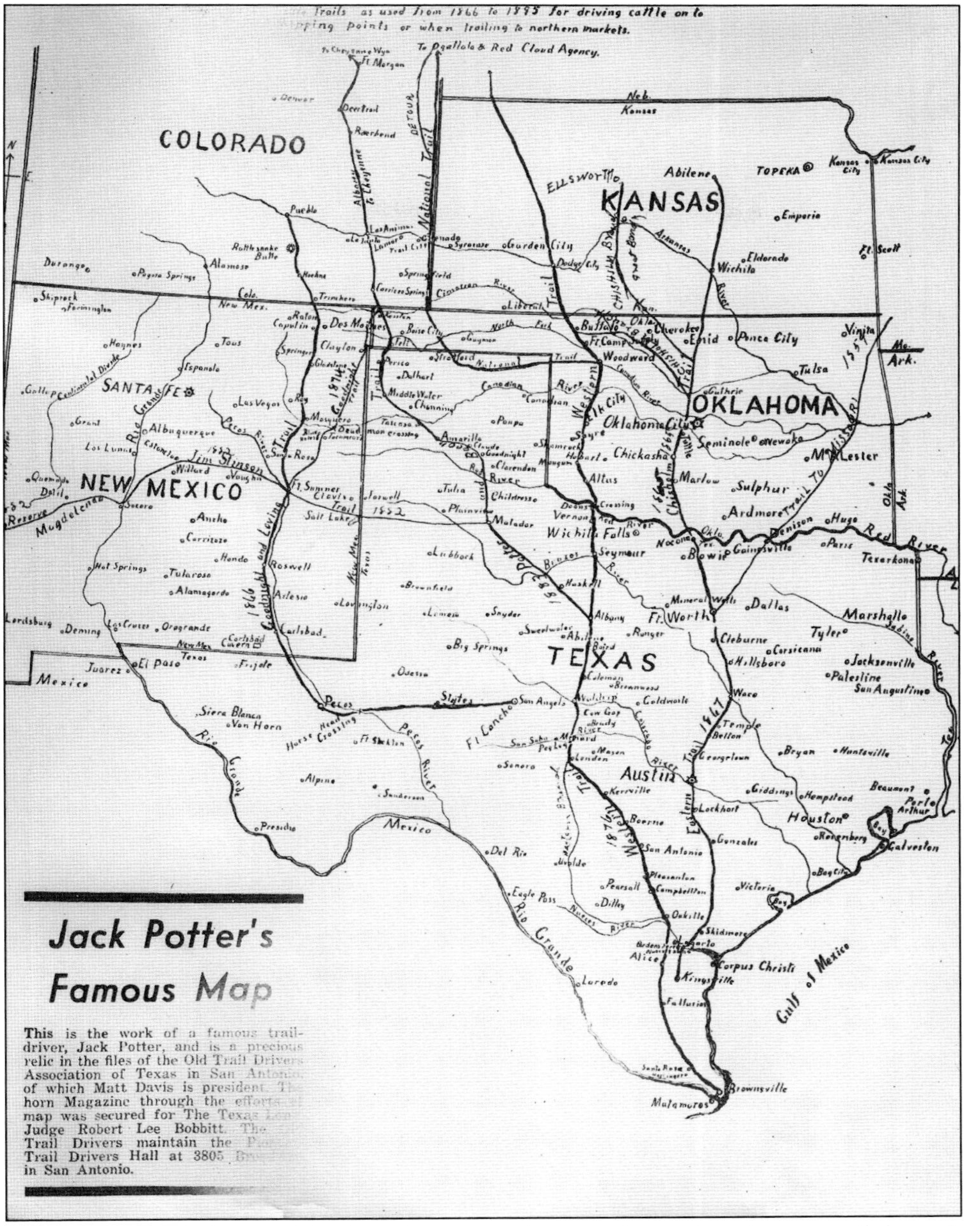

Named "Jack Potter's Famous Map," the key states that it is the work of famous trail driver Jack Potter and is a "precious relic in the files of the Old Trail Drivers Association of Texas in San Antonio." The map depicts cattle trails that were used from 1866 to 1895. In 1866, Lockhart trail drivers began to move herds as large as 3,000 head up the trails. Lockhart resident Col. J.J. Meyers made the first drive from Lockhart after striking a deal with Joseph McCoy, who had stockyards in Kansas and later in Abilene. Hostile Indians, the weather, the rivers and streams to ford, and stampedes made it dangerous, but they could sell the cattle for 10 times the amount they were getting in Lockhart, which was $40 per head versus $4. The drive could take as long as seven months. They would sell their cattle for gold and hopefully return home safely. (Courtesy of the CCHC.)

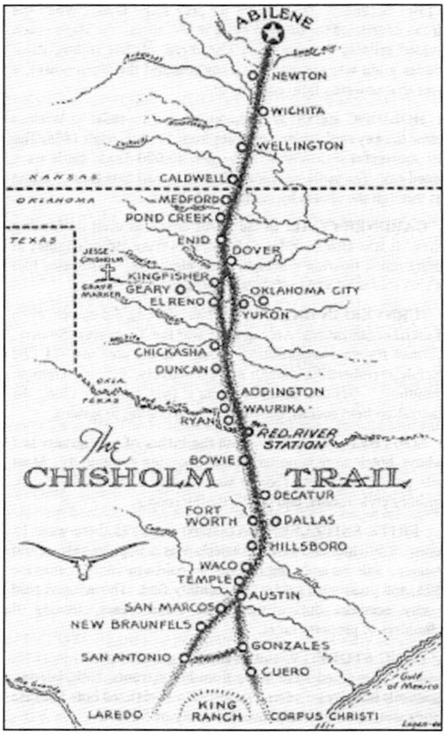

With two trails converging, herds as large as 16,000 head would come through Lockhart. It was not uncommon to see cattle come through the public square, kicking up a dusty trail and trampling local fences and gardens as they left town. Between 1866 and 1890, almost 10 million cattle were driven out of Texas to fetch higher prices in Northern markets, representing the "greatest migration of domestic animals in world history." There were more than 50 trail drivers from Lockhart. Some of the well-known drivers from Lockhart, in addition to Col. J.J. Meyers and Sam Garner, were Mark Withers, Andrew Lee Brock, Noah Ellis, Jesse Blackwell, J.M. Jones, A.M. Cardwell, and Berry Robuck. Below is a rare death notice of driver Noah Ellis (1846–1902), a great-great uncle of the author. (Left, courtesy of the Dickinson County Historical Society; below, courtesy of Ona Anton.)

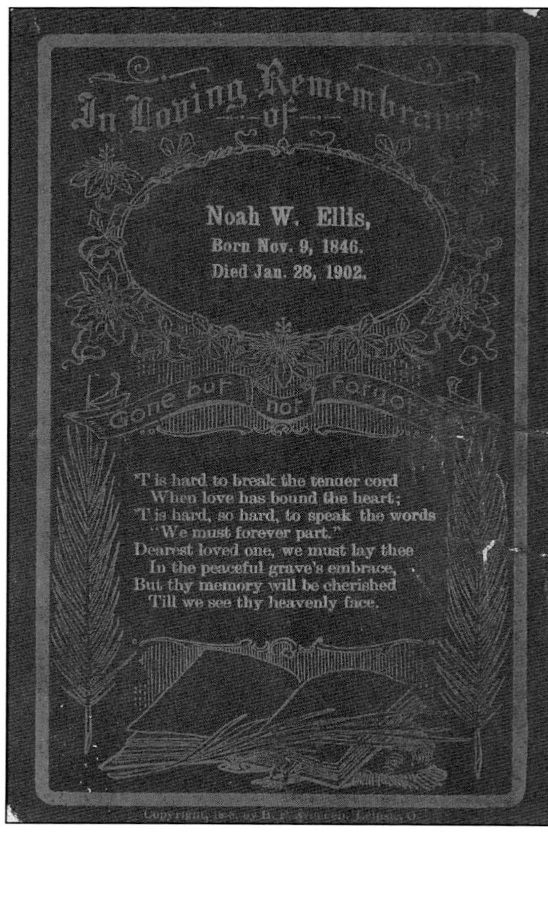

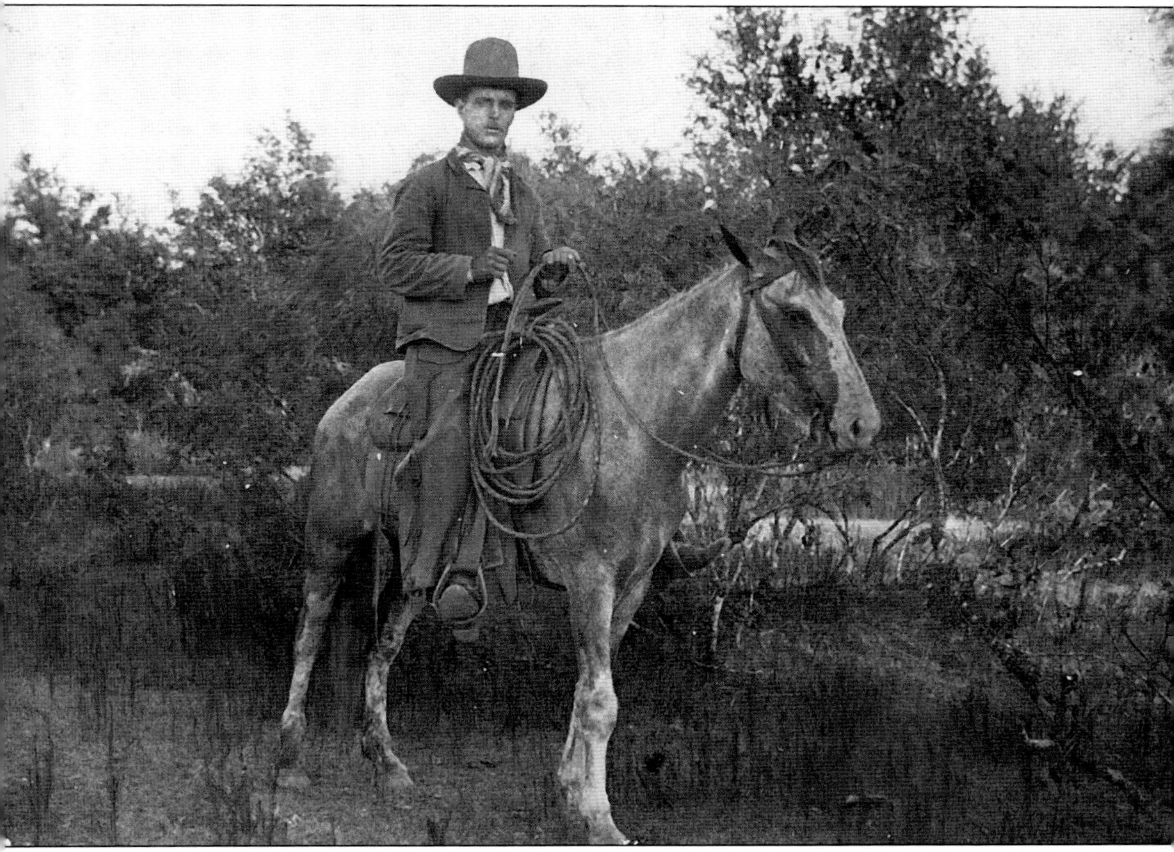

"You must be a cowboy . . . I can tell by your outfit," could be the caption for this postcard-type photograph, taken by Cozby & Son Artists, of an unidentified cowboy. The original image was provided by Joe Henry Bunch whose relatives were great friends with Lockhart cattleman and driver Mark Withers. With the scare of the outbreak of Spanish fever among the Texas herds, business began to suffer, so Abilene stockyard owner Joseph McCoy got creative. He hired Withers and other expert cowboys to rope buffalo in West Texas and load them on a railcar. With long canvas streamers hanging on each side of the car in striking colors and words proclaiming the great cattle bargains at Abilene, the car rolled through St. Louis and on to Chicago. Newspapers hailed the progress of the "buffalo train," and upon the arrival in Chicago, the buffalo were turned out on a grassy field. The clever stunt worked and caused the Chicago buyers to relook at Texas cattle. Many road the train back to Abilene to purchase again. McCoy proclaimed, "Texas cattle suddenly became very popular and in great demand." (Courtesy of Joe Henry Bunch.)

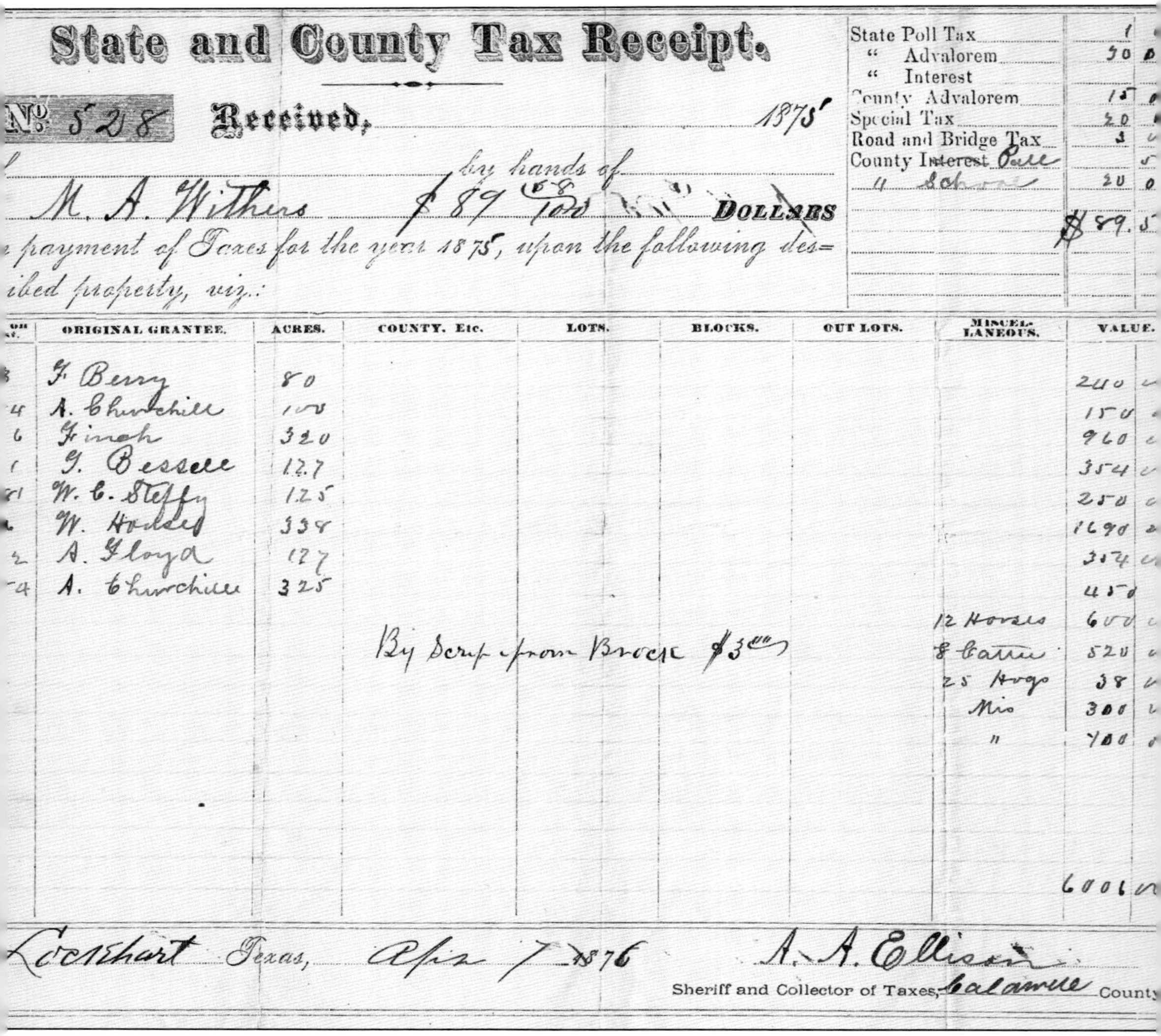

State and County Tax Receipt.

No. 528 Received, 1875

by hands of M. A. Withers $89 58/100 DOLLARS

in payment of Taxes for the year 1875, upon the following described property, viz.:

State Poll Tax	1
" Advalorem	50
" Interest	
County Advalorem	15
Special Tax	20
Road and Bridge Tax	3
County ~~Interest~~ Poll	5
" School	20
	$89.5

Original Grantee	Acres	County, Etc.	Lots	Blocks	Out Lots	Miscellaneous	Value
F. Berry	80						240
A. Churchill	100						150
Finch	320						960
G. Bessell	127						354
W. C. Steffy	125						250
W. Hodsey	338						1690
A. Floyd	127						354
A. Churchill	325						450
						12 Horses	600
		By Scrip from Brock $3.00				8 Cattle	520
						25 Hogs	38
						Mis	300
						"	700
							6006

Lockhart Texas, Apr 7 1876 A. A. Ellison

Sheriff and Collector of Taxes, Caldwell County

Lockhart early settler and cattleman Mark Withers received this tax receipt on April 7, 1875, for paying $89.58 for county taxes on 1,554 acres of land, 12 horses, 8 cattle, 25 hogs, and miscellaneous property he owned. A.A. Ellison, the sheriff and collector of taxes of Caldwell County, signed it. Born in 1846, in Paris, Missouri, Withers came to Texas with his parents and 10 siblings in 1852. He joined the Confederate Army's 36th Texas Cavalry, Company I. After the war was over, he came home to Lockhart where he began driving cattle north for shipment to the Northeast. In 1869, he married Annie Weyland, with whom he had five children. After Annie's death in 1880, he married Mattie Rebecca Bagley in 1888, with whom he had three more children. Withers died in 1937 at his ranch, which was located just outside of Lockhart. The house still stands today at its original site on Borchert Loop. Attempts to make it a museum have failed. It remains vacant. It is owned by Robert and Deborah Marshall. (Courtesy of Gerry and Conrad Ohlendorf.)

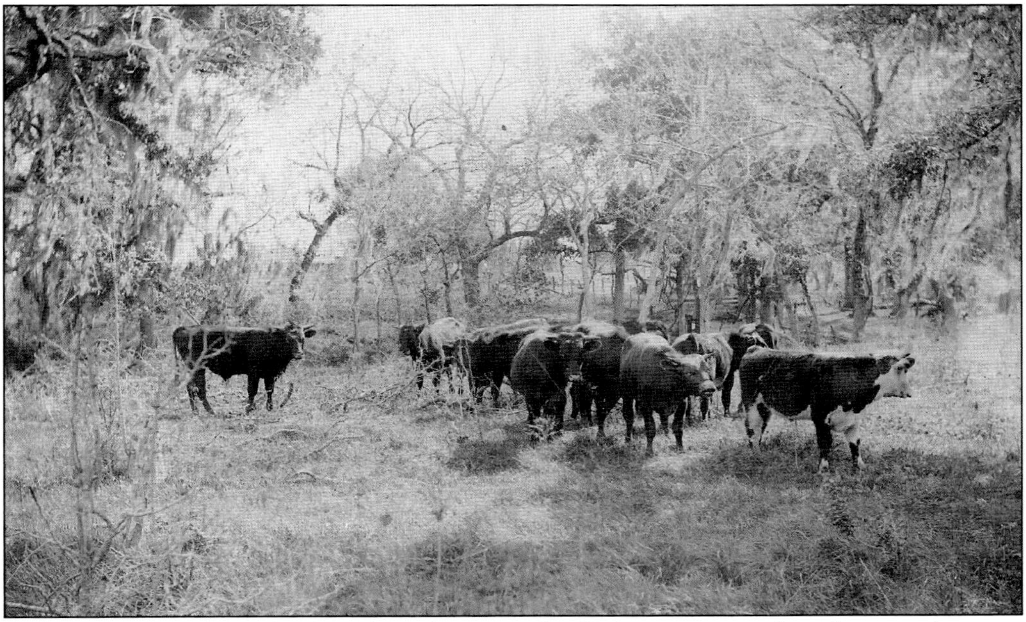

This is a rare photograph of Mark Withers's cattle. Withers once purchased a paint horse in Bastrop before a drive. At the trail's end, he sold the cattle and put the gold in his saddlebags. On the way home, the horse spooked and bolted. Upon Withers's return to Lockhart, he got word the runaway horse had returned to Bastrop. Arriving there, the stable owner told Withers the horse rode in with the saddle still on his back. Withers rushed over to see the saddle, and there were the saddlebags with the gold still in them. Below is Withers's $86.54 tax receipt dated March 2, 1877, for 1,642 acres of land, 10 horses, 12 hogs, and 112 cattle, as well as unidentifiable items. (Above, courtesy of Joe Henry Bunch; below, courtesy of Gerry and Conrad Ohlendorf.)

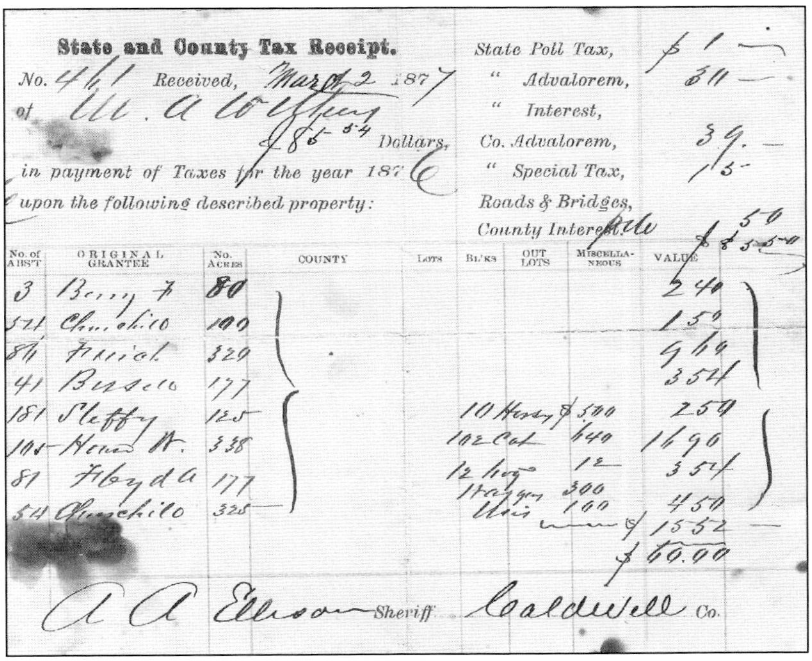

State and County Tax Receipt.

No. 461 Received, March 2 1877

of M. A. Withers

$86.54 Dollars,

in payment of Taxes for the year 1876

upon the following described property:

State Poll Tax, $1

" Advalorem, 311

" Interest,

Co. Advalorem, 39.

" Special Tax, 15

Roads & Bridges,

County Interest.

No. of Abs't	Original Grantee	No. Acres	County	Lots	Bl'ks	Out Lots	Miscellaneous	Value
3	Berry	80						240
571	Churchillo	100						150
84		329						969
41	Bussell	177						354
181	Steffy	125					10 Horses $500	250
105	Howard	338					102 Cat 440	1690
81	Floyd	177					12 hogs 12	354
54	Churchillo	325					300	450
							100	1552

A A Ellison Sheriff Caldwell Co.

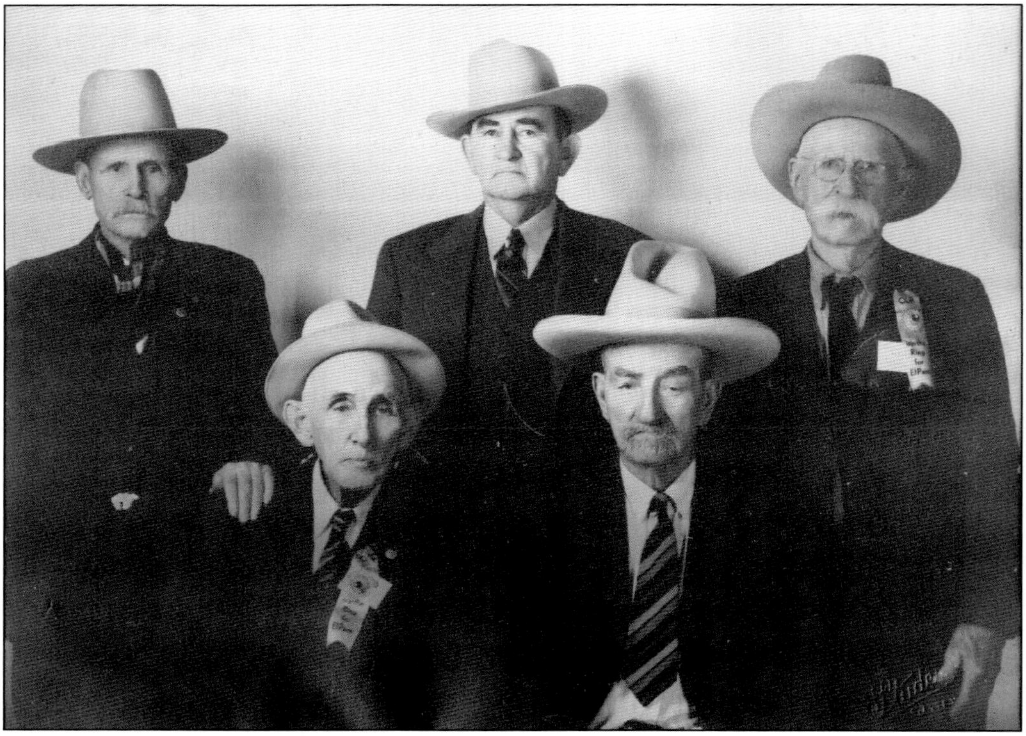

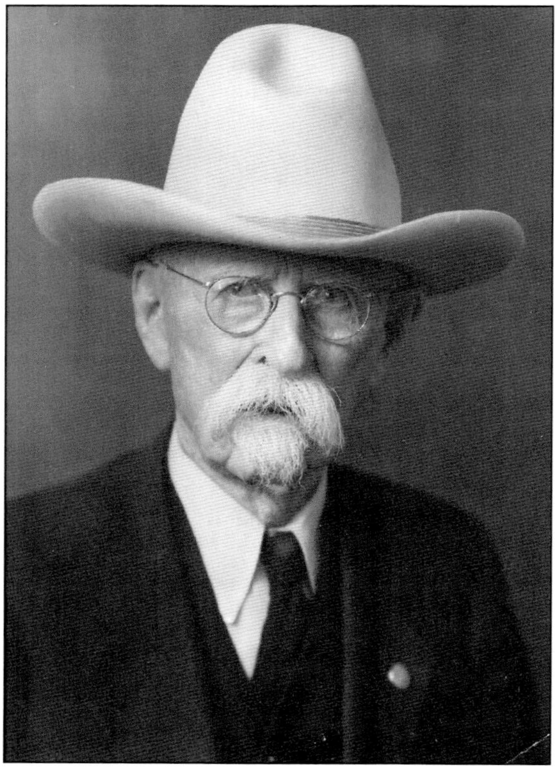

This portrait of five trail drivers was taken in San Antonio, Texas, in 1941. Pictured here are, from left to right, (first row) Mr. Hargus from San Antonio and Ab Blocker from Crystal City; (second row) Jess Blackwell from Lockhart, Tom Johnson from Johnson City, and E.A. Robuck from Lockhart. Conditions on the trail were rough from sudden stampedes, hazardous river crossings, and Indian attacks. Robuck and Hargus experienced the freeze of April 8, 1873, when cattle froze to death, men's boots froze to their stirrups, and sleet was four- to six-inches deep on the ground. Almost all 254 counties in Texas claim the Chisholm Trail (named after Jesse Chisholm) went through their land. Today, there remains confusion as to where it began. Johnson is the brother of Pres. Lyndon B. Johnson. Robuck rode his horse in the Battle of Flowers Parade in San Antonio on April 21, 1941, during the annual Fiesta celebration. (Both, courtesy of the CCHC.)

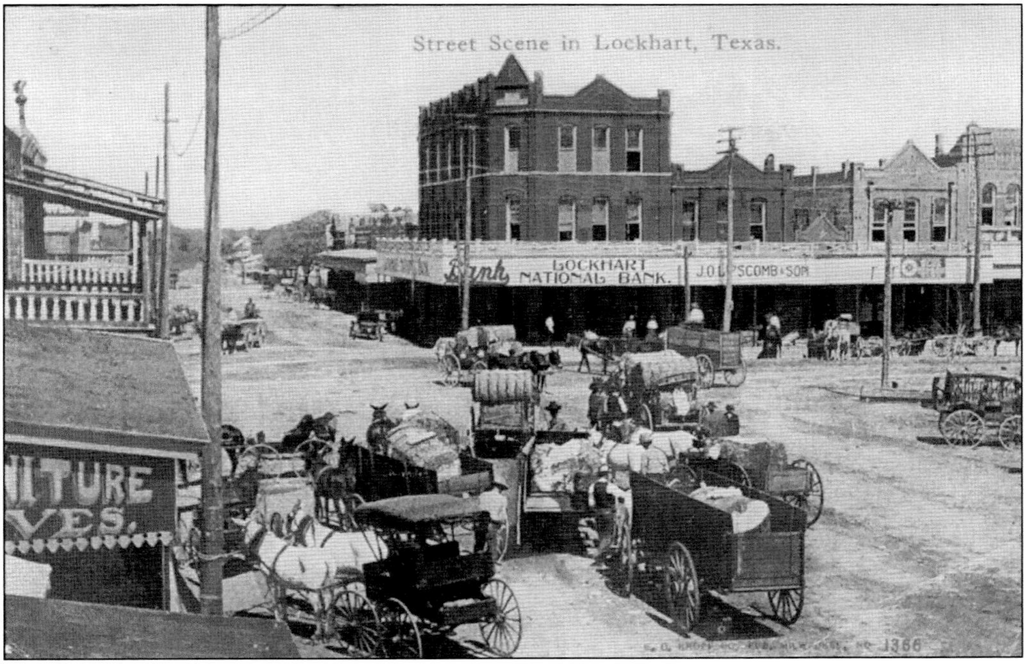

As cattle drives faded out due to the advent of the rail and barbed-wire fencing, Lockhart turned to cotton production. Cotton gins began to pop up, offering employment to area residents. Postcard photographers captured early scenes, like this one taken about 1900 on the public square depicting cotton bales being hauled to market. Looking up Main Street to the northwest corner of the square (above), this photograph shows cotton being hauled by horse-drawn wagons. The bird's–eye view is from the Wm. Blanks's Grocery store. Shown below, a team of oxen is pulling the trailer full of baled cotton in front of Crews Furniture Company and Undertaking on South Main Street. (Above, courtesy of Ronda A. Reagan; below, courtesy of the CCHC.)

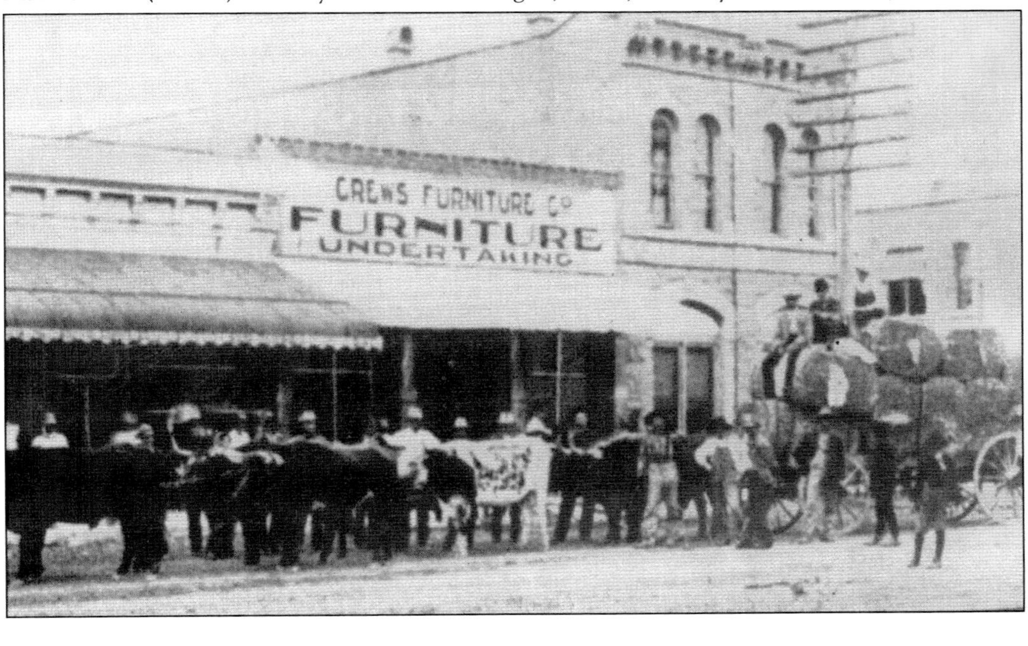

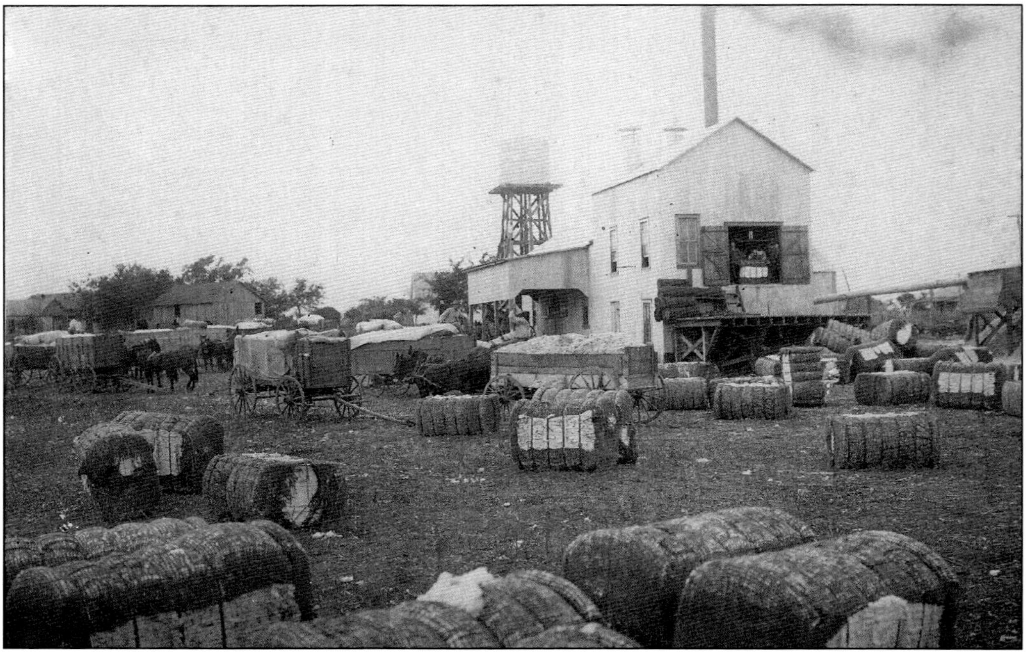

Cotton blossomed in Lockhart around 1880. At one time, there were at least 17 operating cotton gins within the town's boundaries and more operating in the county like the one above near Reedville. By 1900, cotton was king, and the king was Lockhart's own cotton breeder, A.D. Mebane, shown in the photograph below on the right. He was born in Mebane, North Carolina, on April 8, 1855, of Scottish-Irish stock. After the Civil War, the Mebane's brought their young family to Texas for a better life, settling first in Hays County and later in Lockhart where they lived in a two-room log cabin. Mebane married Sara Owen in 1904. His success was evidenced by the grand, redbrick home they lived in on what is now State Park Road. Mebane died on April 30, 1923. (Above, courtesy of Janet Christian; below, courtesy of Gerry and Conrad Ohlendorf.)

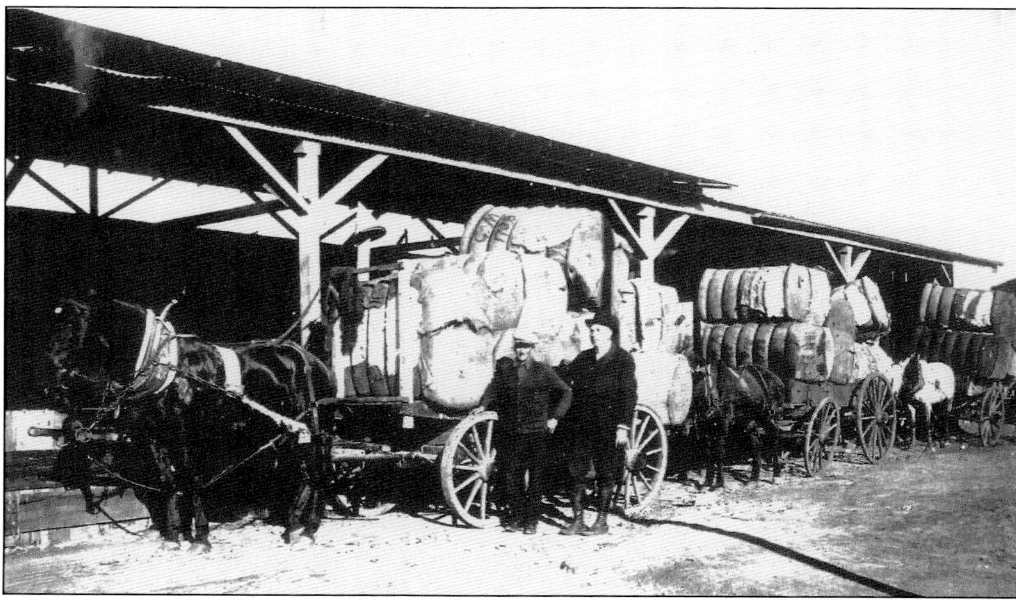

With only an elementary school education, A.D. Mebane began experimenting with selecting the best cotton plants and crossbreeding them to get a better strain of cotton. By 1900, he had created "Mebane Triumph" cottonseed. Other cottonseed developers and growers were the White brothers, who owned and operated White's Lockhart Seed House and W.H. (Tony) Anton of Anton Seed Company. In advertisements, the Mebane Triumph was said to have been bred to produce "strong, stocky, storm-resistant, drought-resistant, high-yield, true-breeding, early maturing plants with large, easy-to-pick bolls having a long lint, an increased lint-to-seed ratio, and easily separated seeds." During the peak production years, sale of Mebane seeds approached $1 million annually. After his death, his associates continued the breeding and improvements so that cotton remained a leading staple in Lockhart. The invoice below on Mebane letterhead shows a shipment to Coahuila, Mexico, in 1923. (Both, courtesy of Ronda A. Reagan.)

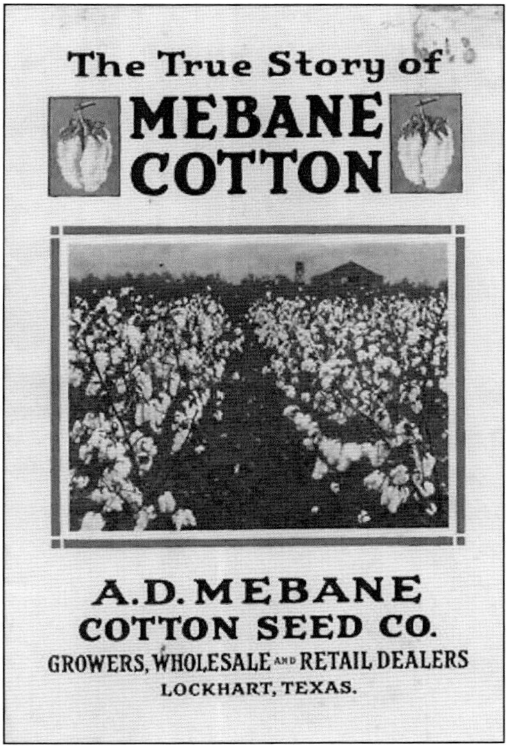

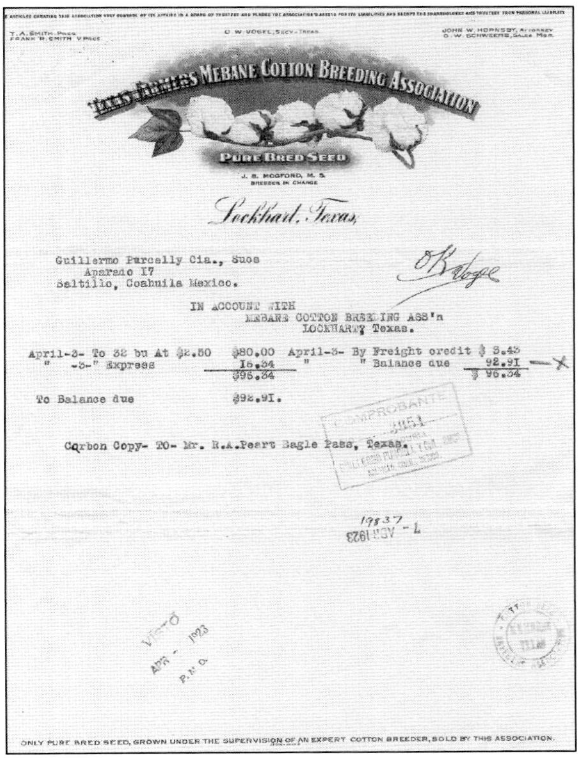

T. A. SMITH, Pres.
FRANK R. SMITH, V. Pres.

C. W. VOGEL, Secy.-Treas.

JOHN W. HORNSBY, Attorney
O. W. SCHWEERS, Sales Mgr.

TEXAS FARMERS MEBANE COTTON BREEDING ASSOCIATION

PURE BRED SEED

J. S. MOGFORD, M. S.
BREEDER IN CHARGE

Lockhart, Texas,

Guillermo Purcelly Cia., Sucs
Aparado I7
Saltillo, Coahuila Mexico.

IN ACCOUNT WITH
MEBANE COTTON BREEDING ASS'n
LOCKHART, Texas.

April-3- To 32 bu At $2.50	$80.00	April-3- By Freight credit	$ 3.43	
" -3-" Express	15.34	" " Balance due	92.91	X
	$95.34		$ 95.34	

To Balance due $92.91.

Carbon Copy- TO- Mr. R.A.Peart Eagle Pass, Texas.

COMPROBANTE
3851

ONLY PURE BRED SEED, GROWN UNDER THE SUPERVISION OF AN EXPERT COTTON BREEDER, SOLD BY THIS ASSOCIATION.

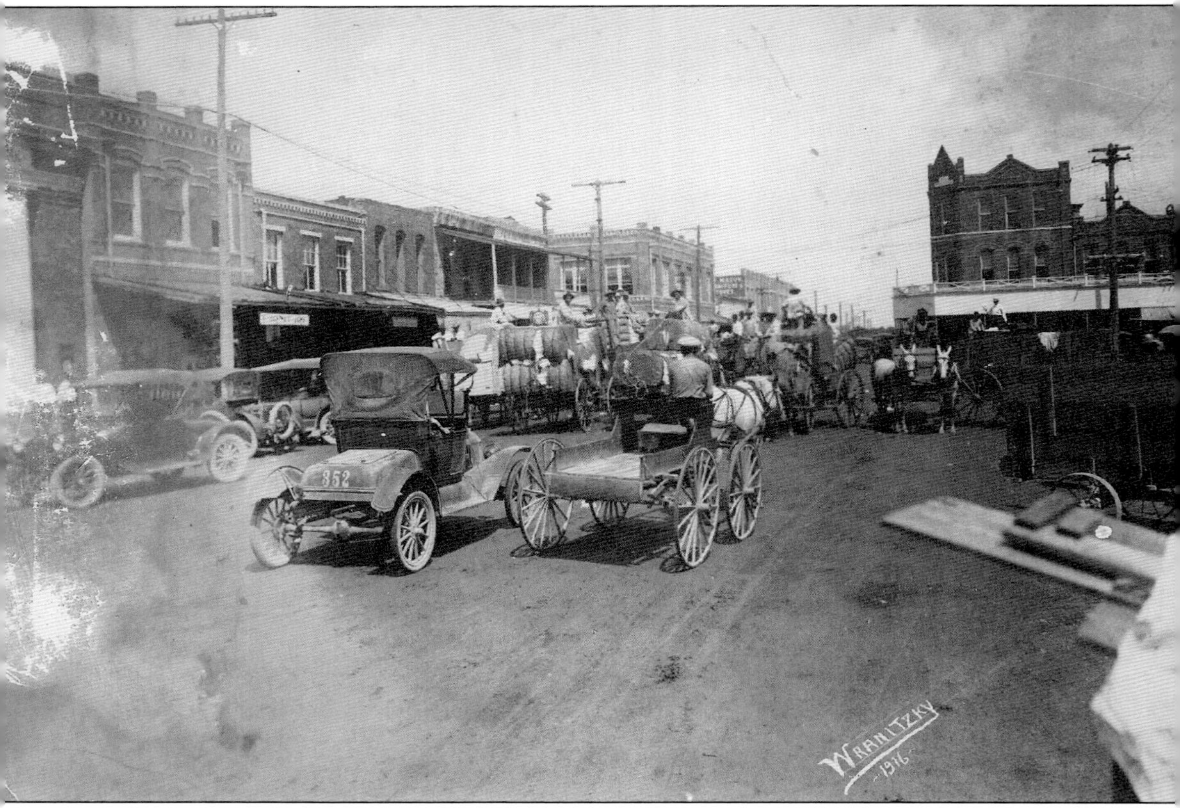

Lockhart farmers found cotton growing to be very lucrative as they produced and shipped cotton and its by-products, cotton seed and cotton seed oil, across the state and country and to Mexico. Cotton oil is used to make soap and cottonseeds are used to make fertilizer. In this 1916 photograph taken on Main Street looking north, one can see some of the town's first automobiles being driven around the public square along with horses and buggies and horse- and mule-drawn wagons loaded with cotton bales. On July 12, 1917, the town celebrated what A.D. Mebane had done for the community with Mebane Day. More than 3,000 attended the huge barbecue. This photograph is by one of Lockhart's many prolific photographers, Wranitzky Bros. (Alfons and Alexandra). (Courtesy of Gerry and Conrad Ohlendorf.)

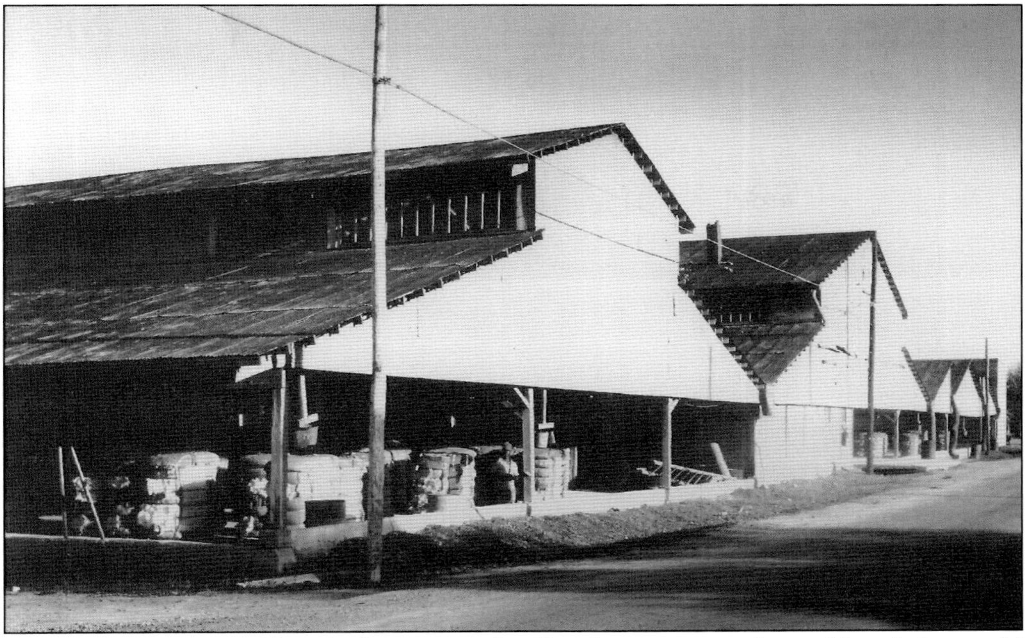

In addition to gins, Lockhart had a cotton oil mill and a cotton warehouse (above) that could hold up to 10,000 bales of cotton. Lockhart's cotton compress (below) was located on what is now State Highway 183 North, next to today's Kreuz's Market. The cotton compress industry revolutionized cotton trade and brought more employment to Lockhart for a time. Compresses reduced bulky bales of cotton produced by gins to roughly one-half their size so that trains could haul them more economically to shipping ports. But by the 1890s, the gins developed their own compress methods, producing high-density bales and making the compresses obsolete. (Above, courtesy of the Eugene Clark Library; below, courtesy of Ronda A. Reagan.)

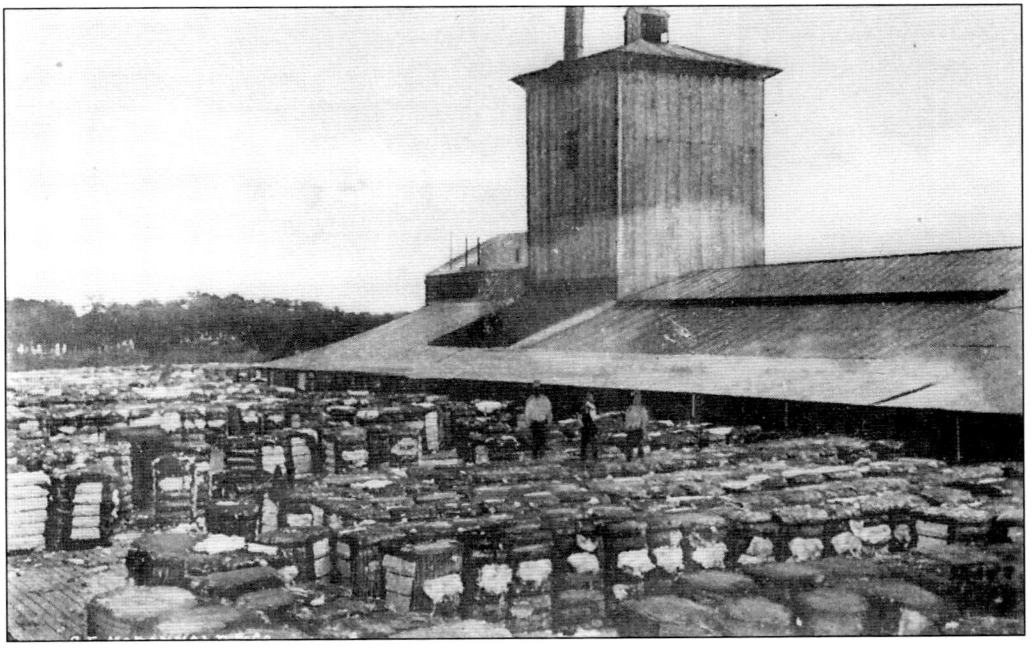

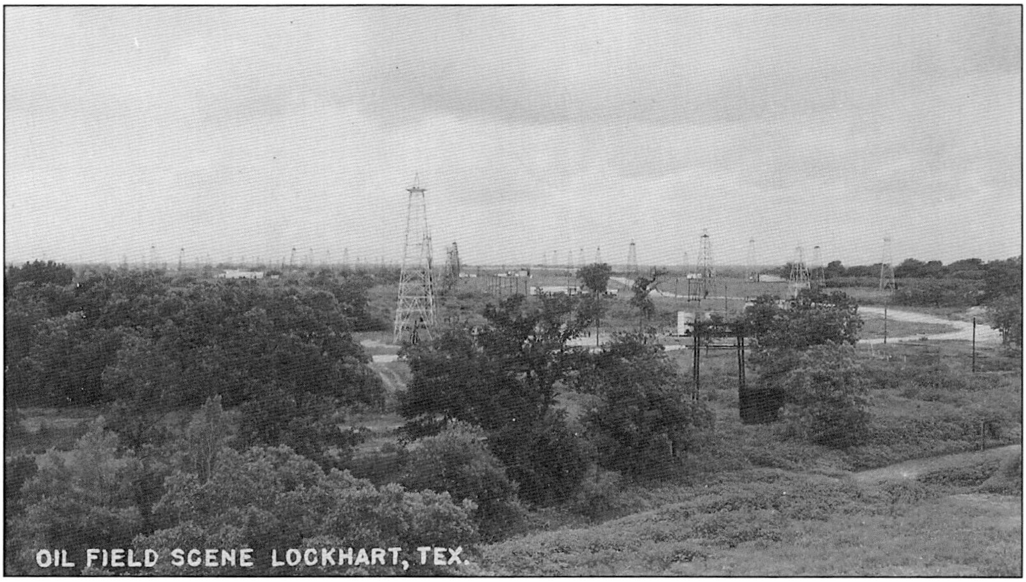

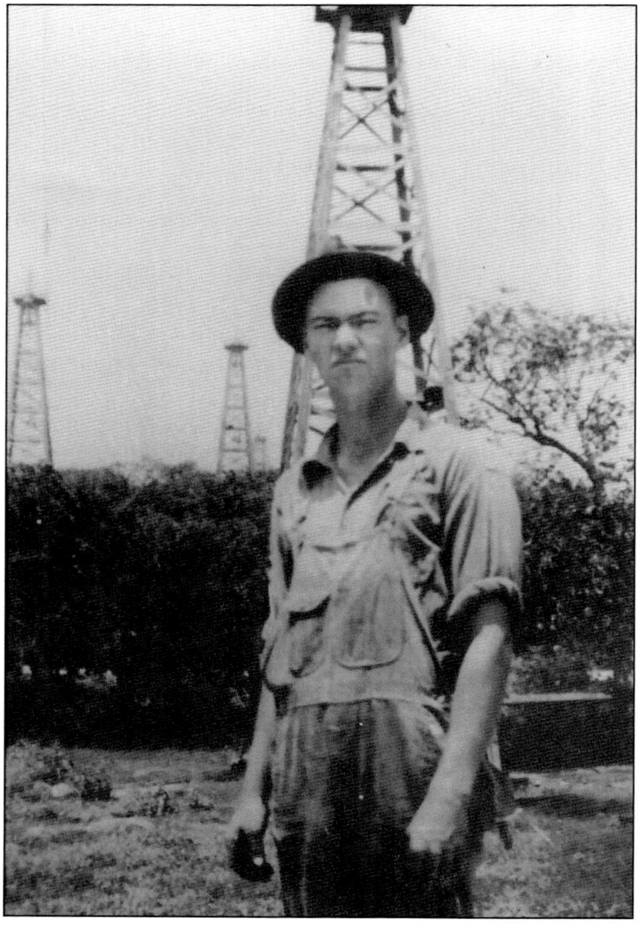

Oil was discovered in several Caldwell County areas in the 1920s. This 1950s postmarked postcard, labeled "Oil Field Scene Lockhart, Tex.," shows numerous oil derricks. The location is not further identified. In the 1920s and 1930s, oil drilling was "pumping" the economy. Oil was discovered in neighboring areas close to Lockhart, including Seawillow, six miles southeast of Lockhart; Dale and Lytton Springs, 10 miles northeast of Lockhart; and in Prairie Lea. Other important fields were the Jolly and Bruner. Luling, to the south, boasted the biggest oil-boom field discovered in 1922, just northwest of the town. The Edgar B. Davis field yielded more than 11 million barrels at its peak in 1924 and leveled its annual production to 2.5 million barrels until the 1930s. The oil man at left is unidentified; the picture was taken in the 1940s at Dale Oil Field. (Above, courtesy of Floyd Wilhelm Jr.; left, courtesy of Gerry and Conrad Ohlendorf.)

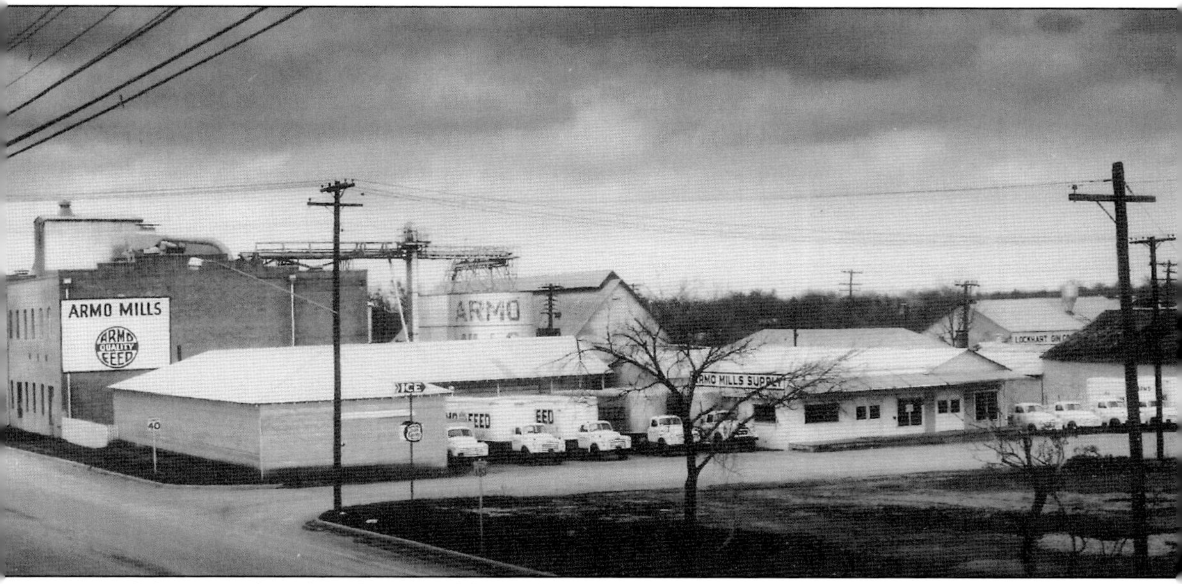

Part of the agricultural trade in Lockhart, this facility, located at 300 North Colorado Street, was once the site of the George H. Mohle's cotton gin. It became Armo Mills in the late 1940s, employing many. Today, it is home of family-run Livengood Feeds. After returning from World War II, Albert Livengood graduated from Texas A&M University with a degree in agriculture. In 1954, he established his first store, Lockhart Farm and Ranch Supply, a retail feed and farm supply. Within six months, he began raising poultry—broilers and turkeys. By 1968, he expanded by starting an egg production business. In 1974, he changed the name of the business to Livengood. Today, his son Burt Livengood runs the family business, based in Lockhart. The feeds are "made for Texans by Texans in Texas." (Courtesy of the Eugene Clark Library.)

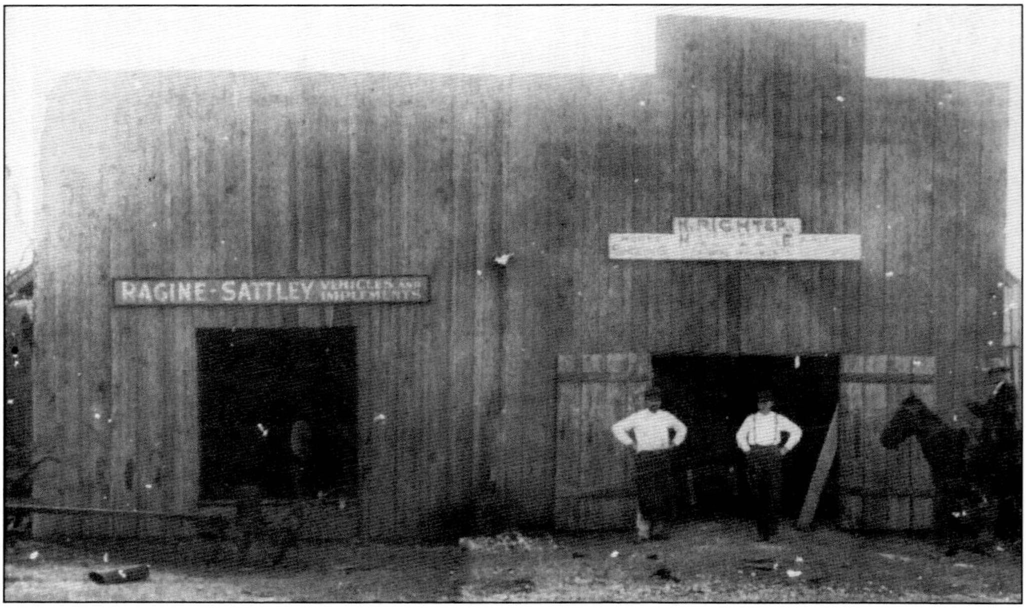

A good horse was most important to the early settlers for many reasons. Many early businesses catered to the farming industry as well as transportation. Shown above are two such stores side by side: the Ragine-Sattley Vehicles and Implements Shop (left) and the M. Richter Blacksmith and Hardware shop, which offered horseshoeing. They were located on Pecos Street. Although the people are unidentified, their clothing depicts the late 1800s to early 1900s, when a horse and buggy were the common mode of transportation. The two-seated buggy below appears to be a surrey with fringe on top from the same period. Two-seated buggies such as these were sold and stored on the second and third floors of the Masur Hardware building at 119 West San Antonio Street. (Above, courtesy of Gerry and Conrad Ohlendorf; below, courtesy of Harry Hilgers Jr.)

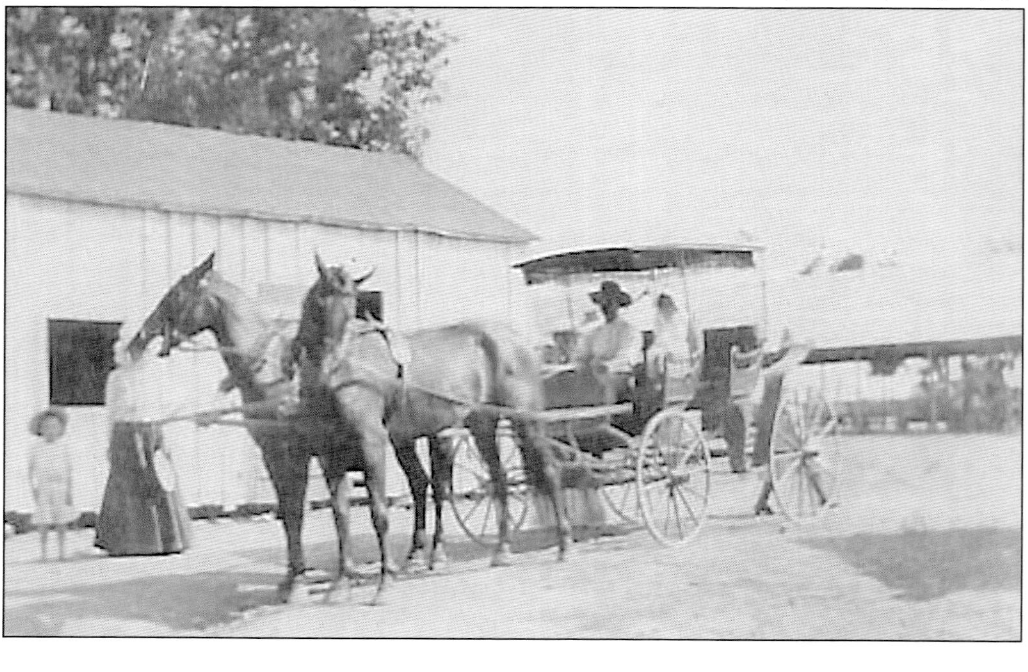

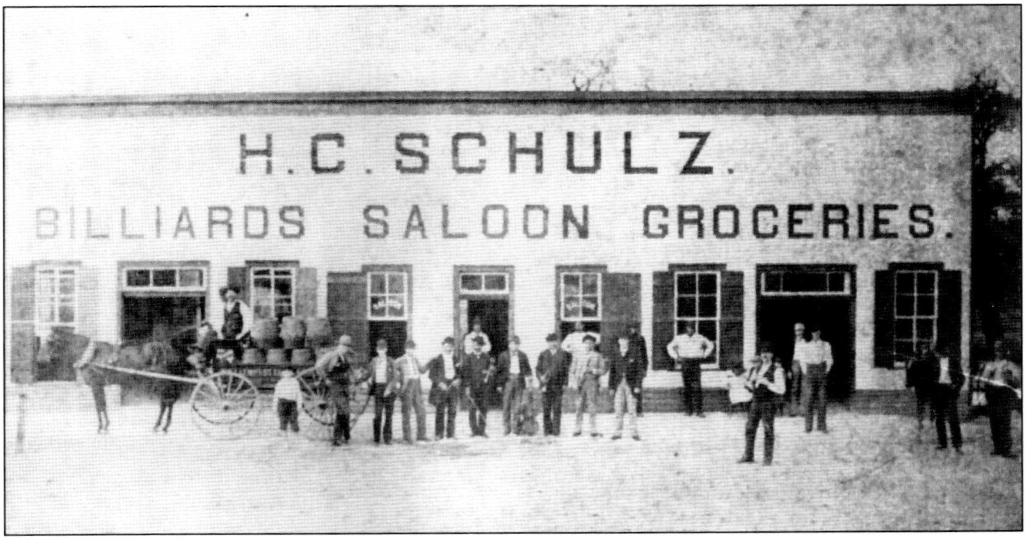

Early grocery stores, which were the descendants of trading posts, and saloons were the predominant businesses in Lockhart in the late 1800s. The H.C. Schulz Grocery and Saloon was one of many. It stood off Pecos Street between the spring and the railroad tracks. Such grocery stores handled dry goods that were impossible to produce economically at home. Staples like flour, sugar, baking soda, dry beans, syrup, salt, tea, coffee, tobacco, spices, and fabrics were popular stock items. Local merchants often sold their goods on credit (a system of trust) until crops came in and accounts could then be paid. The image to the right was taken inside Schulz's saloon. Note the deer antlers on display along the ceiling and the spittoon on the floor. The man in the middle is Schulz; the other two are unidentified. (Both, courtesy of Gerry and Conrad Ohlendorf.)

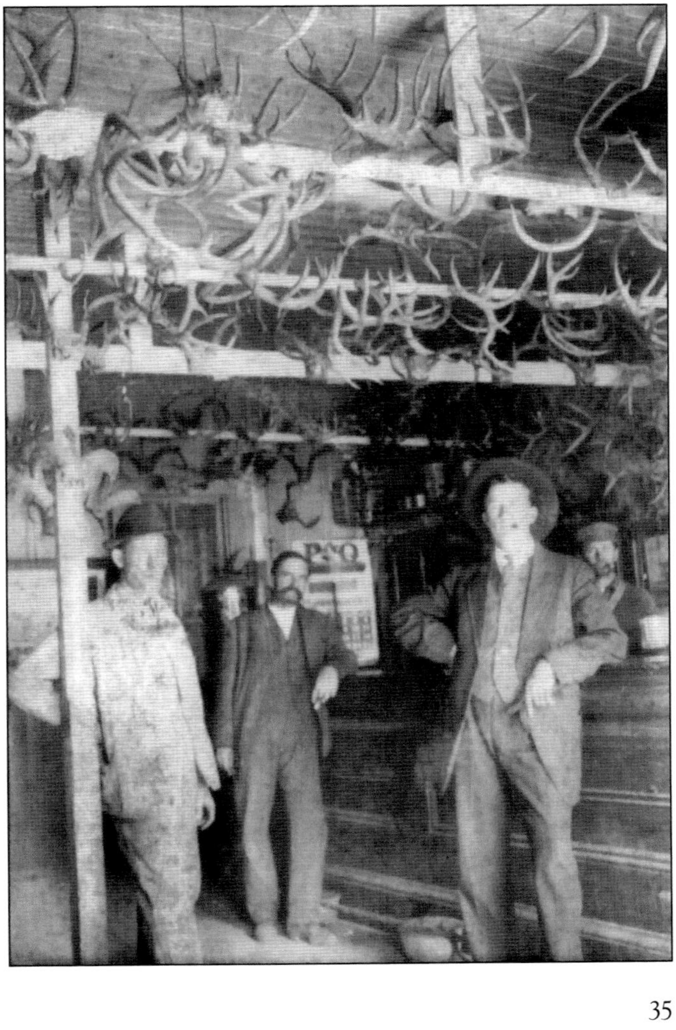

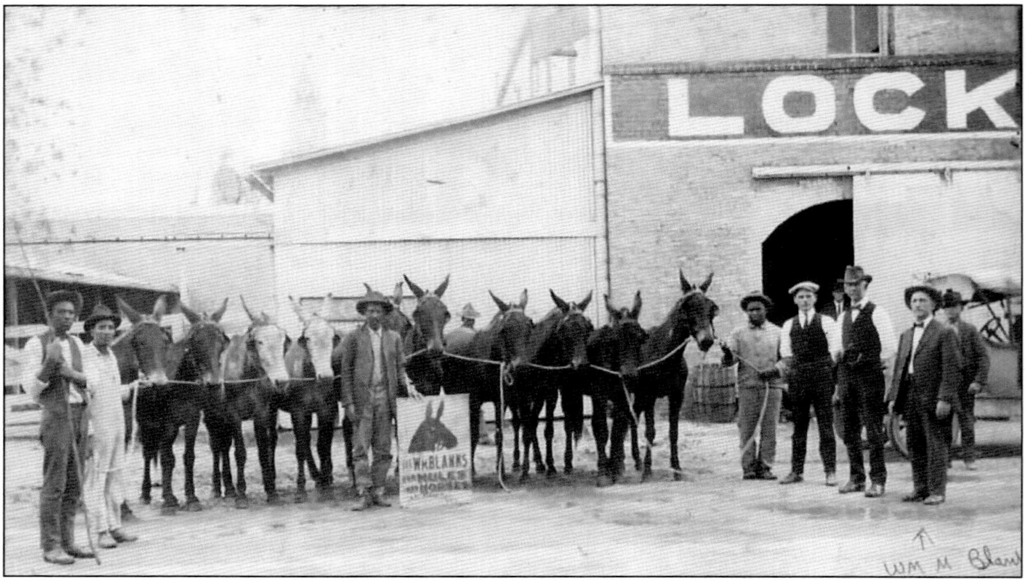

The principal mode of travel in early Texas towns, like Lockhart, was provided by mules and horses paired with buggies and wagons. Few roads existed in Lockhart's early days. They were more like trails—rough and dusty during dry weather and almost impassable in wet weather. One Lockhart businessman, William M. Blanks, shown above on the right, operated Wm. Blanks Mules and Horses. Pictured are, from left to right, two unidentified workers, employees Levi and Neiman, Ed Horne, A.D. Mebane, and Blanks. Blanks went to Kentucky to purchase his mares and took them to Kyle, Texas, to breed them with Max Michalis's jacks. Delivering laundry on Church Street in a horse-drawn wagon, shown below, is Norman Dubois. (Above, courtesy of Harry Hilgers Jr.; below, courtesy of the CCHC.)

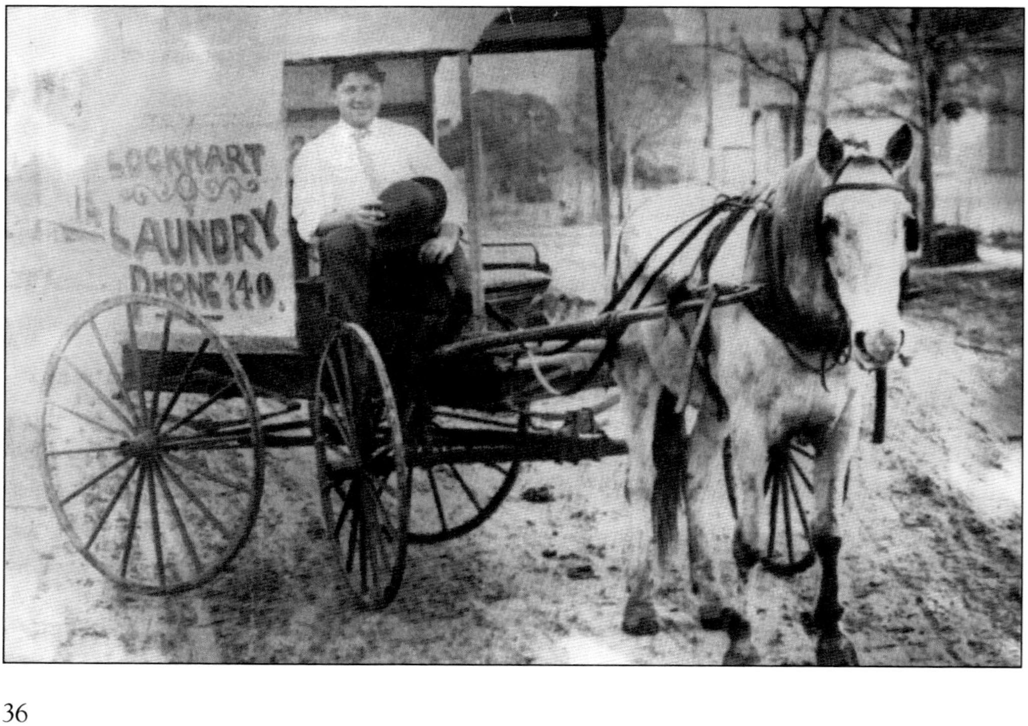

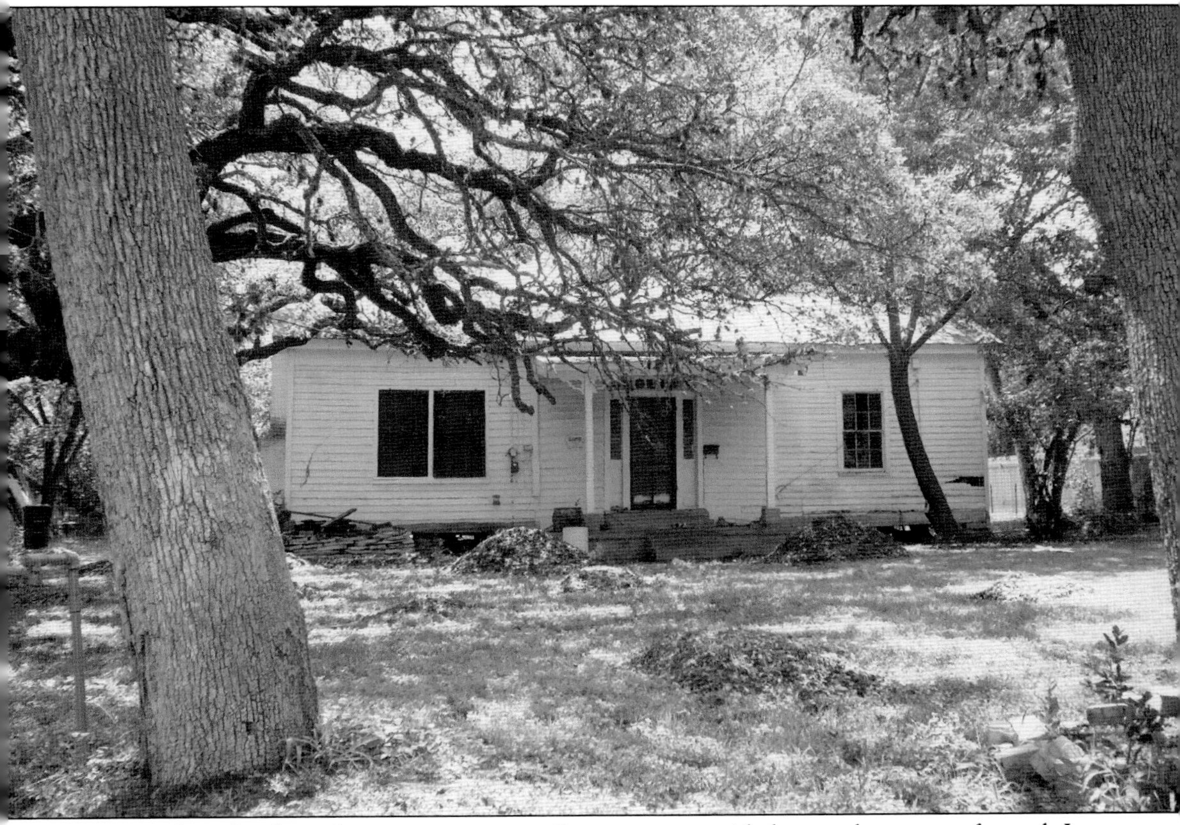

Stagecoaches closely tied to government mail contracts provided an early means of travel. In 1845, biweekly service ran from Houston to Austin via Washington, Independence, LaGrange, and Bastrop. After the Civil War, there were stage routes between almost every small town in Central Texas. Local historians report that Lockhart was included in the run between Gonzales and Austin in the following: "They'd run the horses fast and stop outside Lockhart near Plum Creek to change the team, then again in Lockhart where they'd circle behind this old stagecoach stop." That stop was located on what is Elm Street today where this home stands. Called a "cradle on wheels" by Mark Twain in 1861 due to its unique construction, the coach rocked as it moved instead of bouncing. Rules of the road included: the best seat is next to the driver; do not talk politics or religion; never travel with tight boots; do not ask how far it is to the next station. Bandits and Indian raiding parties made travel dangerous. With the advent of railroad service, stagecoaches were phased out of service in the 1880s. (Courtesy of Ronda A. Reagan.)

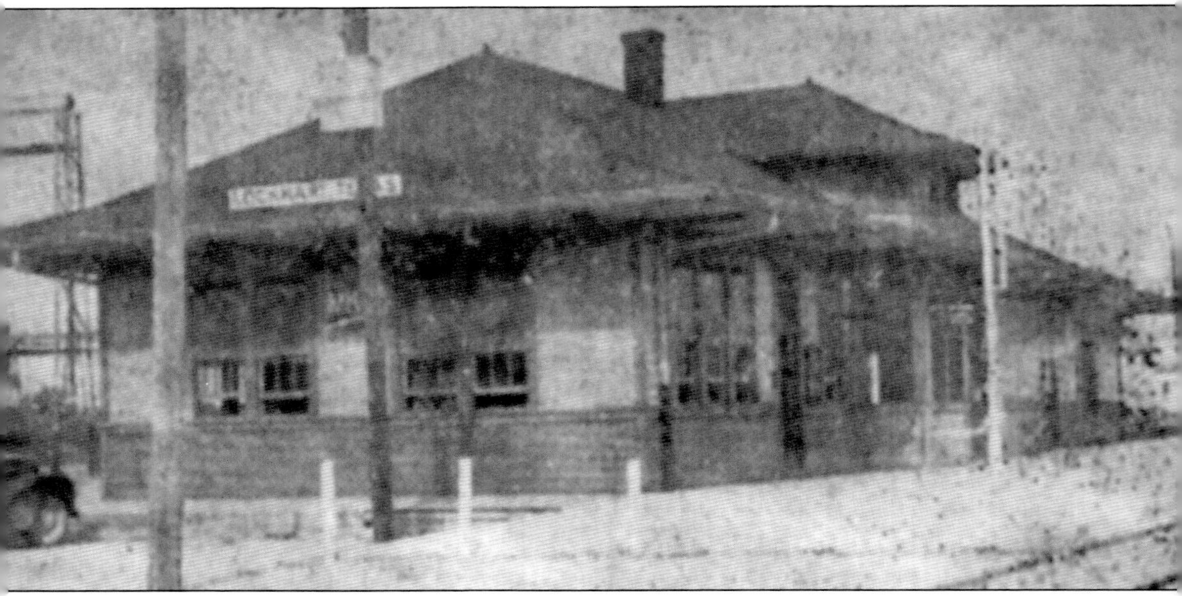

In the 1870s, the first steam locomotive—the great "iron horse"—changed Lockhart's world when it rolled into town. The first line connecting Lockhart was the Missouri-Kansas-Texas (M-K-T) in 1887. Nicknamed the "Katy," the line was advertised as the "gateway to Texas." People in town could set their clocks by it. The railroad connections boosted the economic recovery after the War Between the States. In addition to making shipping cattle and cotton to other markets viable, the rail provided improved transportation for an influx of newcomers from other states and countries. The population increased from 6,572 in 1870 to 11,757 by 1880. The line also hauled oil and other grains as well as passengers. Passengers enjoyed top-of-the-line luxury on the *Texas Special*, the *Bluebonnet*, and the *Katy Flyer*. By World War II, the Katy's prosperity peaked. As years passed, mergers, cutbacks, and much-needed repairs of existing lines led to the ultimate decline of this line, and in 1988, the Interstate Commerce Commission approved the buyout by Union Pacific and its subsidiary, the Missouri Pacific Railroad Company. This picture shows the Katy depot, which was located on Pecos Street next to its successor, the current Union Pacific tracks. The depot was torn down. The area around the old depot is known today as "Tank Town," where grains are stored for loading onto railcars. The Union Pacific is still active today. (Courtesy of the Eugene Clark Library.)

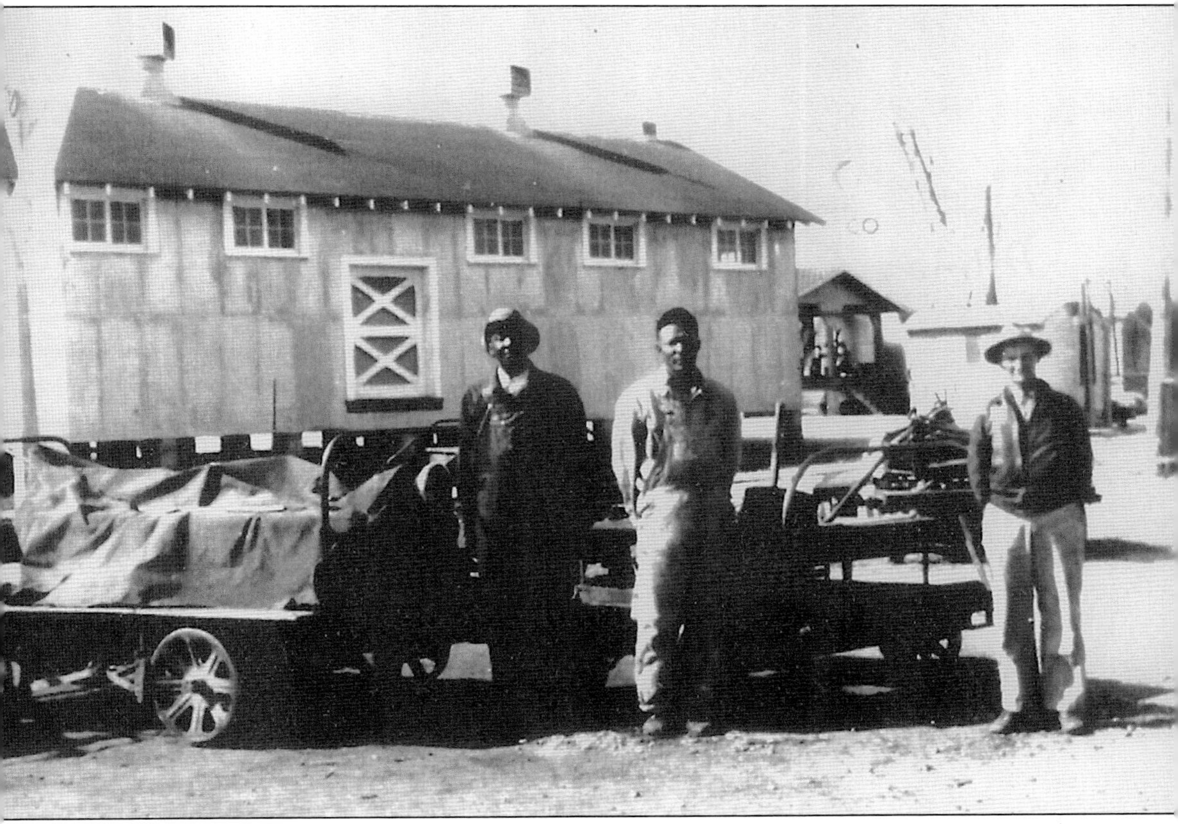

In 1889, the San Antonio & Aransas Pass Railway (SA&AP) laid tracks into Lockhart. The 54-mile branch line ended in Lockhart and connected to Luling, LaGrange, and Shiner. The main SA&AP line connected San Antonio to Aransas Bay. Its tracks were once located parallel to Arkansas, where State Highway 183 is today. Flanking both sides of the rail in the town center were passenger depots and loading docks. Since the SA&AP line ended in Lockhart, the locomotive was literally turned around and pointed back south for the return trip. Parents brought their children to the depot at five o'clock to see it manually turned around on a huge turn table. Locals tell stories of some of the men putting their model Ts and As on the tracks, deflating their tires, and driving seven miles down the tracks to Burditt's Well, a mineral springs resort. "They could really go fast," said Joe Henry Bunch, of Lockhart. With the rail, new towns also sprang up along its routes, like Maxwell, Dale, and Reedville, while others it bypassed faded as people moved away. Hotels were also built to handle the travelers. In this picture are unidentified section workers (left) and their foreman (right) at the Lockhart Depot. The SA&AP terminated the connection between Luling and Shiner in 1933. (Courtesy of the Eugene Clark Library.)

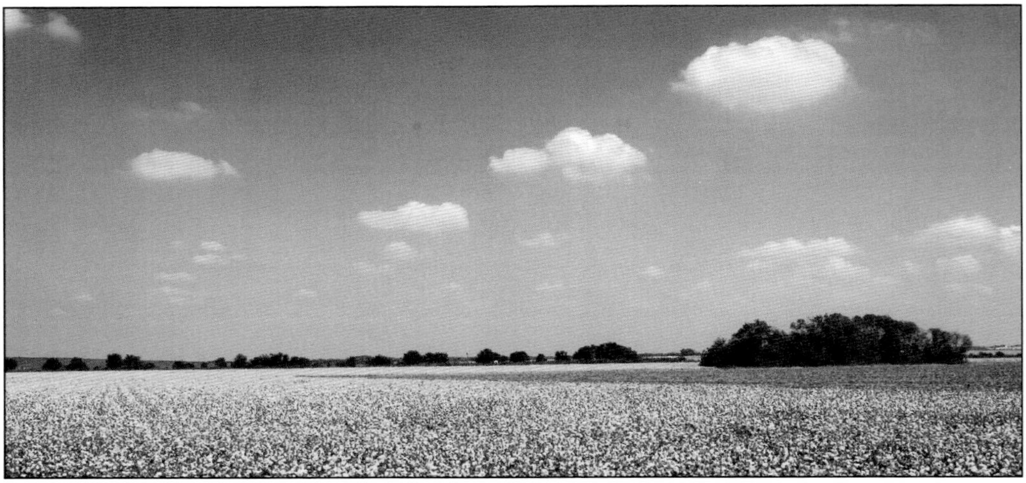

In Caldwell County, cotton is still king. Cotton fields of today are seen to the west and northwest of Lockhart. According to Todd Staples, Texas agriculture commissioner, "The Lone Star State cotton producers make a Texas-sized contribution . . . growing nearly a tenth of [all] the world's cotton." (Courtesy of Ronda A. Reagan.)

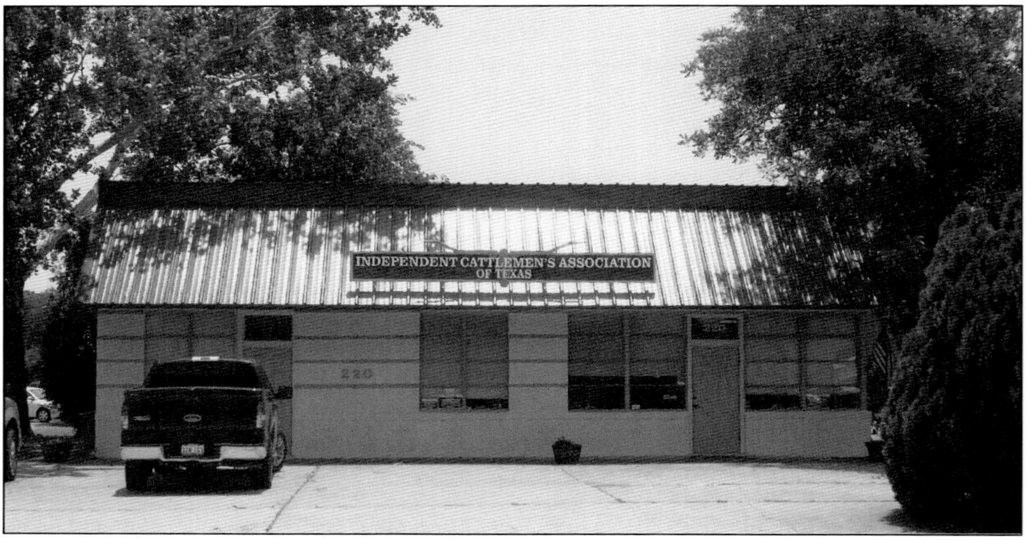

Lockhart cattle production thrives long after the Chisholm Trail days, and Texas leads the nation in beef production. In Lockhart, four barbecue restaurants promote beef by serving up mouth-watering briskets and sausages, making Lockhart the state's favorite place to eat barbecue. The Independent Cattlemen's Association of Texas, headquartered here at 220 West San Antonio Street, just off the town square, is an organization run by and for the benefit of cow-calf producers, keeping members abreast of their industry and all aspects of ranching. (Courtesy of Ronda A. Reagan.)

Three

Shaping the Public Square

When the county was approved by the state in 1848, residents were all living in crude log homes among the oak and elm trees in the area. The first organizational meeting of the newly formed county took place in a log building on the public square to set up the county government and lay out plans for the county's future. The county judge and the newly appointed commissioners divided the county into four districts and set the development of roads to Austin, Bastrop, Gonzales, and San Marcos as their first major project. Meeting in church basements and other stores, they commissioned the construction of the first Caldwell County Courthouse, a small wooden structure built in 1848 at a cost of $200.

Outgrowing the first one, a larger courthouse of limestone brick was built a decade later in 1858 on the same spot. It was 65 feet by 40 feet wide. The third and current courthouse, which was started in 1893, has been featured on the front cover of *The Courthouses of Texas*, Second Edition, published by Texas A&M University Press, and it is known as the most photographed courthouse in Texas. It was completed in 1894 and is still in use today. Built of Muldoon blue limestone trimmed with Pecos red sandstone, the Second Empire masterpiece is three stories with a mansard roof and a dominating, high central tower that features a "four-way" Seth Thomas clock facing north, south, east and west, and a 900-pound bell. The north and south sides feature two secondary towers flanking arches over the main entrance. Most say the design was by architect Alfred Giles, but it is more likely that it was by Henry E.M. Guidon with Giles and Guidon. The same plans were sold to Goliad shortly after Guidon rejoined the Giles firm. Guidon thusly claims that both Goliad and Caldwell designs are his.

It was renovated in 2000 with a $2-million grant and more than $60,000 in funds raised on the grassroots level by local citizens. Then-governor George W. Bush, who later was elected president of the United States, came to Lockhart for the rededication ceremony. At the time of this publication, additional restoration maintenance is ongoing.

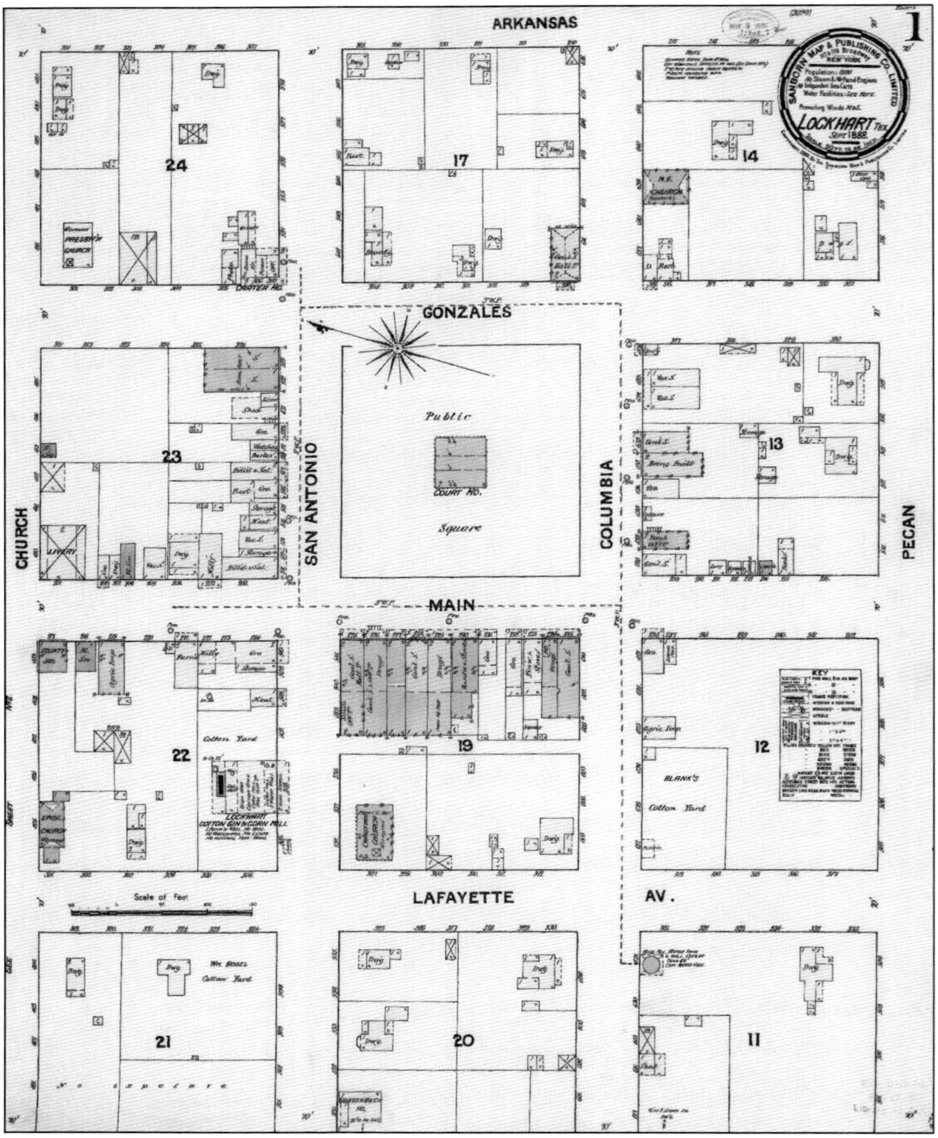

The Sanborn Map Company created thousands of maps of more than 12,000 towns and cities in the United States from 1867 to 1970 to assess fire insurance liability. Typically shown are building construction materials as well as details of the town's fire department, like the sizes and types of fire trucks and the number of personnel. These maps, which are now primarily archived but are available digitally, have become invaluable resources for historians. They are great resources for historic preservation and restoration. This one of Lockhart's center of town is dated September 1888 and it, along with earlier and later maps, helps to show the shaping of the town center. Most of the street names have been changed with the exception of San Antonio Street and Main Street, which is where one can see livery stables, billiards and saloons, meat markets, grocery, drugstores, barbershops, banks, and shops that sold watches. Also shown are William Bogel's and William M. Blanks's two cotton yards. Lockhart's Cotton Gin and Corn Mill is on San Antonio Street across from the First Christian Church. Some structures are labeled "being built" and some are vacant. (Courtesy of the Dolph Briscoe Center for American History, University of Texas Libraries.)

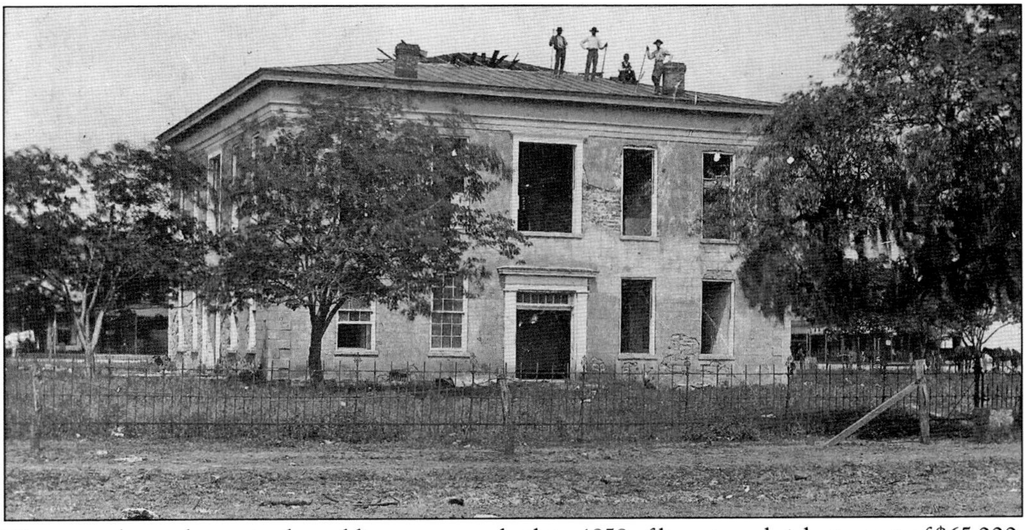

The second courthouse in the public square was built in 1858 of limestone brick at a cost of $65,000. It was taken down to make way for Lockhart's grand, new courthouse, which was scheduled to begin construction in 1893. In this picture postcard documented by Cozby & Son Artists, workers are shown taking down the roof. A wrought iron fence is visible around the courthouse. (Nora Lee Magee Collection, courtesy of Dianne Stevenson.)

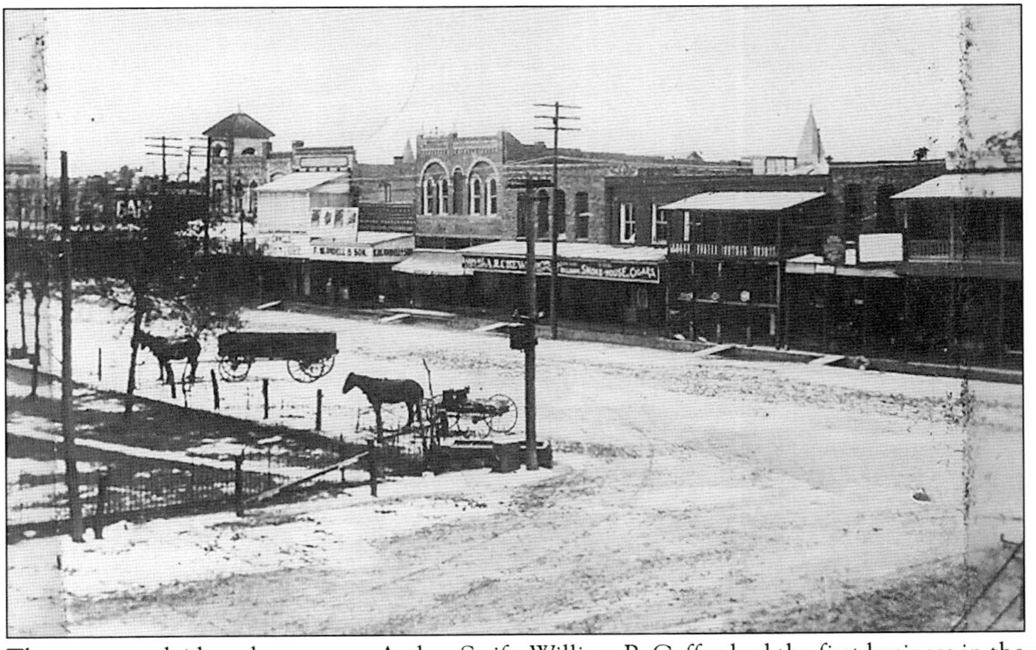

The town was laid out by surveyor Arthur Swift. William B. Coffee had the first business in the area in 1848; it was on what was to be named Main Street on the south side of the square. The crude Plum Creek Post Office, operated east of town on postmaster Isham Good's property, was closed, and a new one opened in town with James Daugherty as postmaster. This early photograph, believed to be taken around 1900, shows Main Street on the square full with shops and a bank as well as the corner of the courthouse lawn with a fence and hitching posts. What is unusual about this image? There is snow on the ground. (Courtesy of the CCHC.)

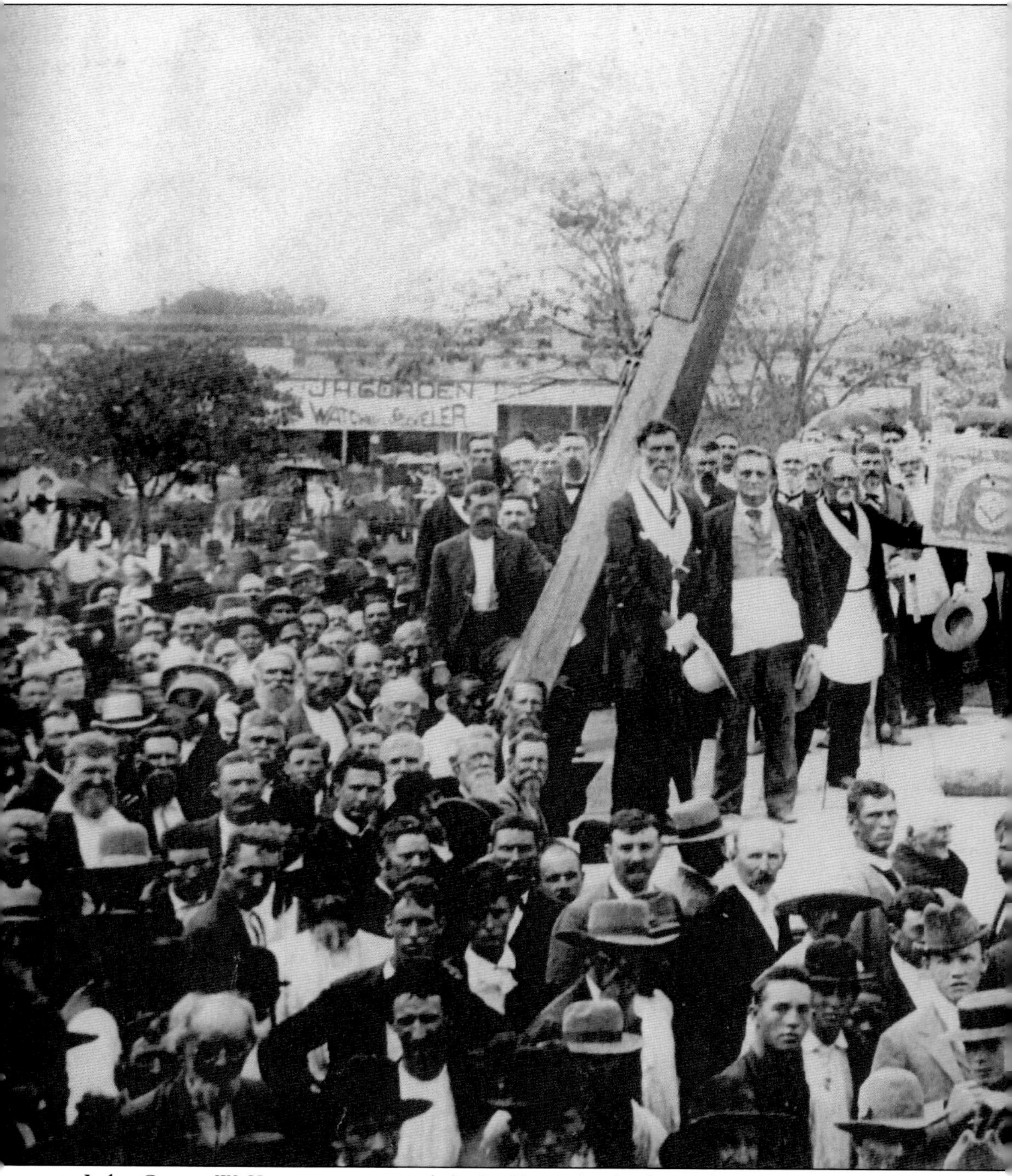

Judge George W. Kyser commissioned the building of a third courthouse in March 1892. The historic event was recorded in this image showing the laying of the cornerstone on August 15, 1893. Conducting the ceremony was Lockhart Masonic Lodge No. 690 grand master John Orchard and deputy grand master W.W. Carpenter. County commissioners J.H. Jolley, First Precinct; R.A. Tiller, Second Precinct; C.R. Smith, Third Precinct; and G.A. McGee (author's great-grandfather),

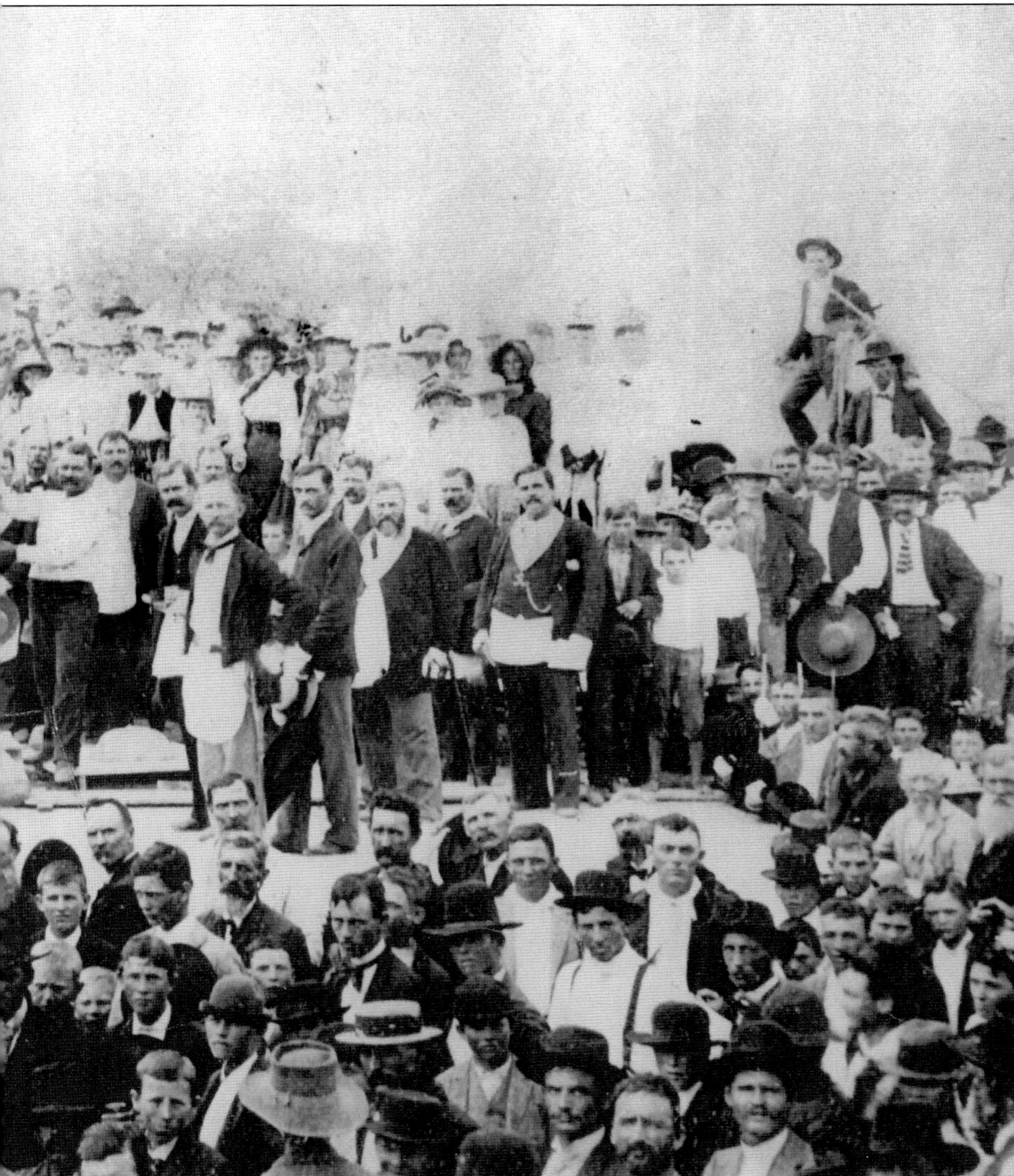

Fourth Precinct were all present. To fund the new building, the county commission sold the old building to Masur Brothers for $151, sold $54,350 in six-percent bonds, and levied a 20¢ per $100 valuation on property. During the construction, commissioners' court was held in the old Thompson Building. (Courtesy of Gerry and Conrad Ohlendorf.)

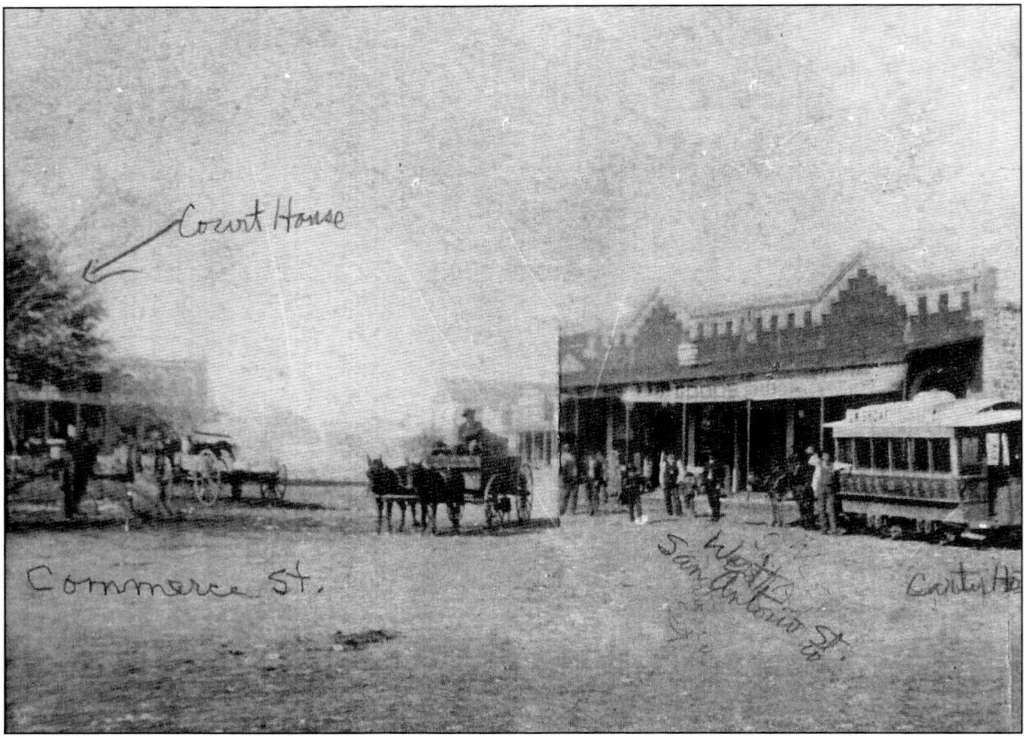

This historical image, taken in 1901, has seen a lot of wear and tear. Someone has written on it noting the courthouse location on the left side, today's Commerce Street in the foreground, San Antonio Street, and the Carter Hotel to the right corner. The mule-drawn trolley was operated by Jonathan Nix and ran to and from both depots. (Courtesy of the Eugene Clark Library.)

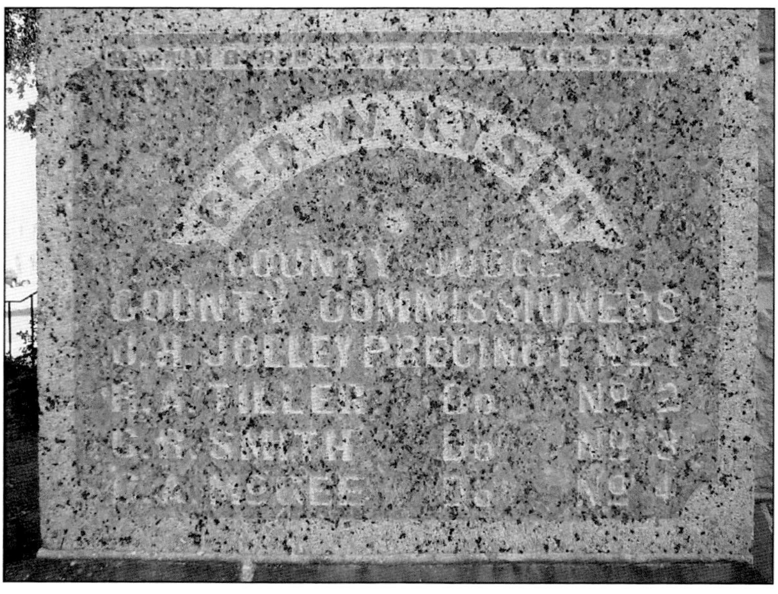

The cornerstone of the Caldwell County Courthouse, ceremoniously laid in 1893, is of Texas Hill Country Burnet red granite. Reports estimate a huge crowd gathered for the event and that between 3,000 and 5,000 enjoyed a barbecue afterwards at the Storey pasture north of town. (Courtesy of Ronda A. Reagan.)

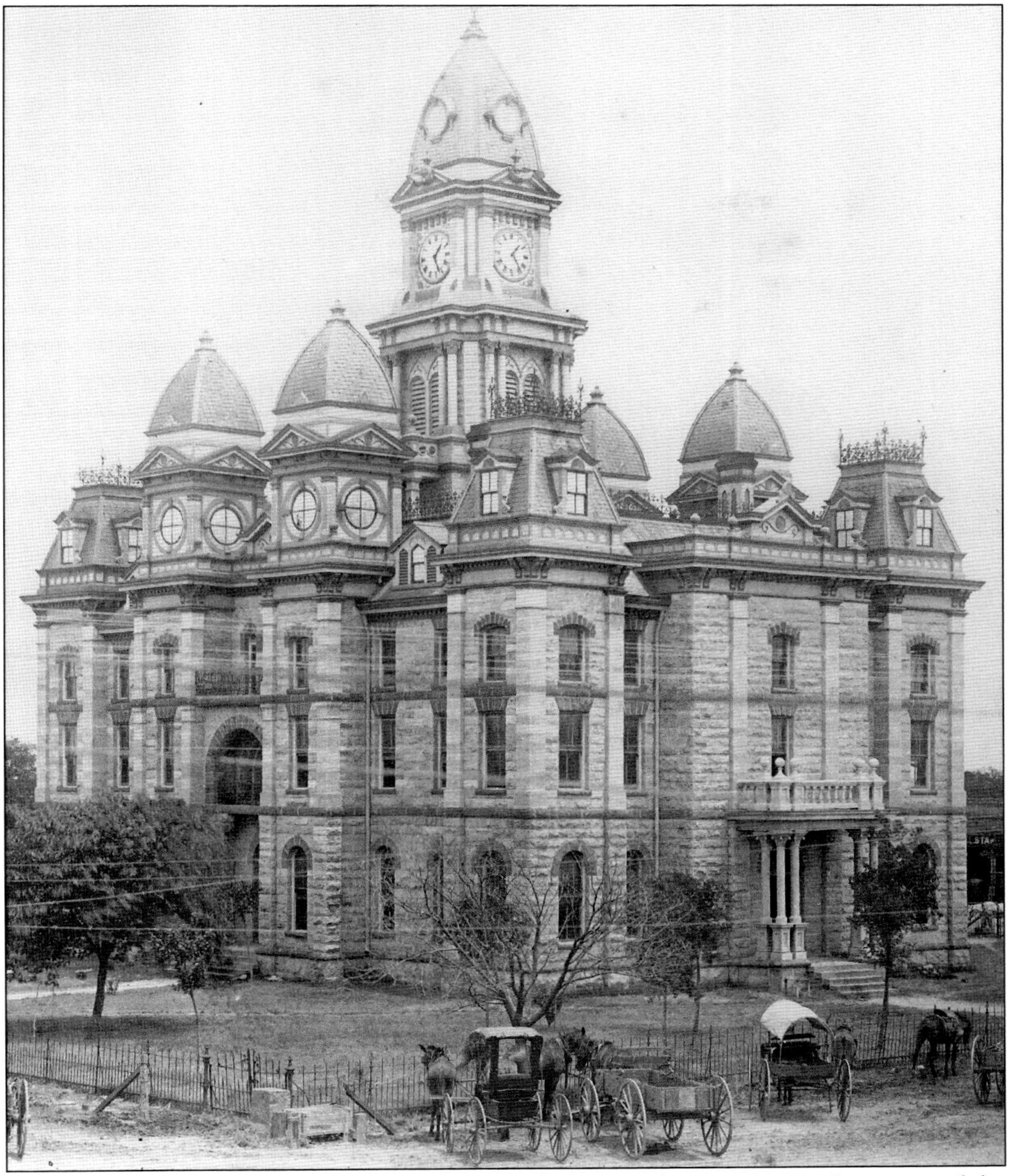

Since 1848, Caldwell County has had three courthouses on the same site in the center of the public square. The most spectacular courthouse is the last and current one, shown here in the days of horse-drawn carriages, buggies, and wagons. Note there is a black dog under the wagon. On July 15, 1924, the "biggest thing that ever happened in Lockhart" occurred. The city had wanted to remove the hitching racks in town to make way for automobiles; however, the farmers disagreed. So, in the middle of the night, someone sawed them off to the ground. This caused a major uprising between the farmers and ranchers who could no longer hitch their teams in town and the owners of automobiles who wanted the parking spaces. Records show there were approximately 5,000 cars in the county and six automobile dealers. The wrought iron fence that surrounded the second and the third courthouse, as shown here, was also removed shortly after that event. (Nora Lee Magee Collection, courtesy of Dianne Stevenson.)

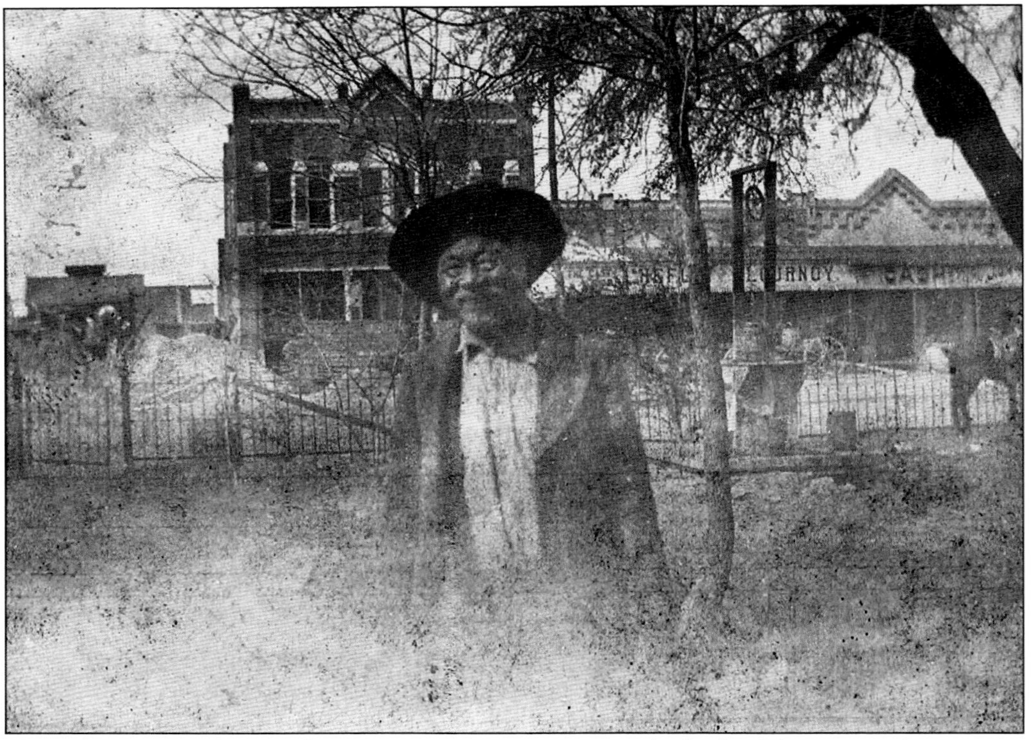

"Courthouse custodian" with no name given is written on the back of this image. A two-story building erected in 1898 is seen in the background on the east side of the square. After the wrought iron fence's removal was ordered, Joseph Masur put 200 feet of it around his Victorian house at the corner of Pecan and Blanco Streets, where it remains today. He reportedly gave half of the fence to his contemporary, Andrew Brock, who placed the balance of it around his new home, a Louisiana Lowcountry style, on 200 acres along Boggy Creek Road west of town. Looking northwest, this postcard shows the streets are still dirt, and the mode of transportation is by horse-drawn wagons and buggies. (Above, Nora Lee Magee Collection, courtesy of Dianne Stevenson; below, courtesy of Ronda A. Reagan.)

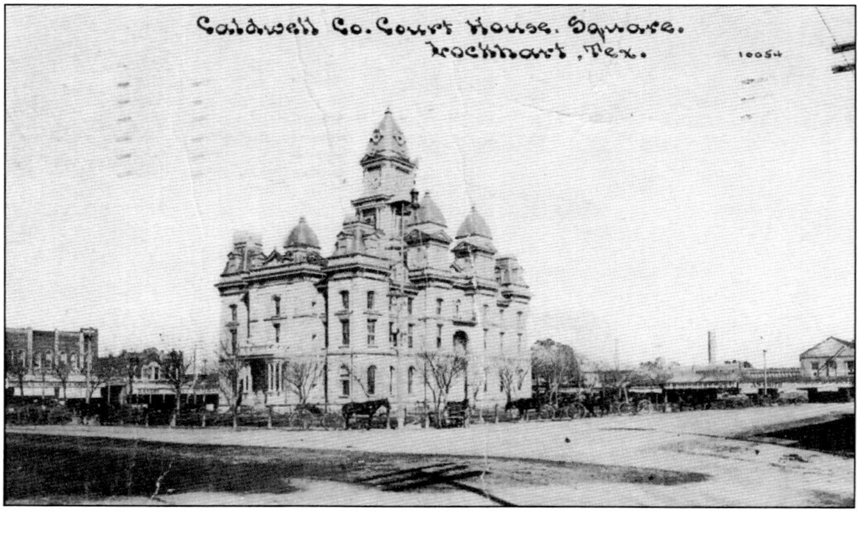

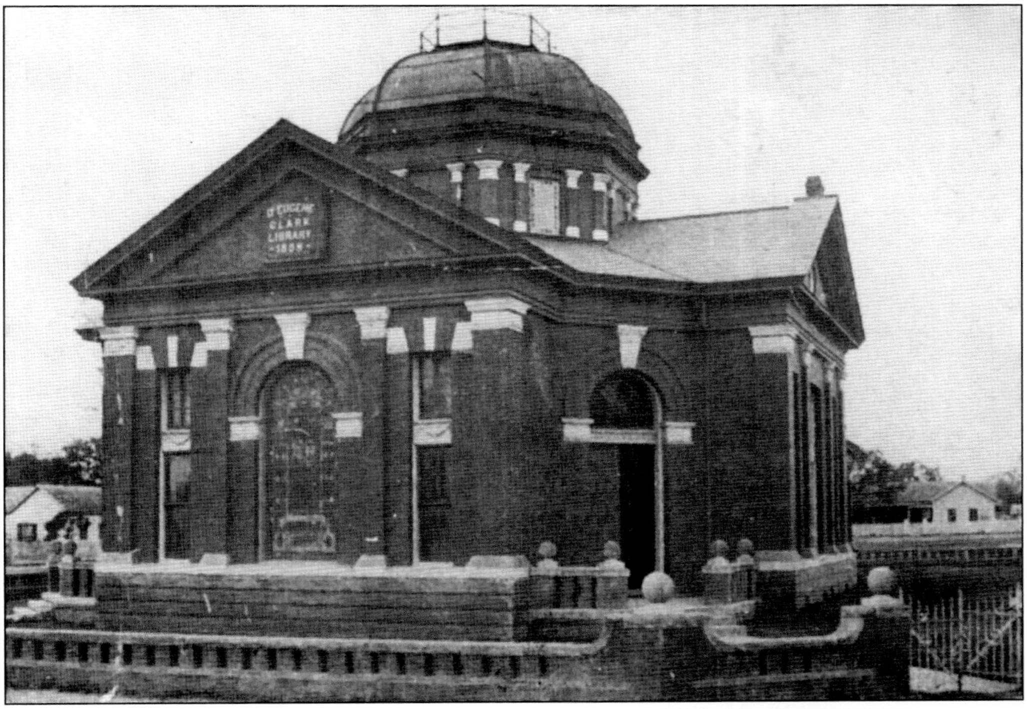

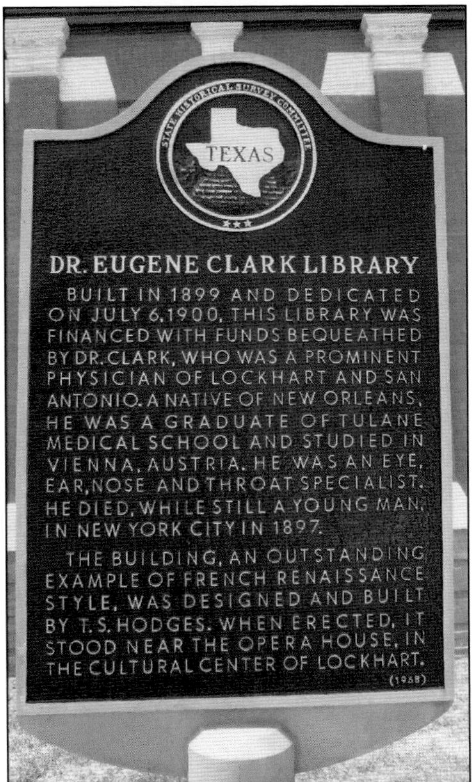

Dr. Eugene Clark Library, located at 217 South Main Street, is the oldest continually run library in the state. Clark, who practiced medicine for 13 years in Lockhart, bequeathed $10,000 in 1897 to Lockhart for a library and lyceum—$6,000 for construction and $1,000 for books. The remainder was placed into a trust for new books and maintenance. Completed in 1899 as designed by architect Thomas Hodges, the two-story library is a Classical Greek Revival modeled after the famed Villa Rotunda in Vicenza, Italy. The redbrick facade with limestone trim has four projecting pediment pavilions. Pilasters and a round keystone arch classically frame a central stained glass memorial window. When built, it originally had auditorium-style seating in the center and on the balcony and was the cultural center for the city. Pres. William Howard Taft spoke from the stage. Today, this historical treasure is a source of beauty and curiosity to visitors in general as well as architects from near and far. (Above, courtesy of Gerry and Conrad Ohlendorf; right, courtesy of Ronda A. Reagan.)

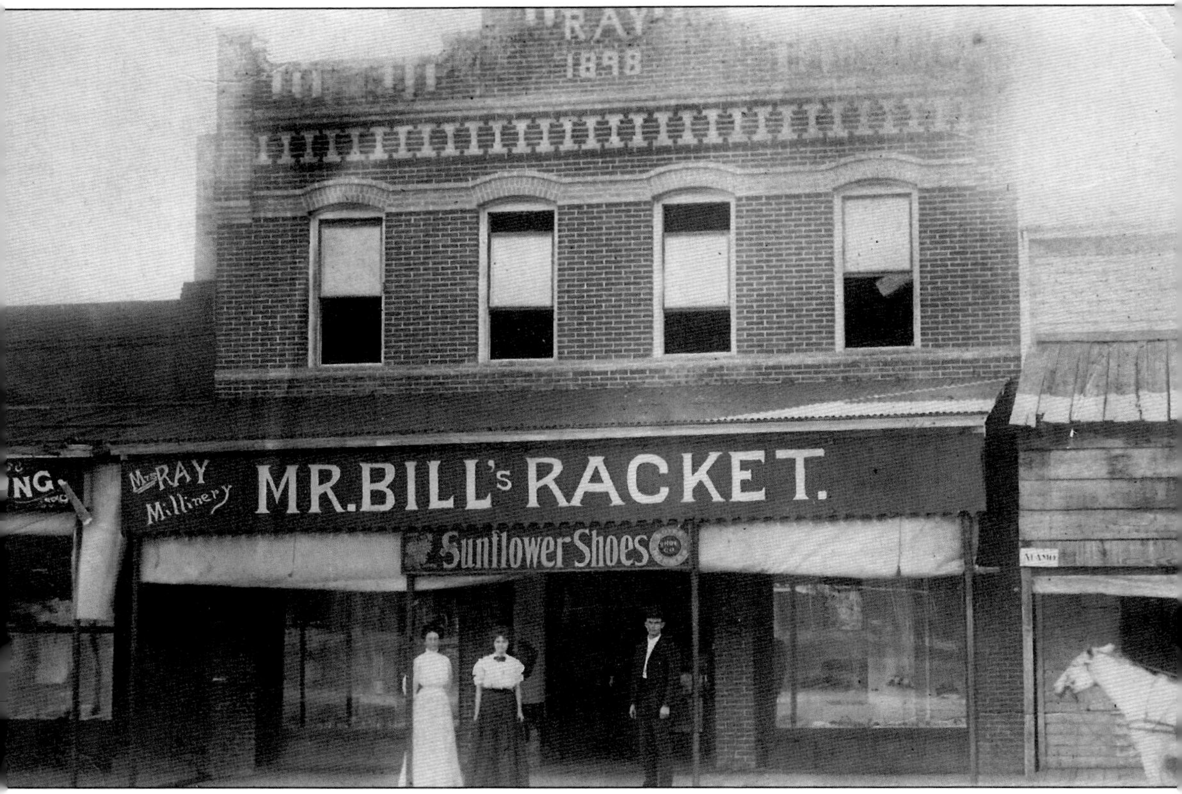

The Ray Building at 104 South Commerce Street was built in 1898 when the street was Gonzales Road. Constructed of red and cream bricks by Birkner Builders, it was designed as a dry goods and millinery store for W.M. Ray and Mattie J. Ray. The people in the picture are unidentified, but likely the Rays are seen standing under Mr. Bill's Racket and Sunflower Shoes signs. To the left corner is Mattie Ray's Millinery. Their clothing is indicative of the late 1800s to the early 1900s. In 1918, Mattie Ray, now a widow, sold the store to Dave M. Wolff who renovated the building into an elegant ladies' wear emporium. The Wolff family owned the building until 1961. The building has also housed a bakery, an automobile parts store, and family clothing store. The current owner has altered the first-floor facade from the original storefront windows. (Courtesy of Gerry and Conrad Ohlendorf.)

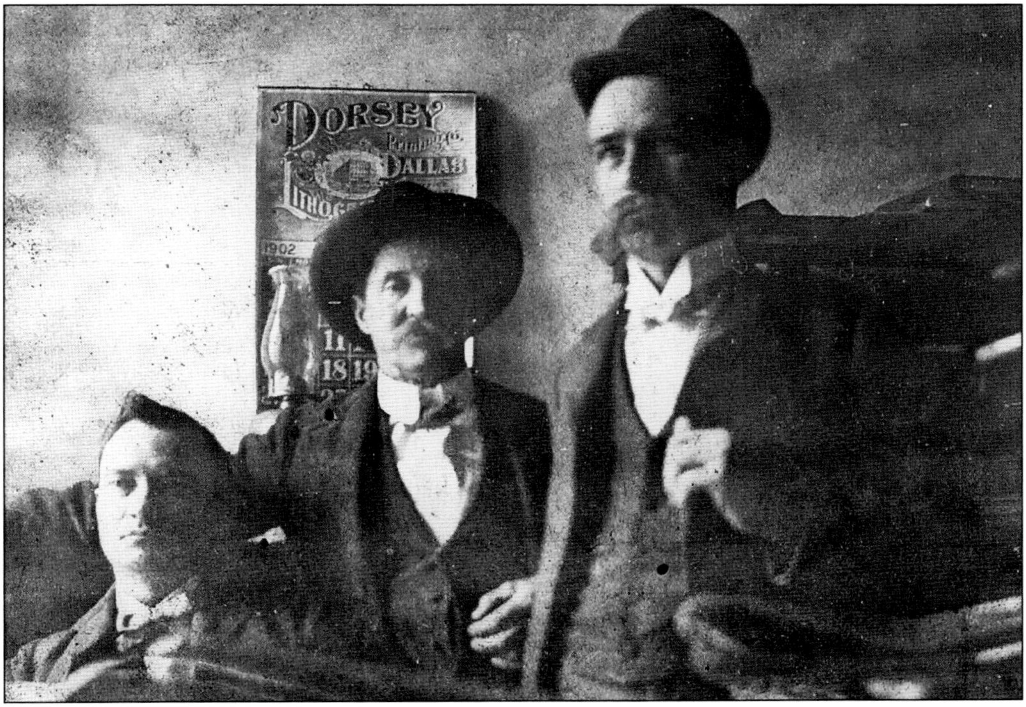

In this photograph, the calendar on the wall is from 1902. From left to right are Lex Magee, Caldwell County tax collector Joseph "Joe" Magee, and Deputy Ell Roy McClain. Joe served as county tax collector from 1882 until his death in 1910. (Nora Lee Magee Collection, courtesy of Dianne Stevenson.)

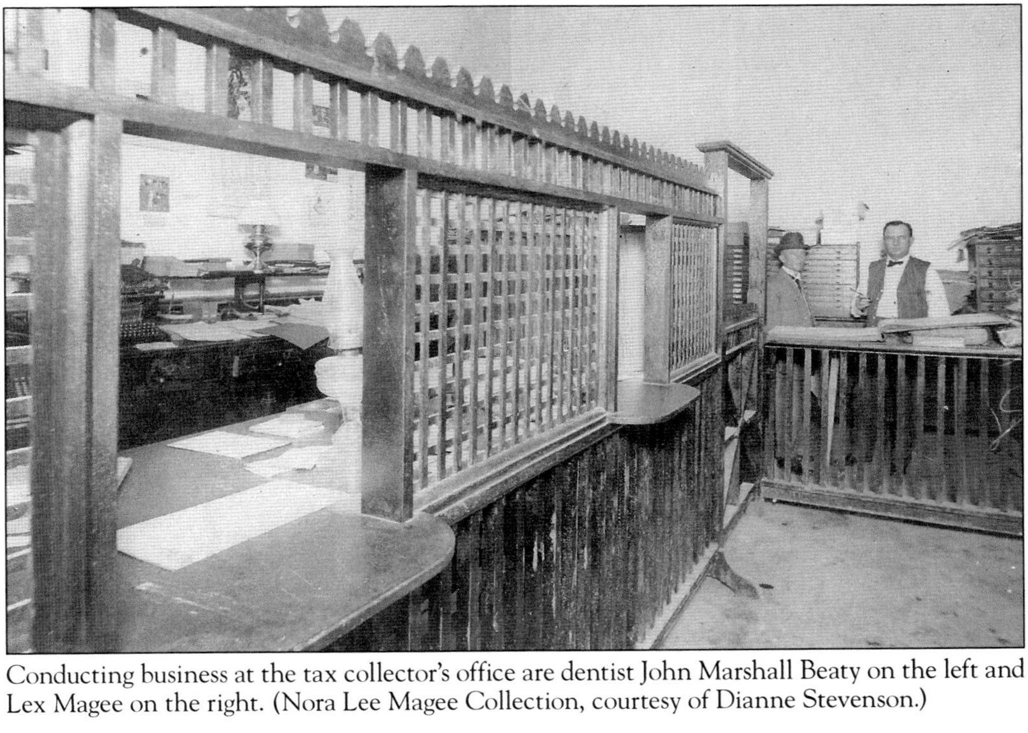

Conducting business at the tax collector's office are dentist John Marshall Beaty on the left and Lex Magee on the right. (Nora Lee Magee Collection, courtesy of Dianne Stevenson.)

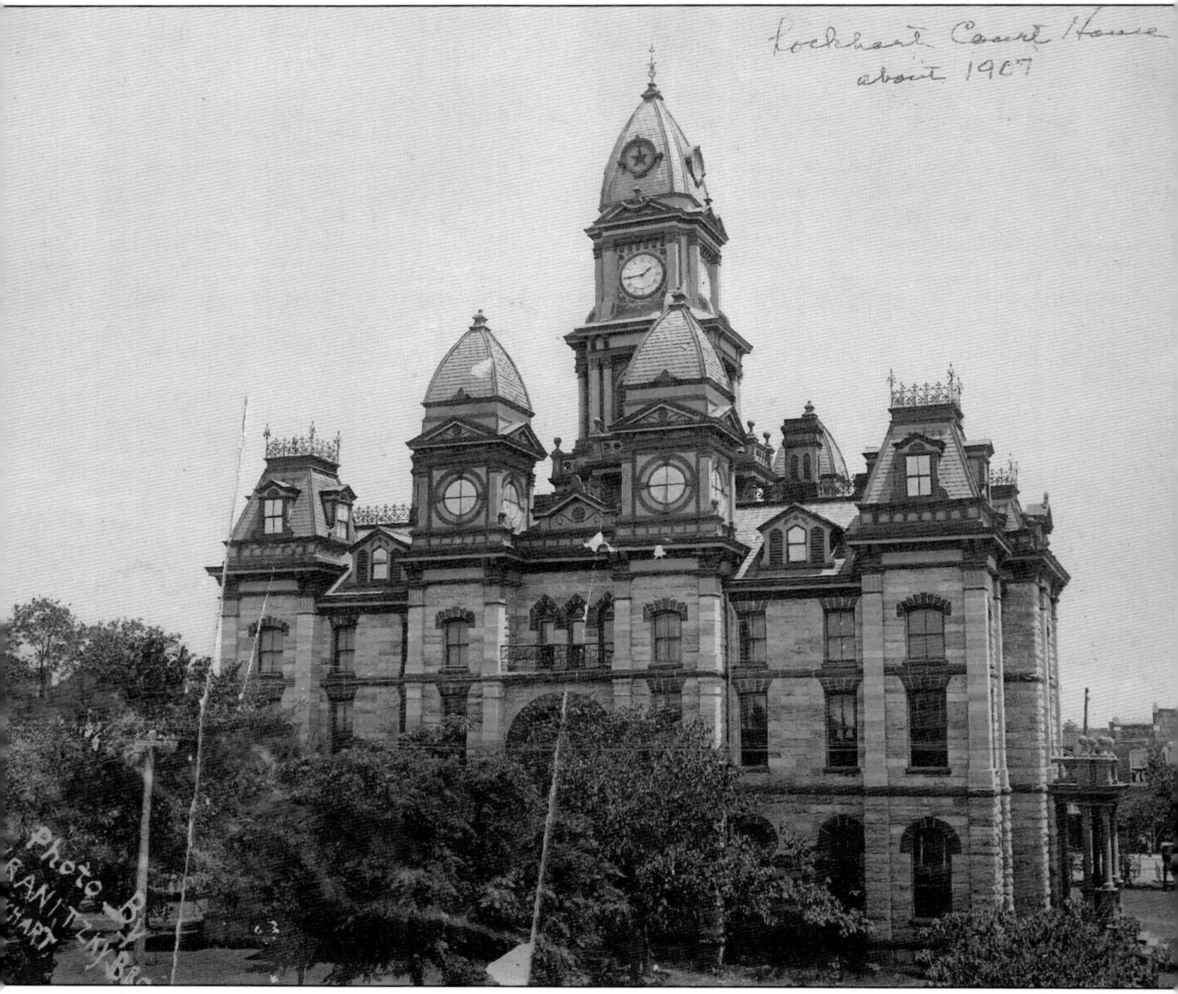

The prolific professional photographers of Lockhart, the Wranitzky Bros., took this beautiful picture of the Caldwell County Courthouse from a second-floor window of their studio on San Antonio Street precisely at 1:45 p.m.—according to the Seth Thomas model No. 16 clock—in 1907. Other than the fact the courthouse was the largest building in Lockhart at the time of its construction, its cornerstone is known to contain a Bible, four newspapers of the county, coins, and other relics. (Courtesy of Gerry and Conrad Ohlendorf.)

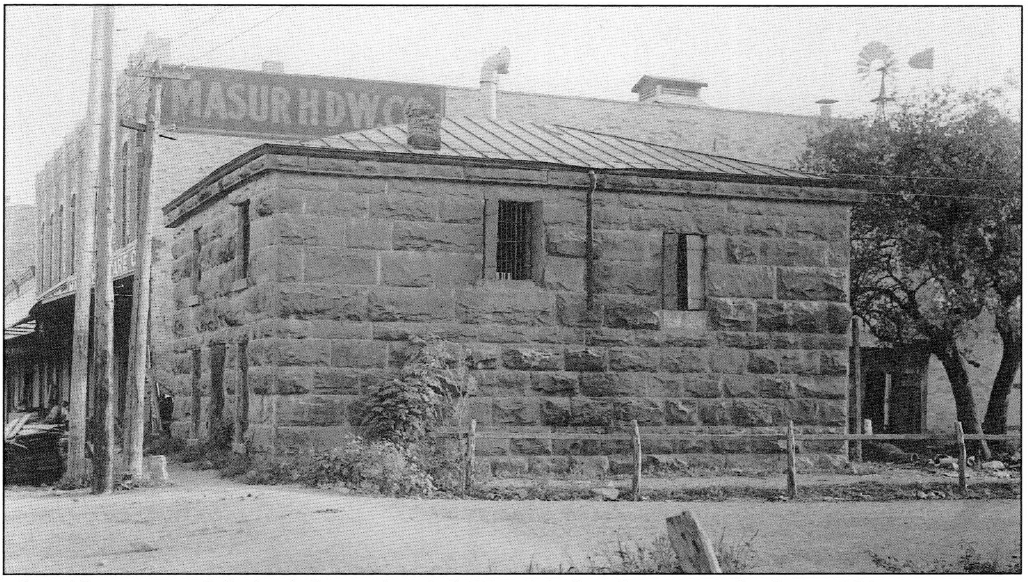

The old county jail (below), located at 315 West Market Street, was built in 1908 at a contract price of $22,480. It is the third jail for Caldwell County. The first one was a log building that burned down in 1858. Prisoners were housed temporarily in the basement of the courthouse, until the second limestone jail (above) was completed in 1873 near the corner of Main and Walnut Streets. But it was soon outdated and deemed too small. Ed Masur purchased the old jail at public auction for $3,502. He dismantled it, recycling the materials to build his hardware store. The jail pictured in the postcard below was used as late as December 1982. The jailer's quarters are on the first floor, and 15 cells of concrete and steel are on the upper floors, including one cell in the center tower. Today, it is the county museum and is a recorded Texas Historic Landmark. (Above, courtesy of the Lockhart Chamber of Commerce; below, courtesy of Ronda A. Reagan.)

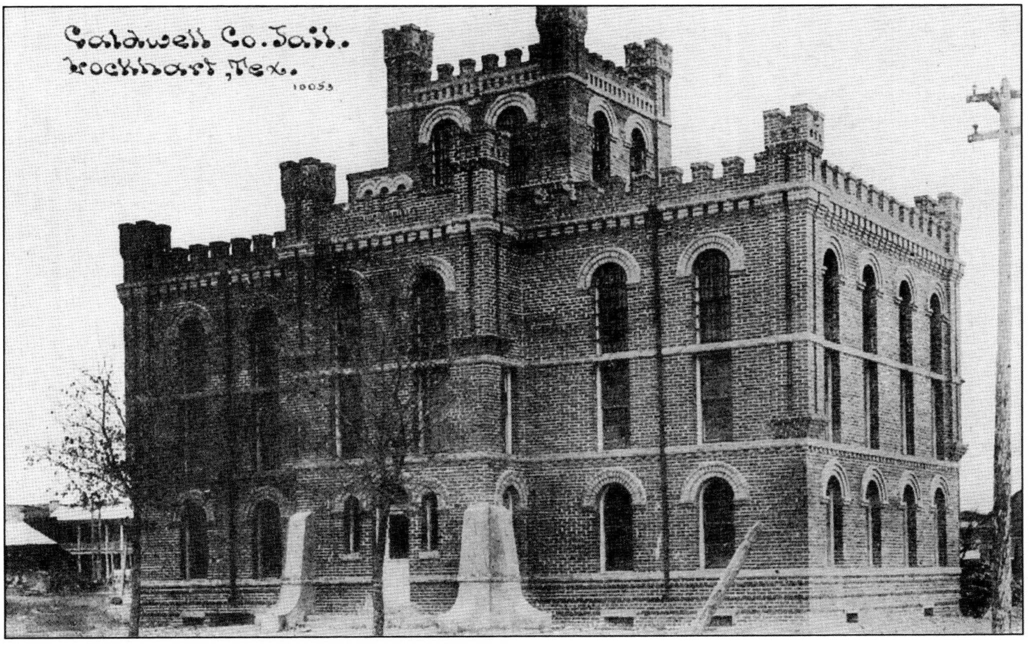

Controversy raged over building this third courthouse. Many thought that $54,350 estimated cost would be a tax burden. However, when the bids came in, Judge George W. Kyser cast the deciding vote to build it and further stated that all the labor and the materials should be first class. Shortly after, the judge got the first water bill after the broom closets were converted to restrooms. Records show that he thought the bill was so high that he ordered them pad-locked.

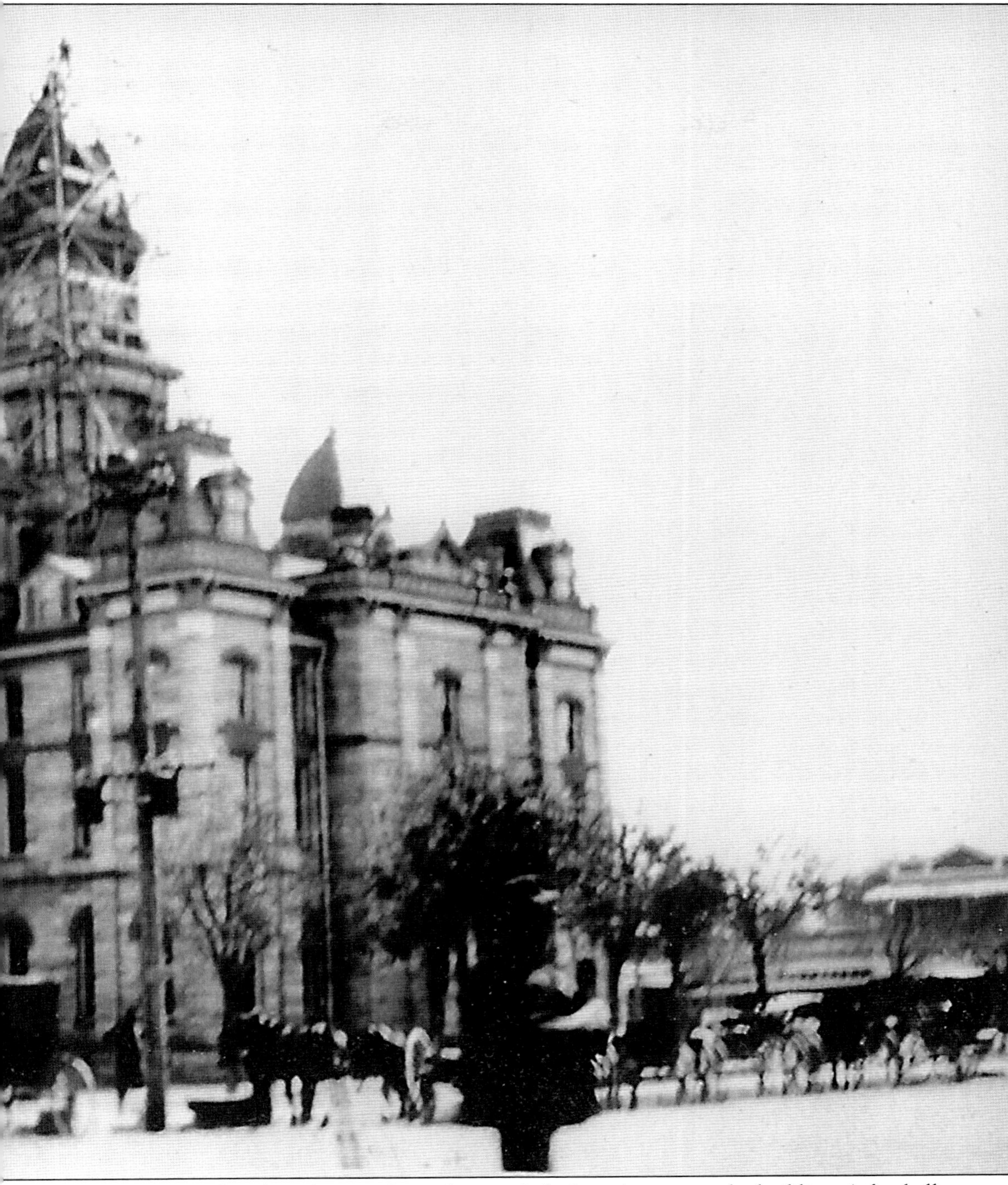

A windmill was placed on the courthouse lawn to help furnish water to the building. A fire bell tower stood on the southwest corner. Today, it is atop the fire station. In this image, horses are tied to a heavy chain that ran between cedar posts around the courthouse's wrought iron fence. (Courtesy of the Eugene Clark Library.)

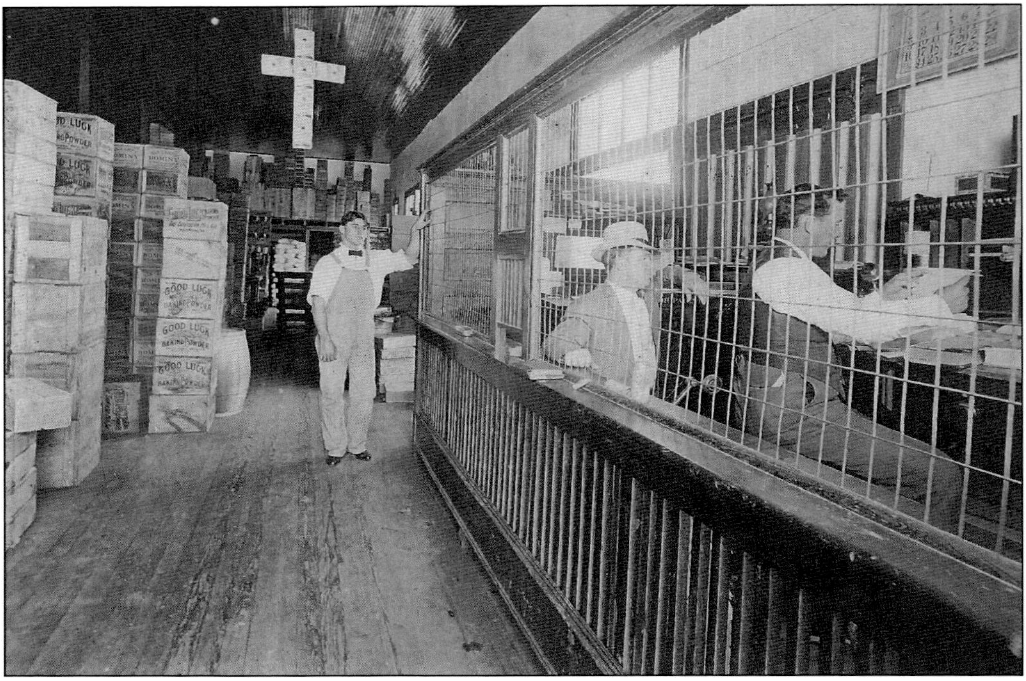

Conducting business as usual is warehouse employee Clyde Smith (left), while Jim Shinn (center) and Ed Shinn run the office from the desk. First cousins Jim and Ed owned and operated this wholesale grocery supply warehouse. Crate boxes of Good Luck Baking Powder and Hominy are stacked on the left. Below is a receipt from Shinn Grocery Company dated February 16, 1923. (Above, Nora Lee Magee Collection, courtesy of Dianne Stevenson; below, courtesy of Ronda A. Reagan.)

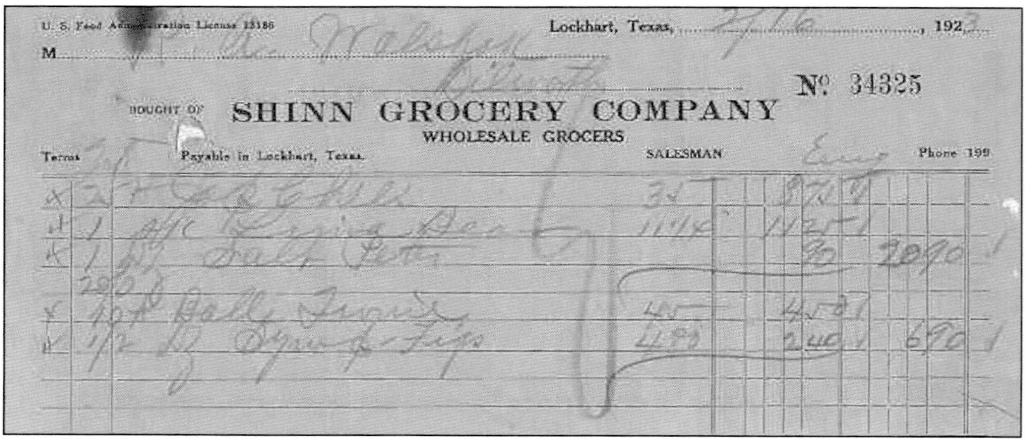

U. S. Food Administration License 13186 Lockhart, Texas, ... 192

M........

No. 34325

BOUGHT OF SHINN GROCERY COMPANY

WHOLESALE GROCERS

Terms .... Payable in Lockhart, Texas. SALESMAN .... Phone 199

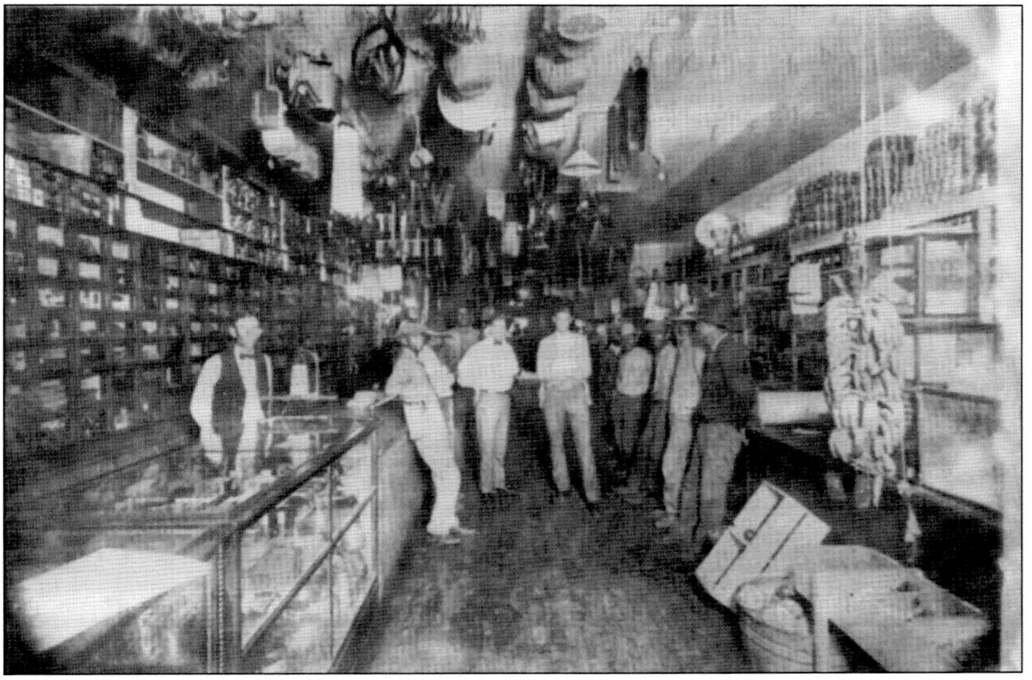

Inside Martin McDowell Hardware and Grocery Store is a group of about a dozen men. New hats are hanging from the ceiling, and the shelving goes from the ground up. The photograph below is in Emmel's Drugstore. Doctor Hardy is far left and Bill Lambe is third from the left. Others are unidentified. (Both, courtesy of the CCHC.)

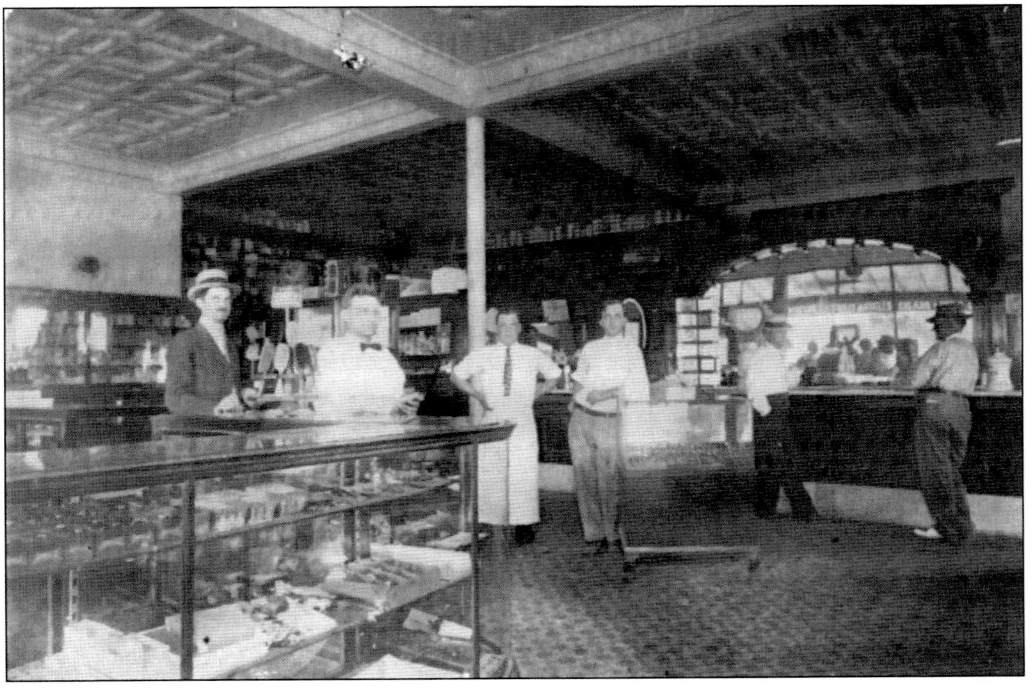

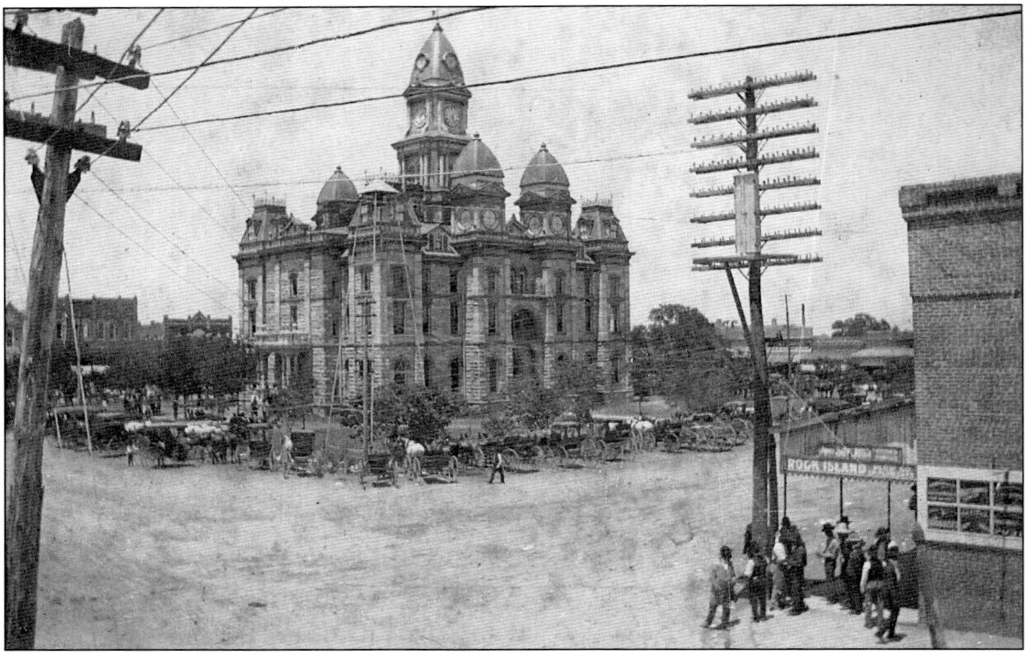

Progress comes to the town center with the introduction of telephone and electrical lines. The streets are still not paved, but cars are parked along the courthouse instead of horse-drawn vehicles. This photograph is taken looking southeast. The building on the right corner still stands today and is a law office. Rock Island is written on the awning. (Courtesy of Gerry and Conrad Ohlendorf.)

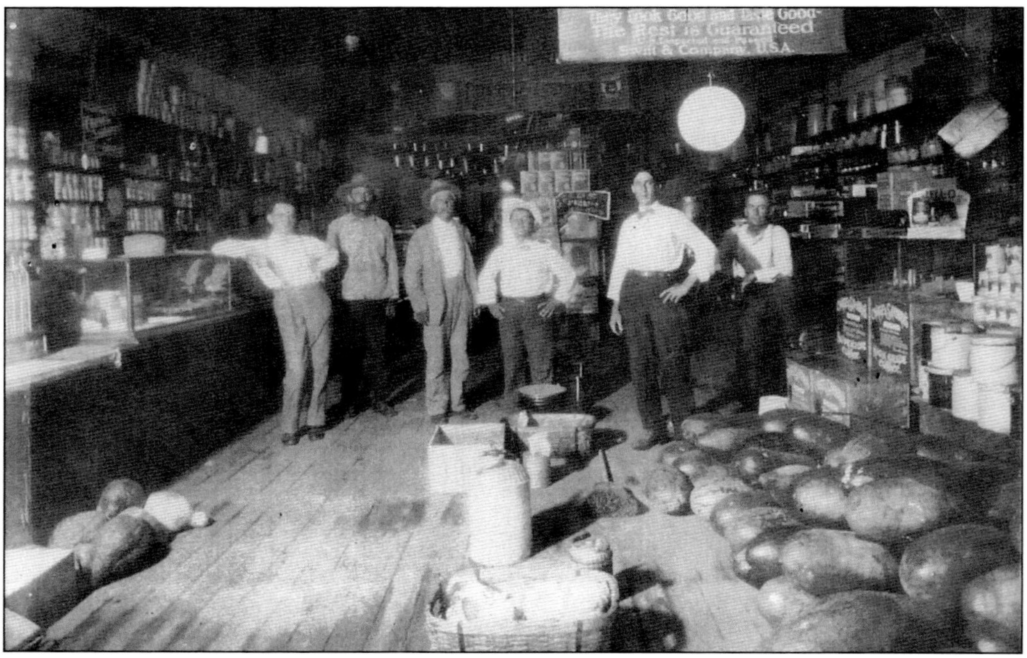
Inside A.W. Smith's Grocery in 1906 are six gentlemen. Watermelons are stacked on the floor to the right. The location was at 116 South Commerce Street. This building was later Glosserman's clothing store. (Courtesy of the Eugene Clark Library.)

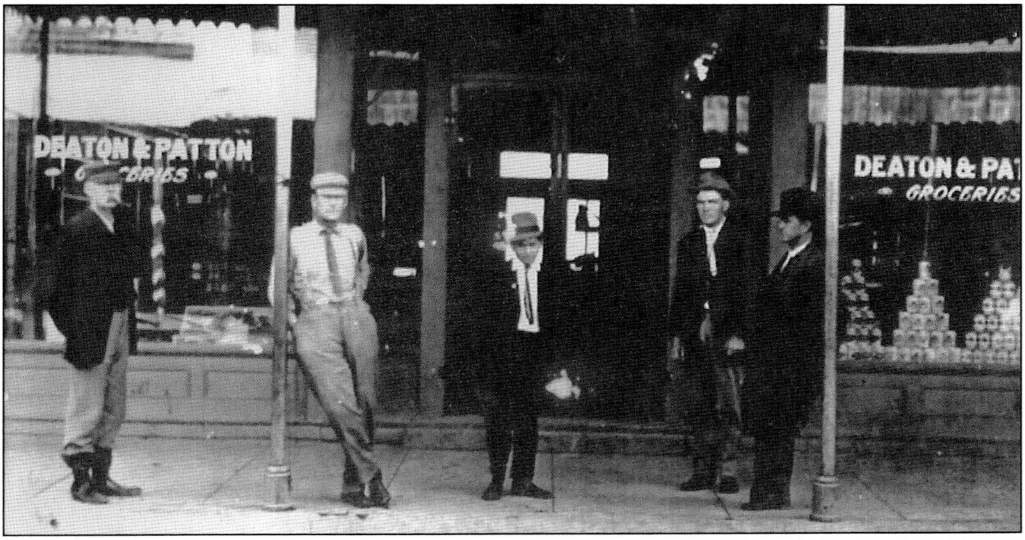

Gathered in front of Deaton & Patton Grocery store in 1908, are, from left to right, Charlie Kreuz, founder of Kreuz' meat market and barbecue; Warren Patton; Will Deaton; and two Kreuz brothers, believed to be Charlie Kreuz Jr. and Alvin Mollie Kreuz. This grocery store location was next door to the former Kreuz Market, now Smitty's Market on South Commerce Street, one block off the east side of the square. In 1907, three of Charlie Kreuz's sons, William (Willie), Theodore (Teddy), and Alvin (Mr. Mollie), purchased the market from their father. (Courtesy Eugene Clark Library.)

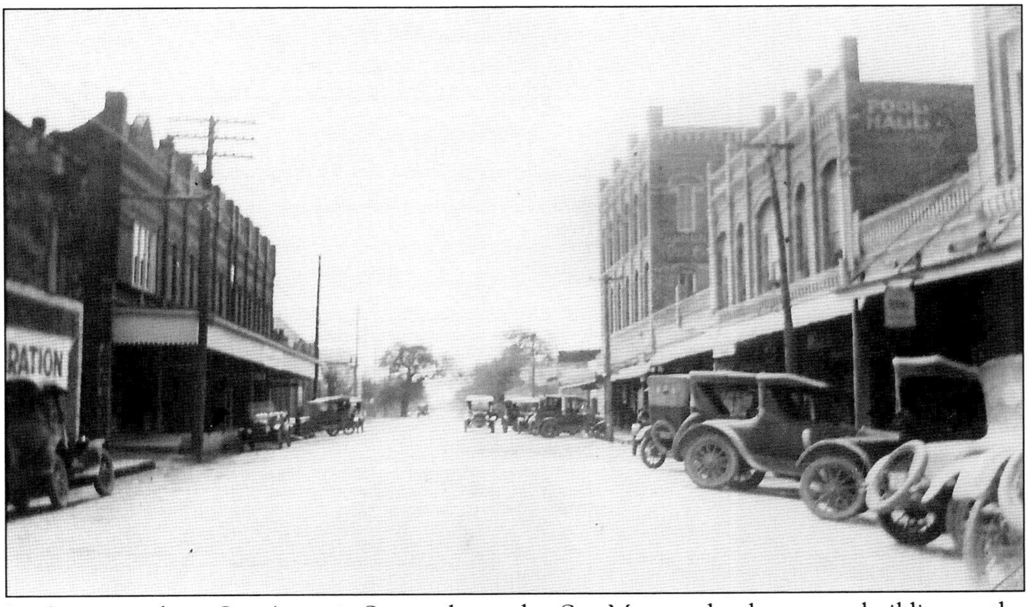

Looking west down San Antonio Street, the road to San Marcos, the three-story building on the right is the Masur Brothers Hardware Building, erected in 1908 with a full basement and more than 19,000 square feet. The building stands today along with the others on the north side of the street (right), but the Vogel Building on the left with the awning no longer exists. Today, it is drive-through bank. (Courtesy of Gerry and Conrad Ohlendorf.)

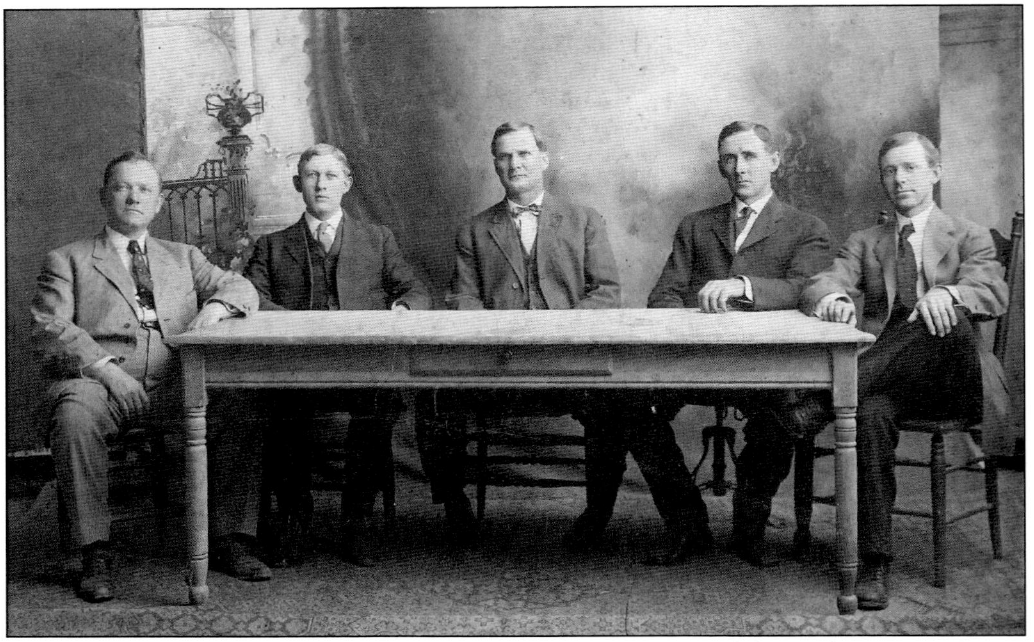

The mayor and council members pose for the Wranitzky Bros. From left to right are A.E. Carter, alderman; J.P. Cardwell, mayor (1912–1914); W.P. Swearingen, alderman; R.A. Beaty, alderman; and Sam Smith, alderman. (Courtesy of the CCHC.)

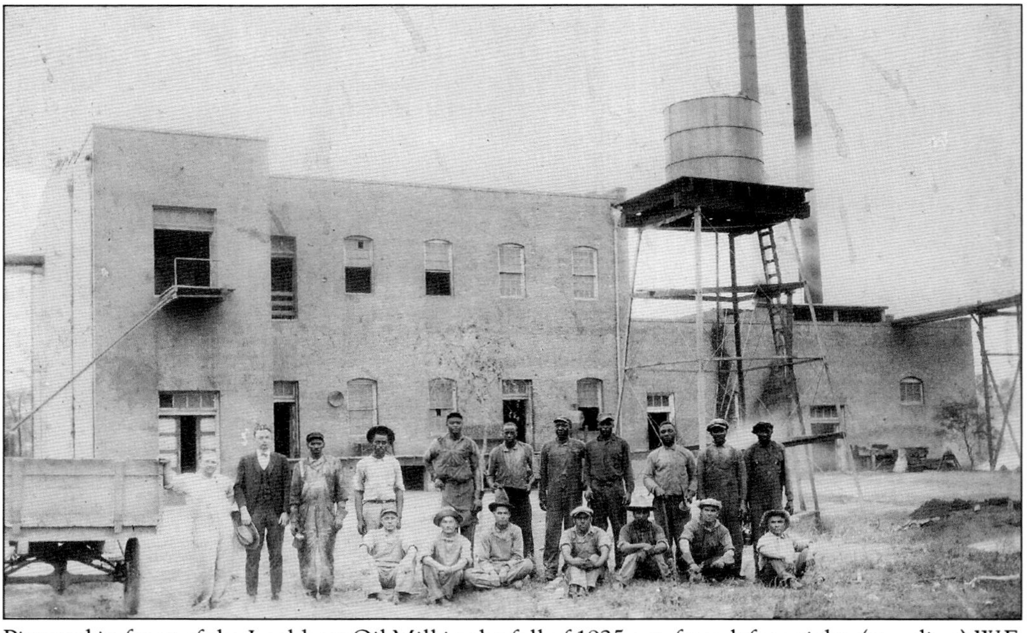

Pictured in front of the Lockhart Oil Mill in the fall of 1925 are, from left to right, (standing) W.F. Morgan, superintendent; L.C. Stokes, bookkeeper; Maynard Gray, fireman; George Sapp; Ben Greenwood; Allie Jones; Tom Jackson; Jessie Green; Willie "Smokie" Greer; McKinley Edwards; and A.J. Warren; (sitting) Elias Flores; Dionisio Hernandez; three unidentified men; Antonio "Pete" Gonzales; and Raphael "Roof" Vasquez. (Courtesy of the CCHC.)

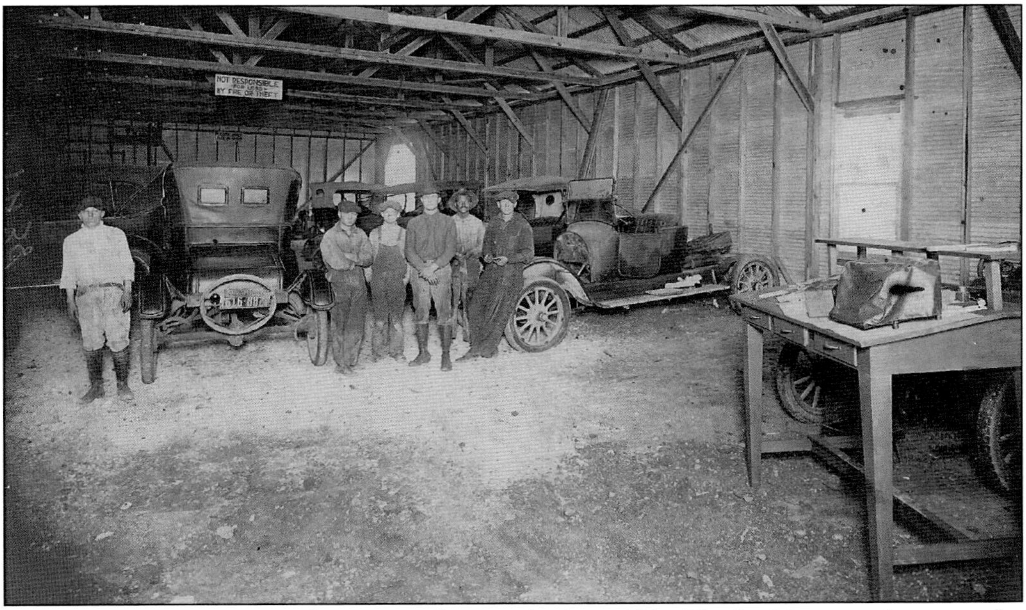

This was Ferd Schaarschmidt's Repair Shop in the late 1920s. The building stood next to the county jail, which is now a museum, on East Market Street. Standing next to the car on the right side is Rudolph Schaarschmidt, and on the left is Hilmer Scheh. (Courtesy of the CCHC.)

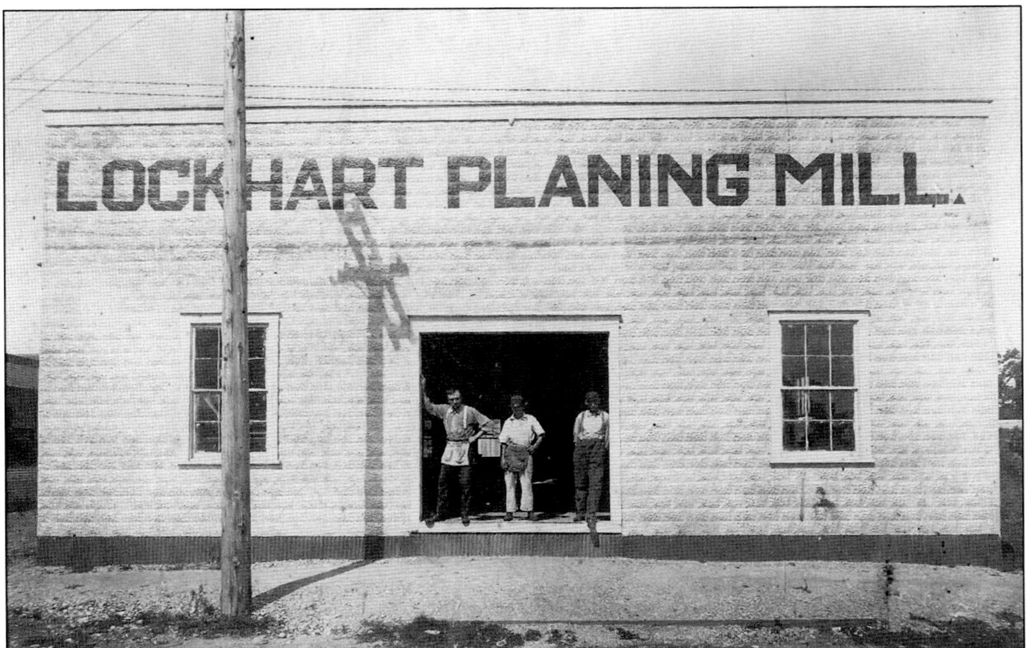

Lockhart Planing Mill helped to build the city, supplying good milled lumber. Three unidentified men pose for a picture in front of the building. Lumber mills began to spring up to support all the economic development of new businesses in the town. (Courtesy of Gerry and Conrad Ohlendorf.)

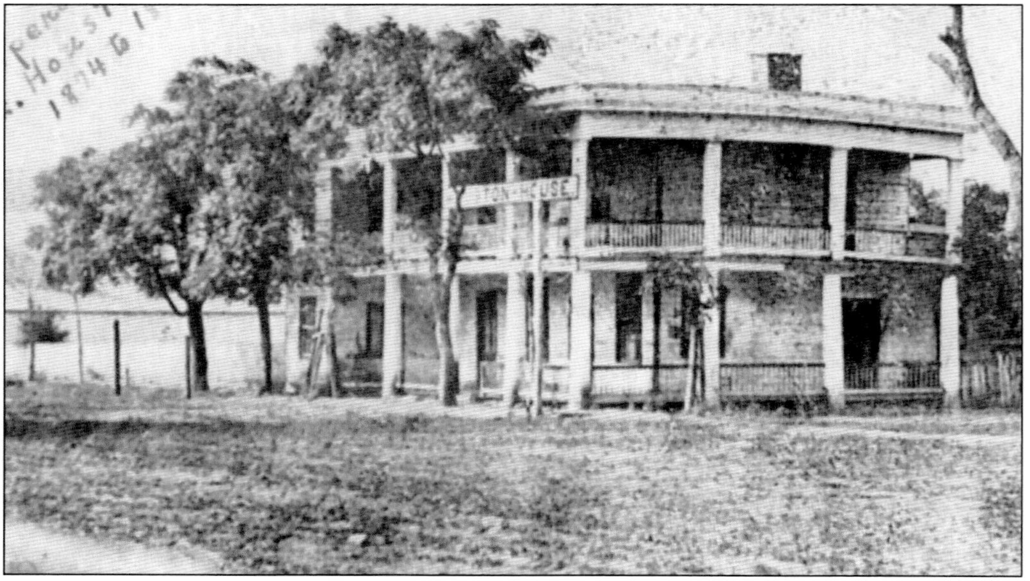

The Houston House Hotel was one of Lockhart's first hotels. It was originally three stories and stood on the northeast corner of the courthouse square near the San Antonio & Aransas Pass Railroad Depot. It was a grand hotel with wraparound verandas to catch the coastal breezes in the evening. But in 1879, a severe storm blew through Lockhart, inflicting major wind damage on the Houston House. It reopened as a two-story building. Lockhart had several other hotels, including the Connolly Hotel at 109 West Walnut; the Moon Hotel, which was later called the Tate Hotel, located where the Ford Motor Company is today; the Griesenbeck Hotel, which had its heyday in 1908, located near where city hall is now; and the Alhambra Hotel, which still stands inoperable across from the Central Fire Station on Market Street. (Courtesy of Gerry and Conrad Ohlendorf.)

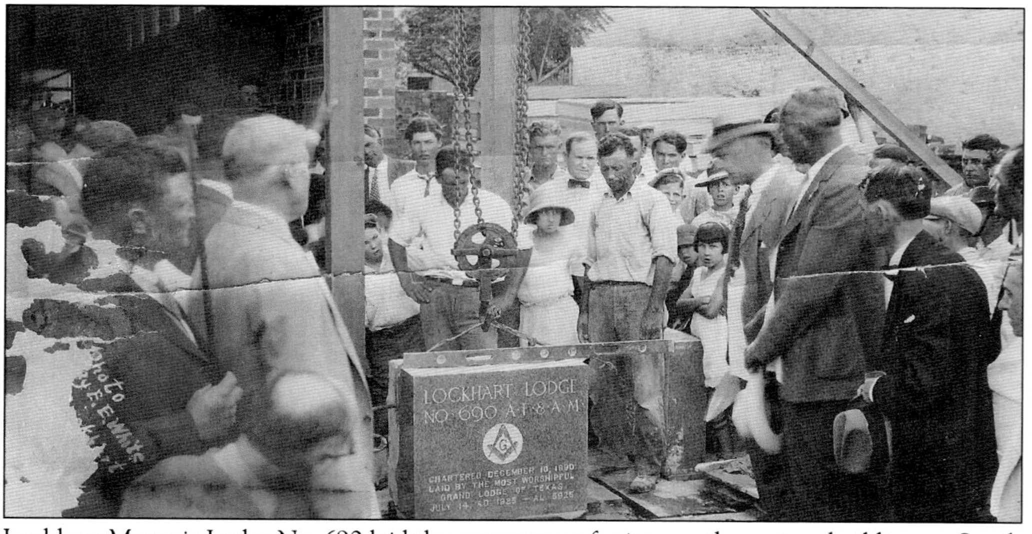

Lockhart Masonic Lodge No. 690 laid the cornerstone for its new three-story building on South Main Street, one block off the square, in 1926. Today, the city has purchased the building as an expansion to the Eugene Clark Library. Under renovation at the time of this publication, the third floor will house new city council chambers, while the library, which is already using the first floor, will also take over the second. (Courtesy of Gerry and Conrad Ohlendorf.)

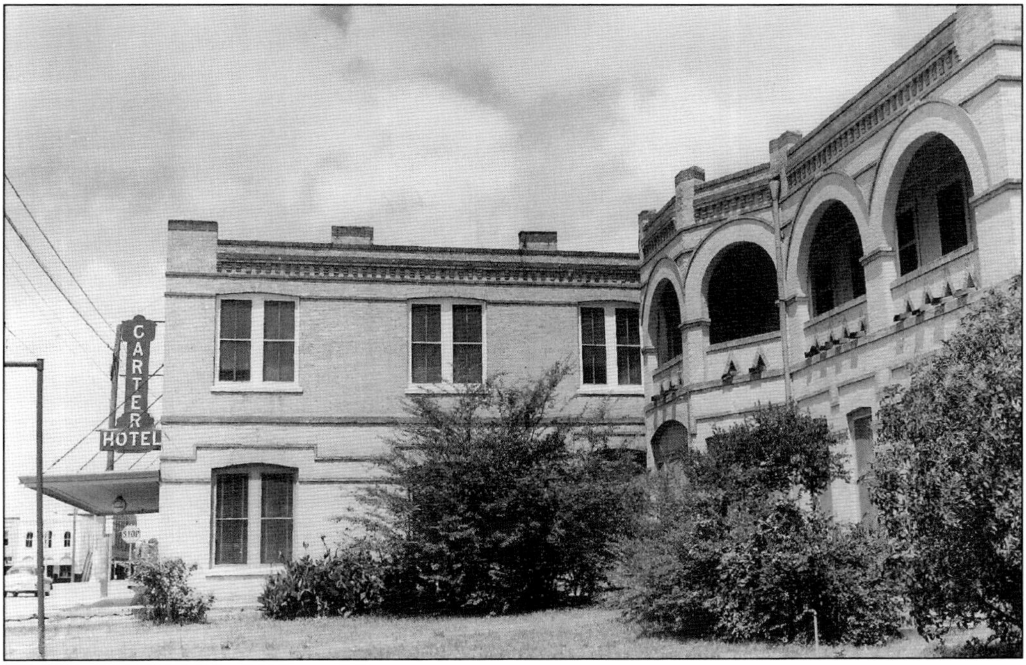

Margaret Carter erected the Carter Hotel in 1897 to replace the old wooden building, which had at one time been a "fine wooden three-story structure," with a new, brick, two-story one. Carter, born in England, came to America in 1877, settling first in nearby Luling. She asked her son-in-law architect Thomas Hodges from Gonzales to design her new hotel. Hodges built it in the Moorish style with five arches and a second-floor gallery. Being located only one block from the railroad depot made it popular for travelers. It also served as a cultural center of Lockhart. It stood on the northeast corner of the square at East San Antonio and Commerce Streets until it was torn down to make way for Lockhart Savings and Loan in 1960. Today, the justice center is housed in the former bank building. (Courtesy of the CCHC.)

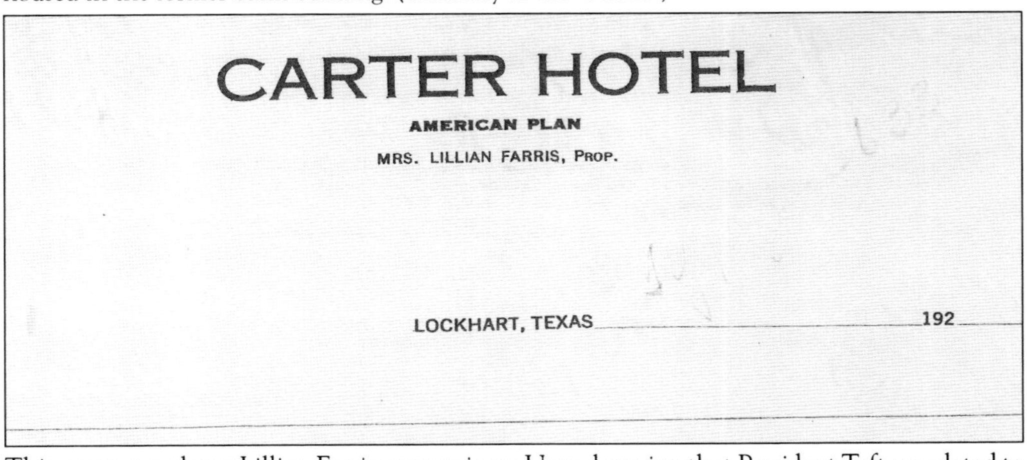

CARTER HOTEL

AMERICAN PLAN

MRS. LILLIAN FARRIS, PROP.

LOCKHART, TEXAS ______________ 192 ____

This notepaper shows Lillian Ferris as proprietor. Upon learning that President Taft was slated to speak at the Eugene Clark Library, Ferris prepared a beautiful meal of fine squabs for the former president, only to discover upon his arrival that he was a vegetarian. Roney R. Roberts provided transportation from the depot to hotels in the early 1900s with his team of horses pulling a fancy wagon. (Courtesy of Ronda A. Reagan.)

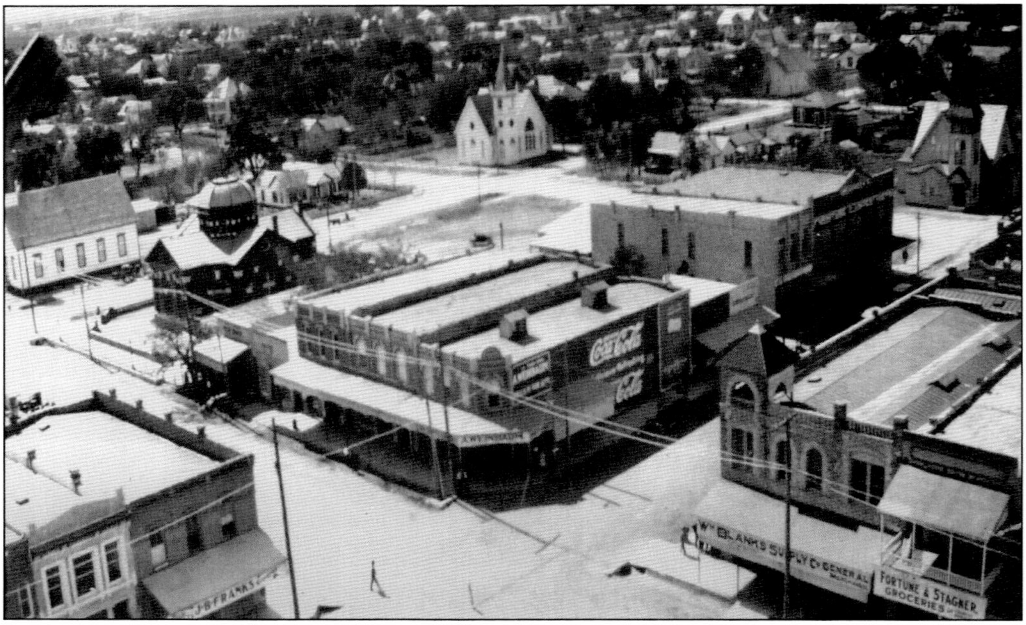

As seen from the courthouse vantage point in 1921, the following four bird's–eye views are of the four corners of the town square. Above is the southwest corner of Main and Market Streets. A Baptist church can be seen in the center background. One can also see the Eugene Clark Library. William M. Blanks's supply and general merchandise store is in the lower right corner. The J.R. Franks Building on the lower left is now the county tax office. (Courtesy of the Eugene Clark Library.)

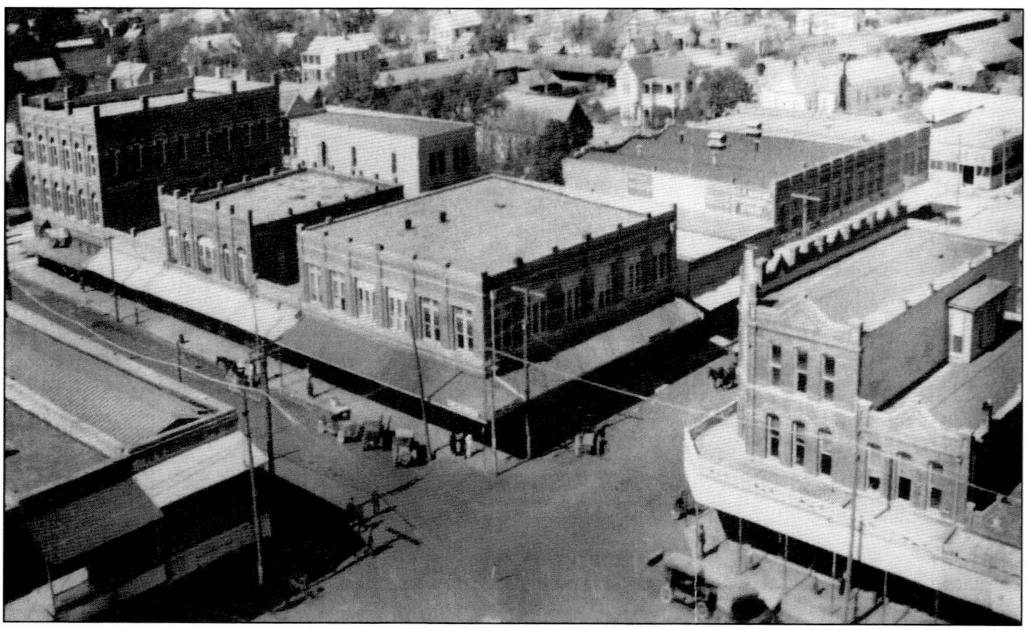

This view is of the northwest corner of the square with the current old Corner Drug Store Building, constructed in 1910, in the middle foreground. On the right corner is the three-story A.L. Brock Building, erected in 1898. Built in 1908, the three-story Masur Hardware Building is on the far left. Note all the awnings. (Courtesy of the Eugene Clark Library.)

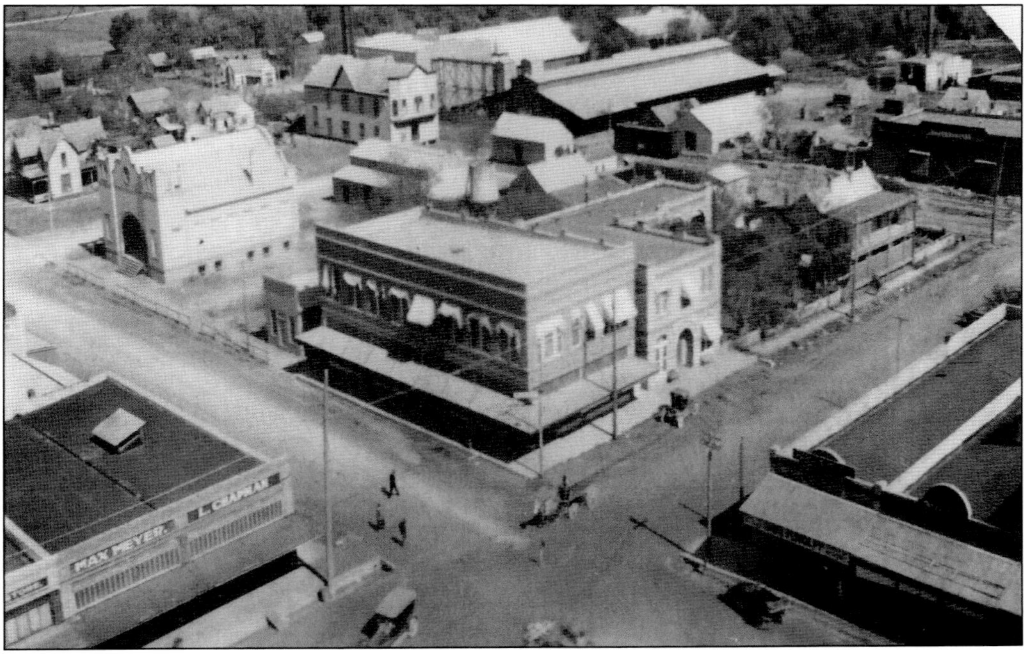

This is the northeast corner of the square. The Carter Hotel and its addition are in the center, and the Presbyterian church is to the left. Commerce Street is to the left, and San Antonio is to the right. The future site for Livengood Feed is at the center in the background. The Max Meyer and L. Chapman Building is in the lower left corner. (Courtesy of the Eugene Clark Library.)

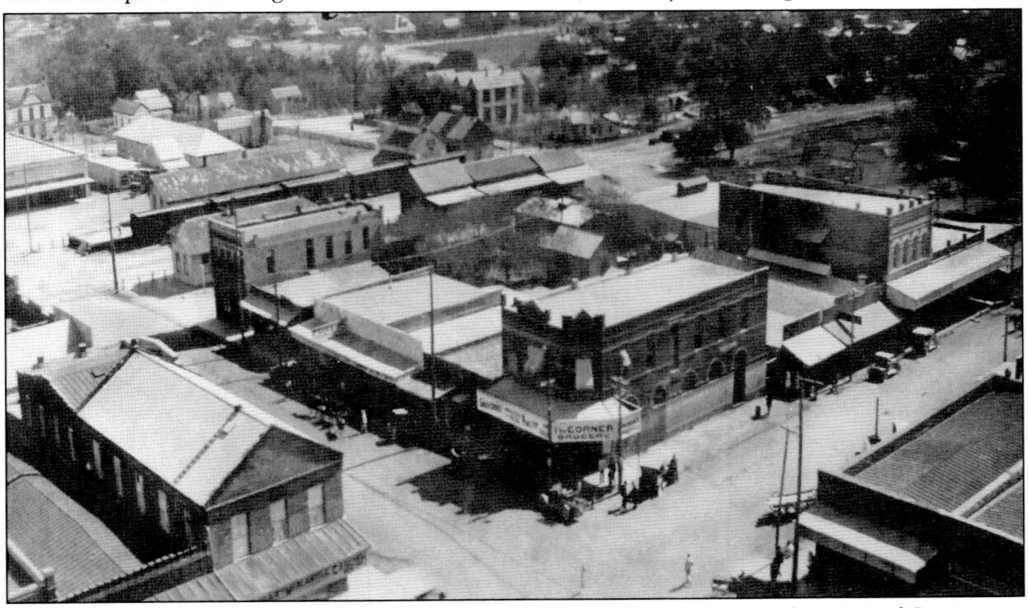

This view is the southeast corner of the square in 1921. The intersection shown is of Commerce Street, which runs north and south, and Market Street, which runs east and west. The building in the center on the corner is the Corner Grocery. To its right on Commerce Street is Smitty's Market, formerly Kreuz's Market. The building on the lower left is the oldest building on the square still standing today. It was built in 1873. (Courtesy of the Eugene Clark Library.)

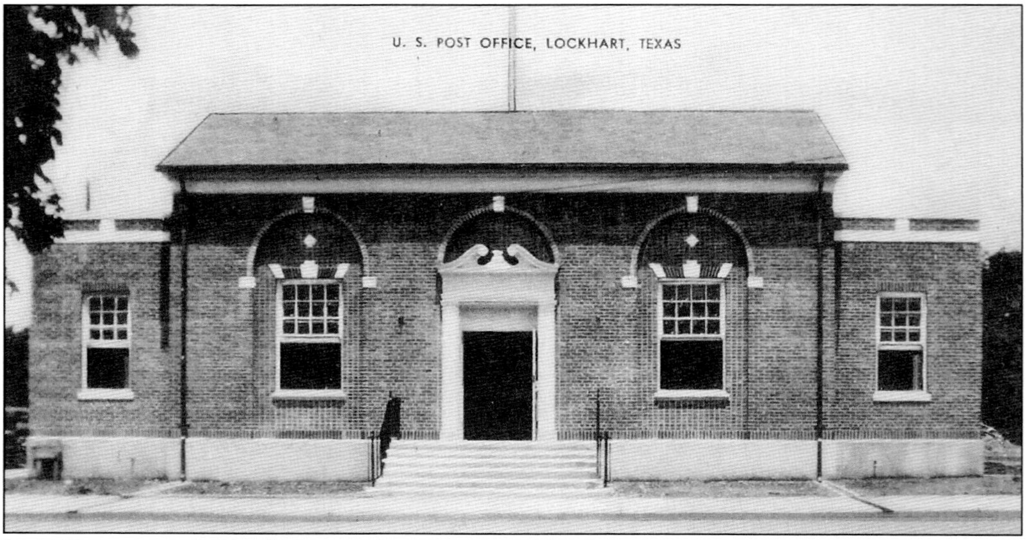

In 1848, prior to Caldwell County being approved by the Texas State Legislature and Lockhart being named the county seat, the area's first post office was called Plum Creek. Postmaster Isham Good operated it out of his home. It was closed and renamed Lockhart Post Office. The location moved about in different buildings until 1936. Mail was delivered by "mail wagon," which was driven by George Dugger starting around 1910. He was paid $900 a year then. Dugger remained the mailman until 1945. Located at 217 West Market Street, the current federal post office building, pictured above, was completed in 1936. In the summer of 1934, the US Treasury Department and Post Office Department at Washington approved a $67,000 allotment for a site and a post office building to be built. Shown below, the vacant lot on West Market Street, owned by Fred Adams, was selected. The lot was a portion of the former site of the Griesenbeck Hotel, which faced north on San Antonio Street. (Both, courtesy of John Baker.)

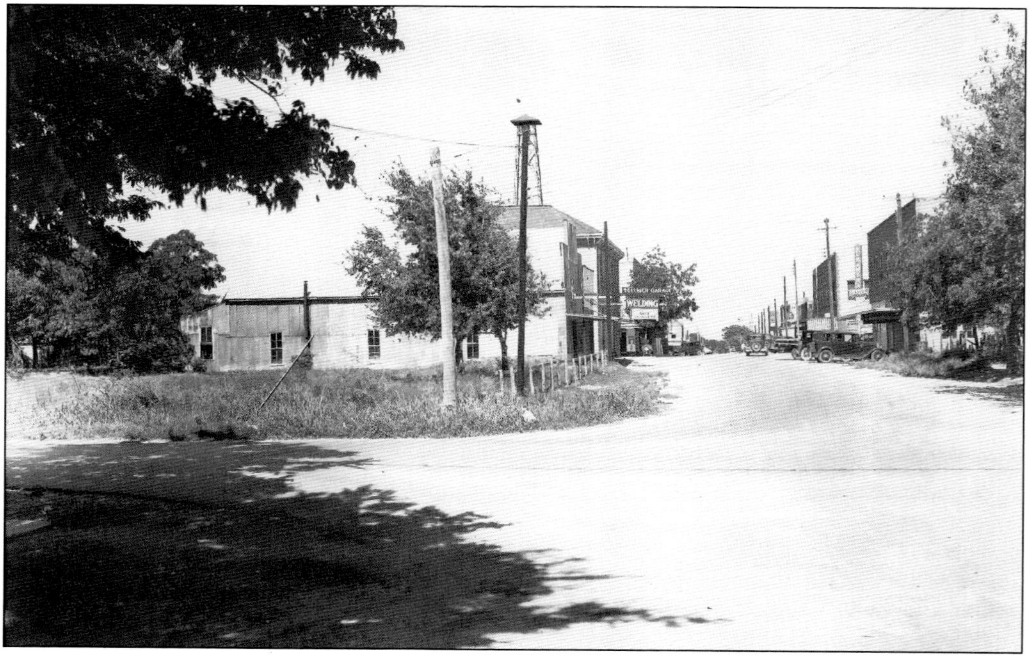

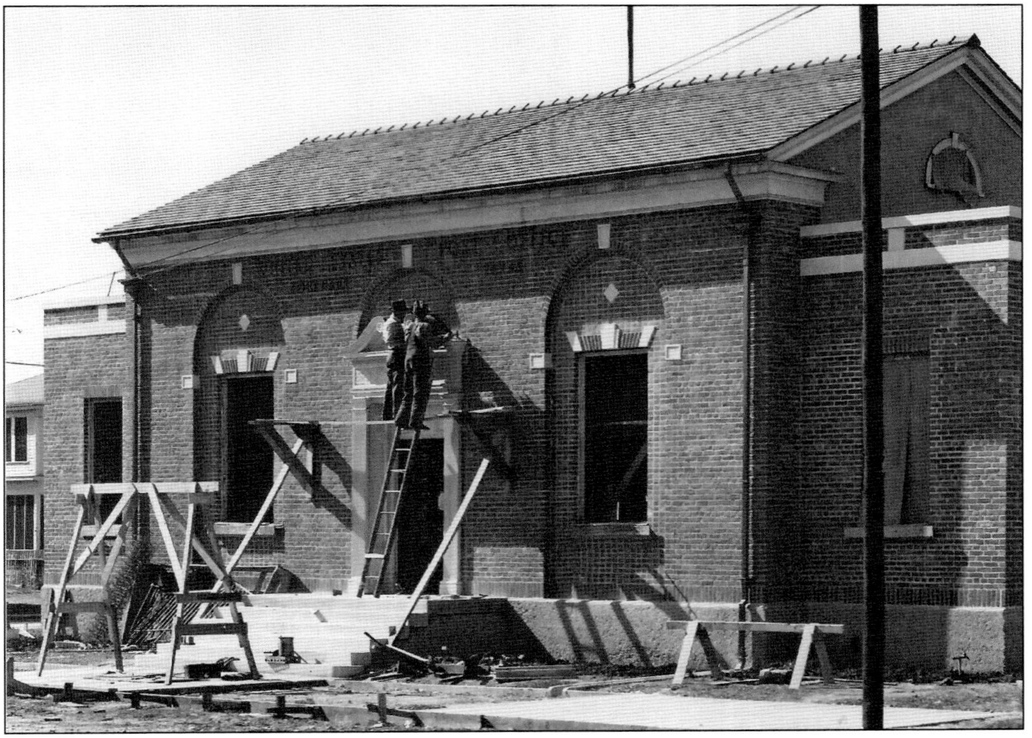

Mail delivery was operated from numerous locations around town prior to construction of this redbrick state-of-the-art post office. More space and larger scales were needed because of the mass amounts of cottonseed that were being mailed out of Lockhart, the "seed bin of the south." After trouble with one contractor going out of business, a second was hired, Walter C. Eeds of Lockhart. The new post office opened June 4, 1936. (Courtesy of John Baker.)

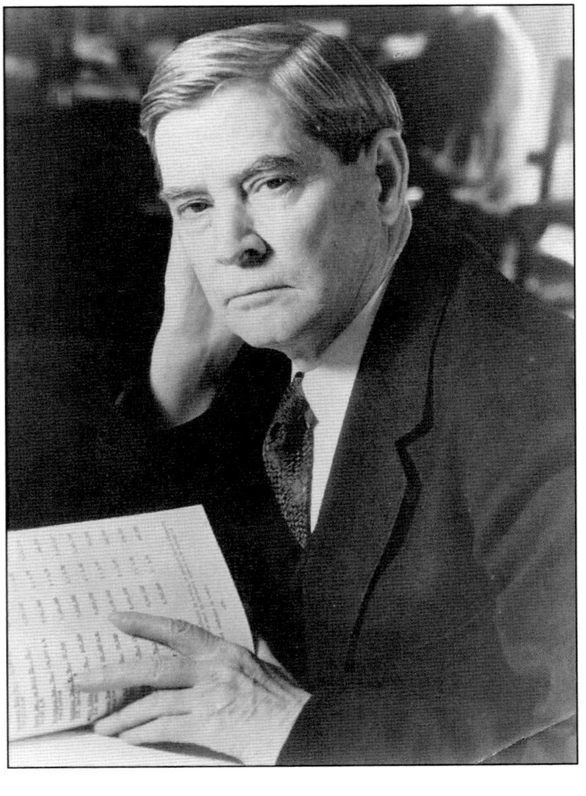

In 1929, Congressman James Paul Buchanan (1867–1937) presented a bill to Congress stating that $100,000 was needed to secure a site and to build a post office in Lockhart. He cited that Lockhart has $40,000 in postal receipts, making it entitled to an "adequate building." It was not until five years later that the $67,000 was finally awarded to the town to purchase the lot and erect a new post office. (Courtesy of John Baker.)

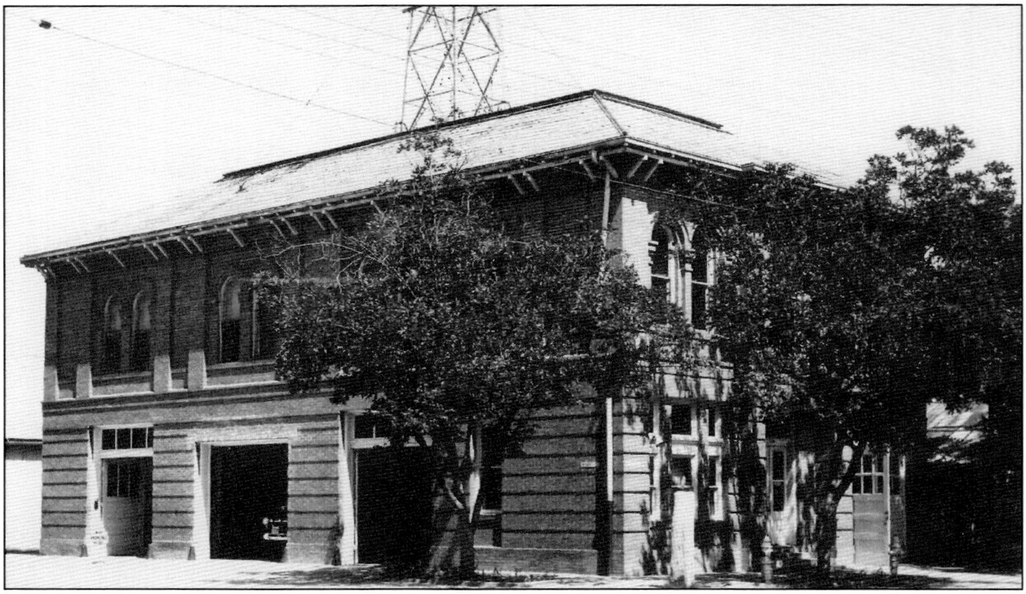

Fire Chief E.B. Coopwood, who served for 29 years, spaded the first shovelful of dirt at the ground breaking for the Lockhart City Hall and Fire Station in 1911. By 1915, according to Sanborn Map Company, the fire department consisted of "2 hose companies of about 20 men each, 1 hook and ladder company of 20 men; 1 paid driver sleeps in station; 2 relief drivers; no horses; 1 American La France Combination Hose and Chemical Truck with [numerous] hoses; a telephone in the station, whistle at the pump station and large bell in the courthouse square." In this later picture, the tower with its fire bell, which was moved from the square, can be seen on the roof of the fire station. Three unidentified men pose in front of a new fire truck, shown below. This brick fire station has been in continuous operation for 100 years. The Lockhart Volunteer Hook and Ladder Company has come a long way since the "Bucket Brigade" of 1888. (Both, courtesy of the Eugene Clark Library.)

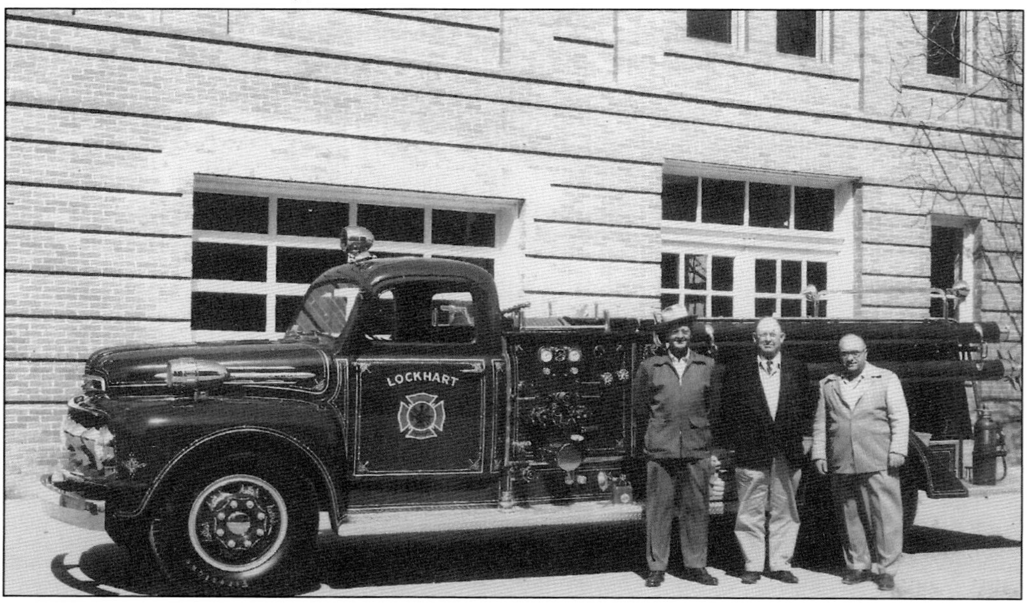

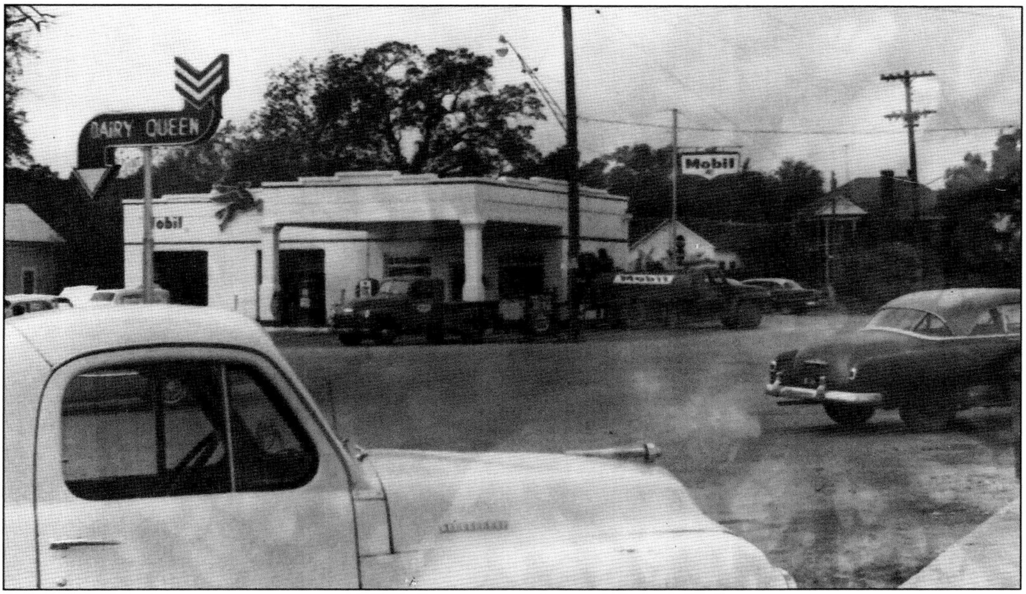

In the good old days, "gas stations," like this Mobil station at the corner of Prairie Lea and Main Streets, offered full service at the pump. Formerly Magnolia Oil, this gas station was built on the site of a former Baptist church. It was owned by Walter Scott. This building, as well as the old DQ (Dairy Queen) across the street, has appeared in at least one of the 30-plus movies that have been filmed in and around Lockhart. (Courtesy of the CCHC.)

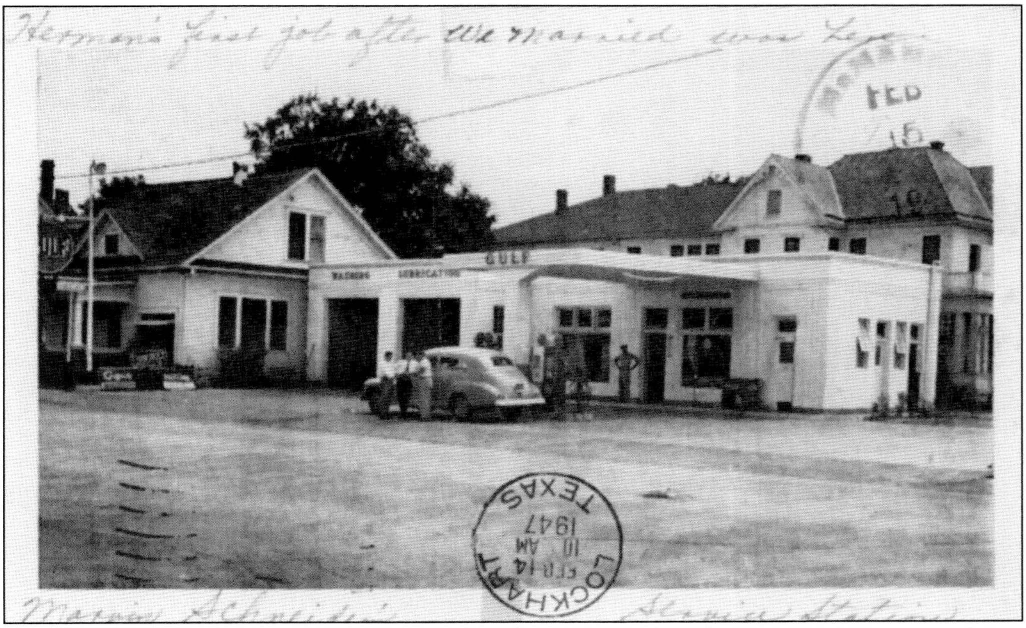

Marvin R. Schneider Service Station (Gulf Oil) was located at the corner of Blanco and San Antonio Street. The message on the back of his picture postcard, postmarked 1927 at Grand Central Station, New York, says, "For best all-around service, you can't beat this place—it's got everything!" The Tate Hotel (formerly the Moon Hotel) is visible in the background. Today, a Ford Motor Company car lot is located here. (Courtesy of Ona Anton.)

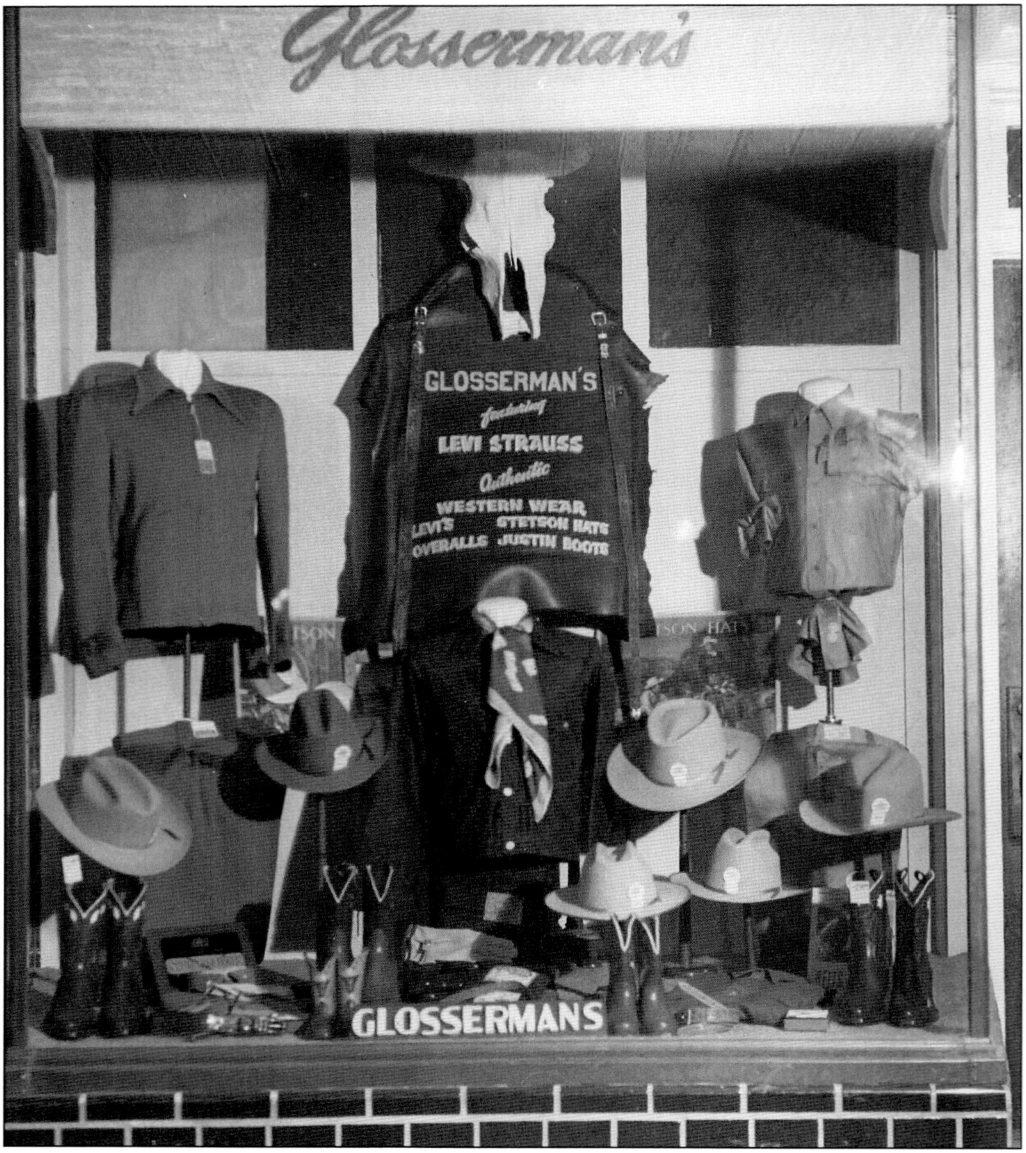

Glosserman's Clothiers store was located on the east side of the square at 116 South Commerce Street. The building, which remains today, was built by well-known German builder Gus Birkner in 1899. It first served as a grocery store operated by A.W. Smith, as well as Shinn & Wisian among others, until Sam Glosserman moved in and opened his clothing store. By mid century, the store featured Levi Strauss authentic Western wear, Stetson felt hats, and leather boots as shown in this picture window. It is reported that a trap door in the floor led to a basement where, during A.W. Smith's ownership, local men played poker. The Glossermans were successful business owners in town. Glosserman Chevrolet was another long-time Lockhart institution. The Glosserman name can still be seen above the door although it is an antique store today. (Courtesy CCHC.)

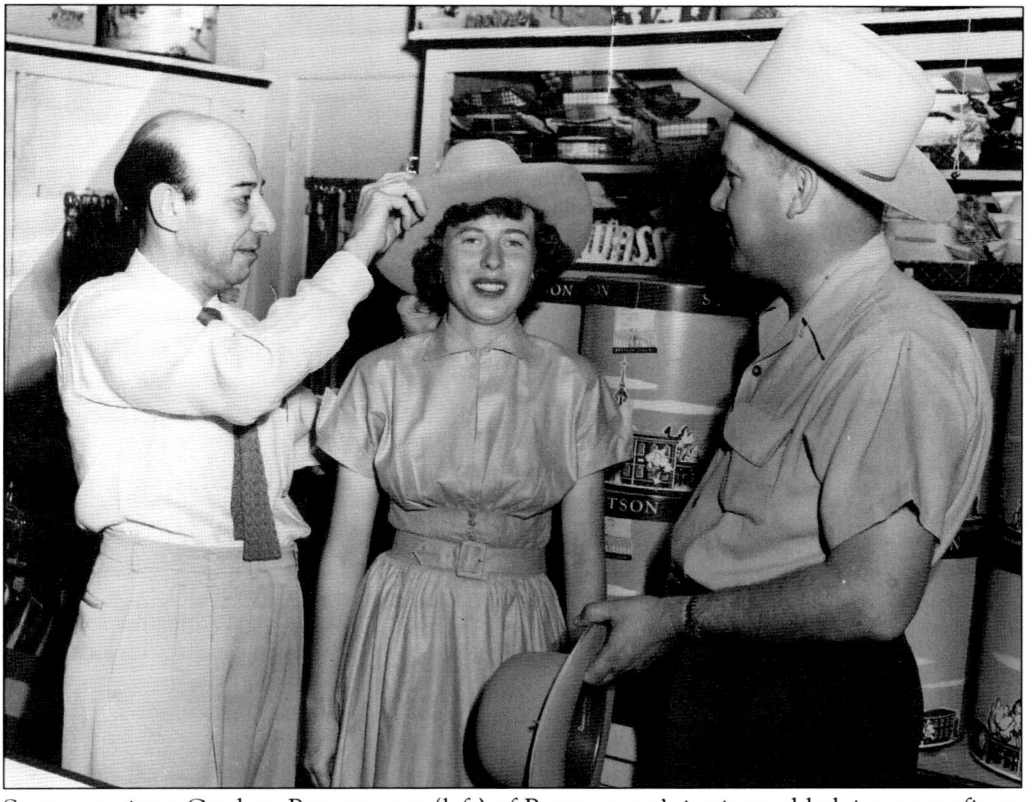

Store proprietor Gershon Rosenwasser (left) of Rosenwasser's is pictured helping to outfit an unidentified young lady with a cowboy hat. The dry goods store was a family business started in 1902 by Morris Rosenwasser, a Jewish immigrant born in Hungary. His ability to speak German and Polish helped him trade with area immigrant farmers. He expanded his shop and moved into two buildings on the north corner of San Antonio Street and the east side of Commerce Street. Sons Gershon and Isadore, who basically grew up in the store, ran it after their father's passing. (Courtesy of the CCHC.)

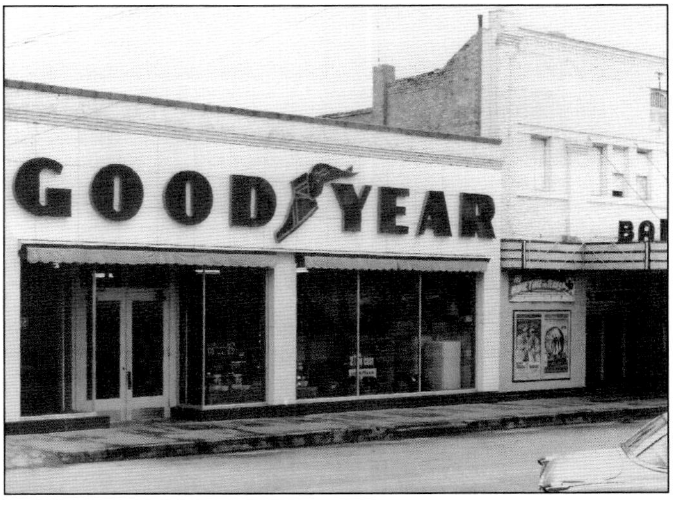

One block off the square at 212 South Main Street was the Goodyear store (1952). In 1892, the post office was here. Next door to the right, at 214 South Main Street, was the Baker Theatre. It was built in 1920 for A.D. Baker to show motion pictures indoors. Matinee movie prices were 20¢ for adults and 10¢ for children; evening shows were 25¢. The building is open today with both live theater performances as well as live music. (Courtesy of the Eugene Clark Library.)

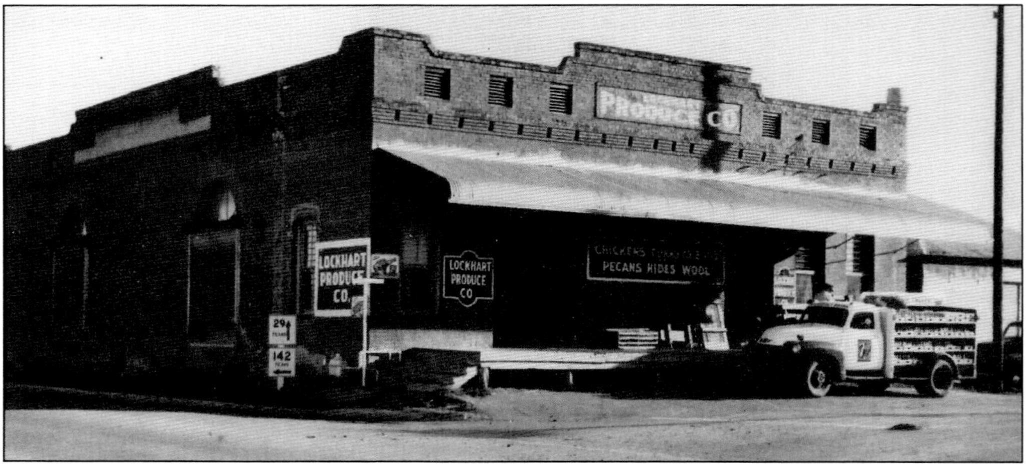

A wholesale grocery, the Lockhart Produce Company, was built at the turn of the 20th century on East San Antonio Street and Aransas (now State Highway 183). The brick building, which still exists today, has a full basement. In this 1940s photograph, a 7 Up delivery truck is parked outside. The store also sold chickens, turkeys, eggs, pecans, hides, and wool. (Courtesy of the Eugene Clark Library.)

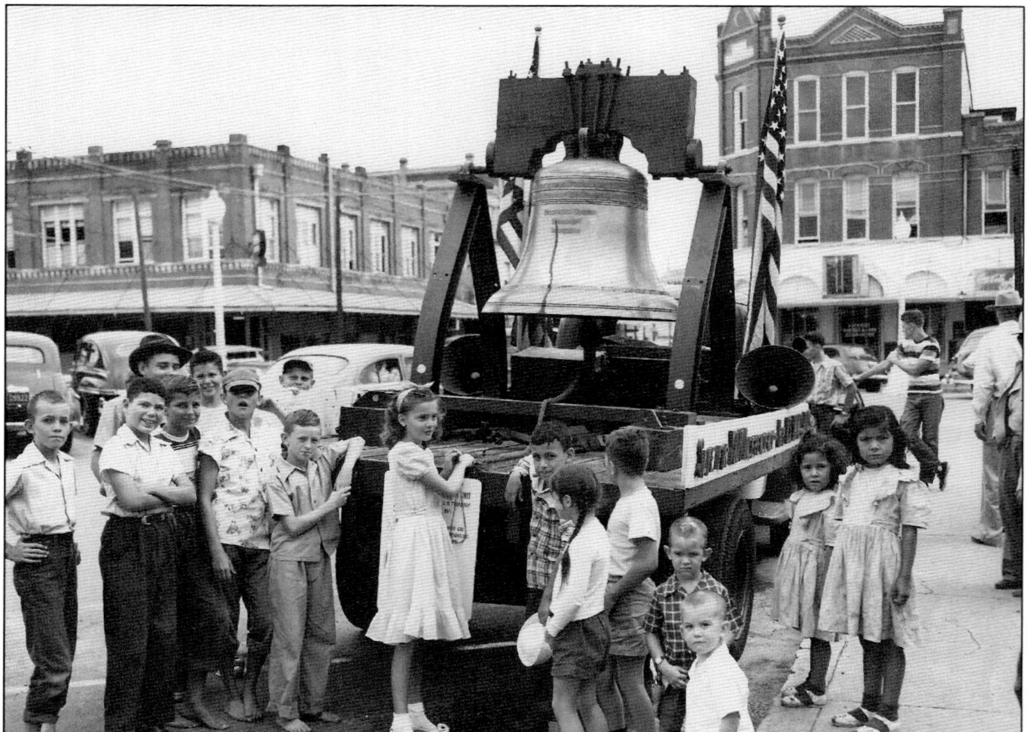

A replica of the Liberty Bell toured the country, coming to Lockhart's town square. Crowds gathered on Main Street to take a close look, including Hunter Hill (far left) and several other unidentified children. Most of the boys are barefoot. In the background is the three-story A.L. Brock Building on the right and the Corner Drugstore on the left. (Courtesy of Gerry and Conrad Ohlendorf.)

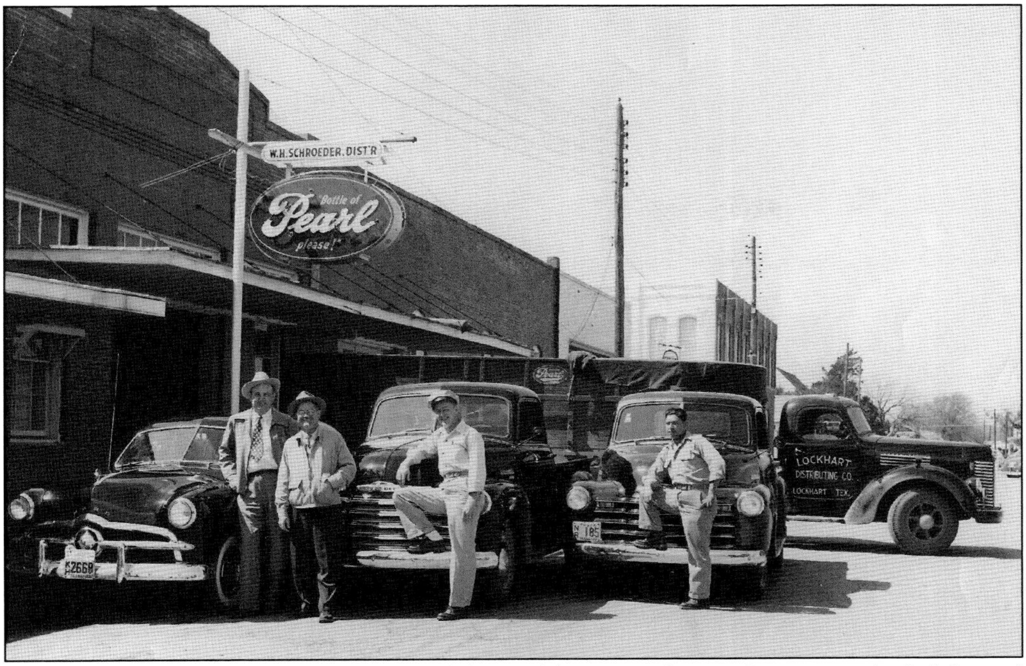

W.H. Schroeder (left) owned and operated the Lockhart Distributing Company, which delivered San Antonio Brewing Company's Pearl Beer and Southern Select throughout the area, including all the way to Shiner. One of the long-haul and short-delivery drivers was a Lockhart native and the father of the author of this book, Herman W. Anton, posing third from the left. (Courtesy of Ona Anton.)

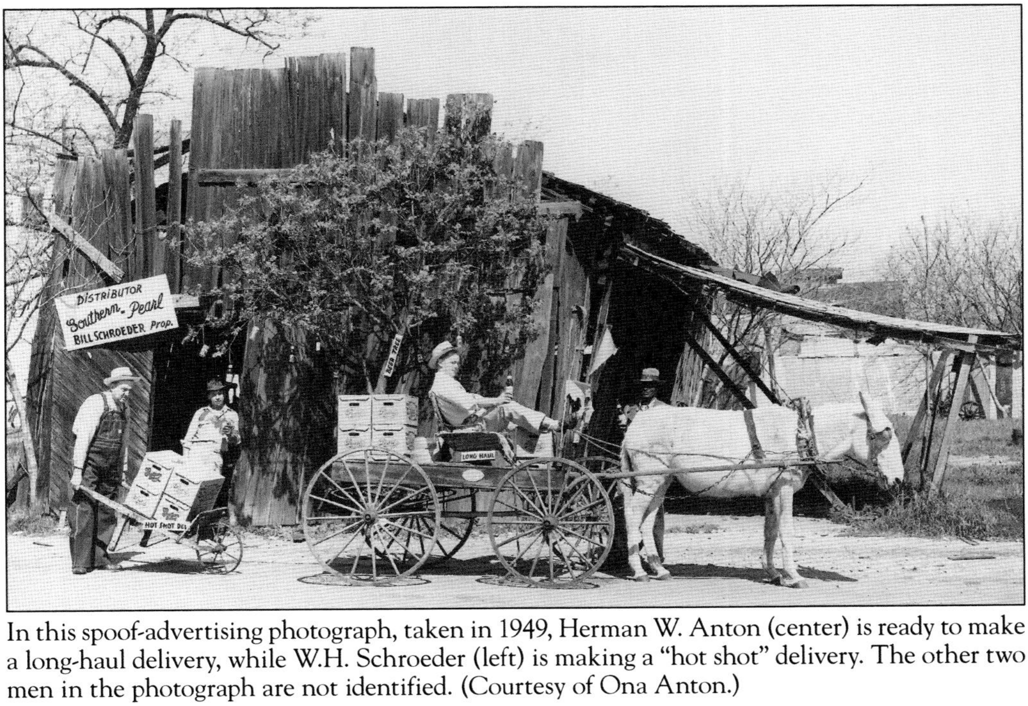

In this spoof-advertising photograph, taken in 1949, Herman W. Anton (center) is ready to make a long-haul delivery, while W.H. Schroeder (left) is making a "hot shot" delivery. The other two men in the photograph are not identified. (Courtesy of Ona Anton.)

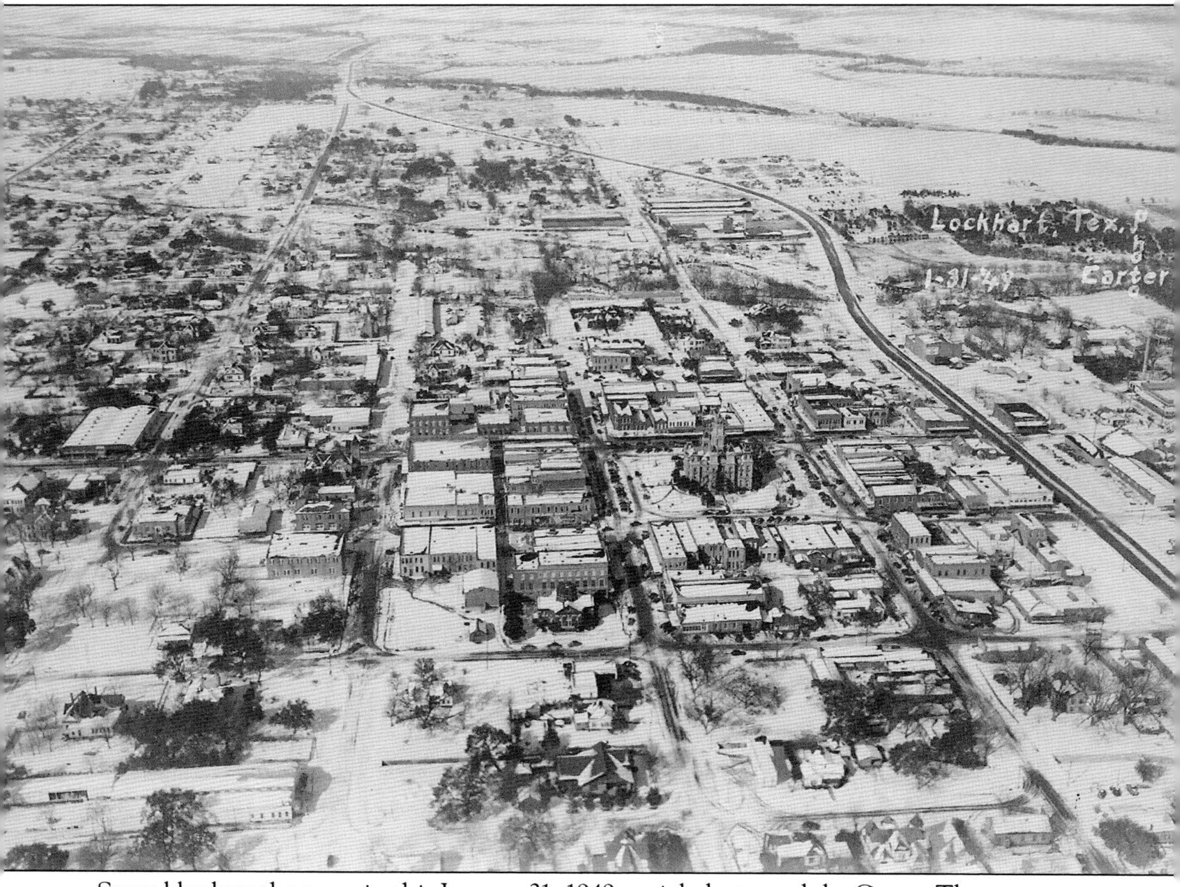

Snow blankets the town in this January 31, 1949, aerial photograph by Carter. The town square was in its 101st year of development by then, with Lockhart having grown from a population of "1055 free residents and approximately 200 slaves" in 1850 to about 5,000. The town saw many changes, outgrowing two courthouses and building a third magnificent centerpiece on the square in 1894. Primitive log cabin shelters became a thing of the past as they were replaced by stick-built homes made with sawmill lumber. Lockhart's reputation of being a lawless community changed to that of a civil, religious one. The original wooden stores on the public square were replaced with masonry buildings by 1901, many of which stand today. From dirt trails to paved roads, the town took shape. From cattle drives to cotton, the economy remains based primarily on agriculture as citizens adopted ranching and farming as primary trades. Travel by horse and buggy gave way to automobiles and automotive steam engines and to a time when the town had four automobile dealers. (Courtesy of Gerry and Conrad Ohlendorf.)

Four

Families and Homes

Texas is the largest state in geography, diversity of people, and cultures. In the mid–19th century, most Texas settlers were of European descent. Lockhart was a true "melting pot." Though the people that settled here had different cultures, they all seemed to share an attitude that has come to be known as that true Texas spirit—tenacity in the face of adversity or a "do-or-die" temperament—which is both courageous and stubborn. This was the unsettled Wild West, so they had to be strong spirited. In the early days, Texans of German descent made up the state's largest ethnic group, behind Anglos, Hispanics, and African Americans. Germans and many other immigrants sailed from their homeland for six long weeks, landing in Galveston and Indianola. From there, they either walked or rode in wagons or on horseback to Lockhart and other nearby towns, like New Braunfels. They brought with them strong work ethics, customs, dialects, good food, sausage making, a love for music, and a dream for a better life. The French, Poles, Czechs, and Creoles were also among the immigrants. The Czechs also brought music and instruments, like brass horns and accordions, which became popular with Mexicans. Today, these sounds are the basis for Tejano music. And what small Texas town does not have a bake shop that sells *kolaches*? Black Texans who fought alongside the Union Army during the Civil War were nicknamed "buffalo soldiers" by the Cheyenne and the Comanche Indians. African American cowboys were fairly common throughout the cattle kingdom era.

Texans had one more thing in common . . . a knack for "braggin'." For example, "everything is bigger and better in Texas." And, they were hospitable. The South has long been noted for large family get-togethers. But it extended beyond relations. On the open range and in the new town of Lockhart, it was not uncommon to welcome road-weary travelers, who might be complete strangers, into their humble homes for a warm meal and soft bed in which to sleep. These virtues remain true today.

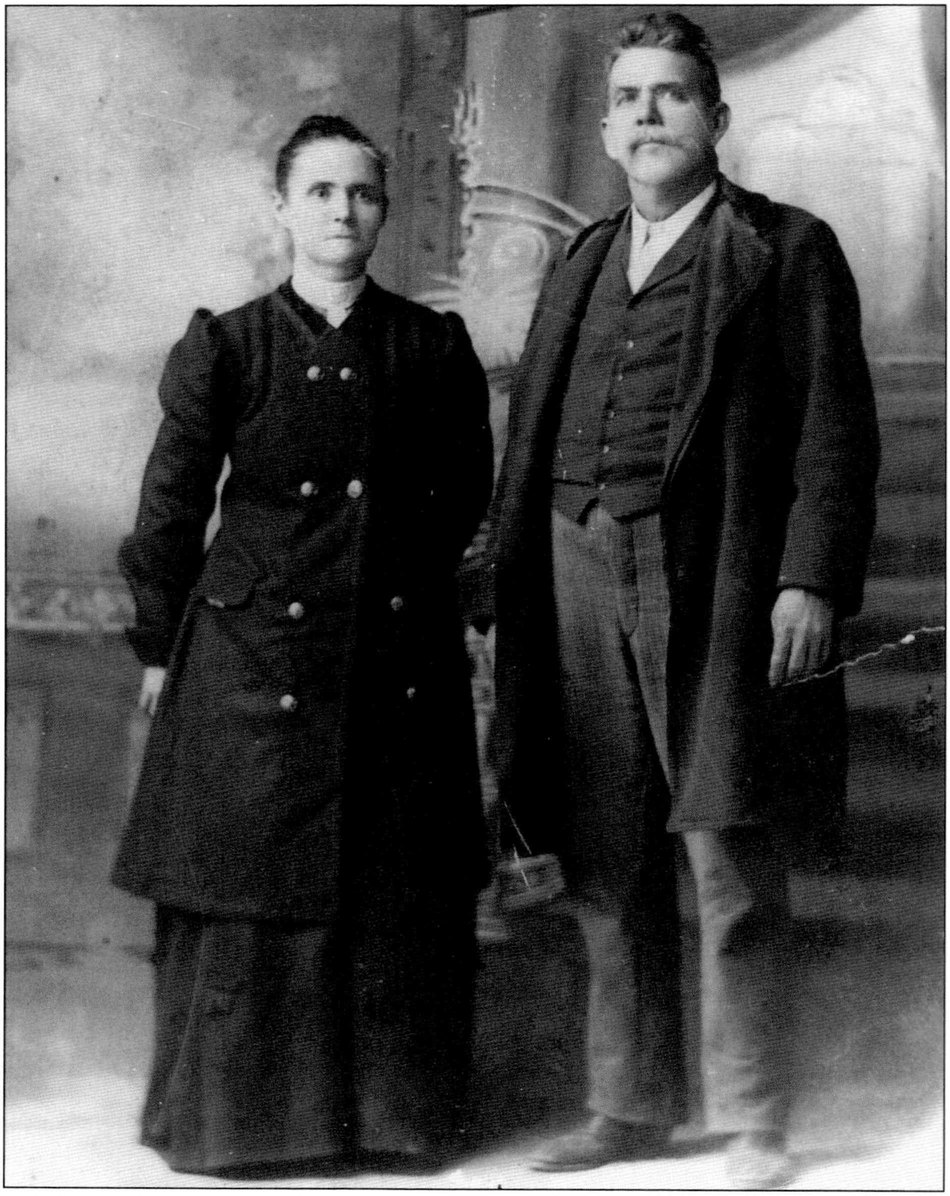

One of the area's earliest Anglo settlers was German-born Ambrose Tinney (who is also the author's maternal great-great-great-great-grandfather). Tinney arrived in Texas in 1830. In 1832, he received a Spanish Land Grant, signed by impresario Green DeWitt, for a league of land (4,428 acres) in "Coahuila y Texas." The territory surveyed by Byrd Lockhart on July 25, 1833, would later become part of eastern Caldwell County in 1848. He settled there and raised a family. The area, which held the name of Tinney Creek until being renamed McMahan, was located at the Lockhart and LaGrange crossroad. A true Texan, Tinney volunteered to serve in the Texas army west of the Brazos River at Washington. Records show that he "mustered up" in Gonzales on June 30, 1836. His granddaughter Sarah Tinney is pictured with her husband, David Lafayette Ellis, who owned the first store in McMahan. The store was called Wild Cat, a name the town's famous baseball team later adopted. (Courtesy of Ona Anton.)

Born August 22, 1861, in Germany, Heinrich Jacob Anton (pictured) came to Texas landing at Indianola in 1881. He walked to Lockhart with all his possessions in a handkerchief and spent the first night in a livery stable. He married German immigrant Augusta Maria Germer (seated) on January 1, 1893, in Maxwell, with Rev. T.K. Poch officiating. Her mother is standing in the back. A son, Hermann Jacob Anton (center), was born on June 28, 1894. He is the paternal grandfather of this book's author. Heinrich (Henry) Anton petitioned for US naturalization in July 1892, with Emil Seeliger, blacksmith, and H.F. Masur, merchant, attesting to his character and residency. The petition was dismissed when it was discovered that Masur was not a citizen and could not legally sign the affidavit. Anton was eventually naturalized in 1913. (Courtesy of Ona Anton.)

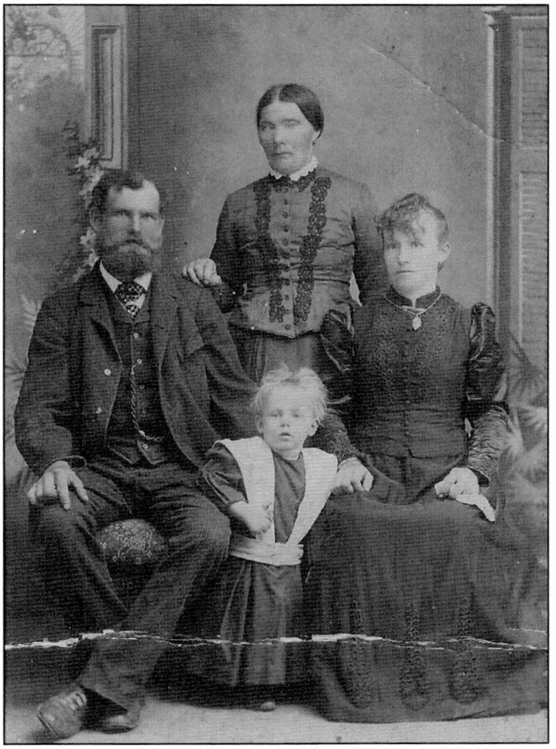

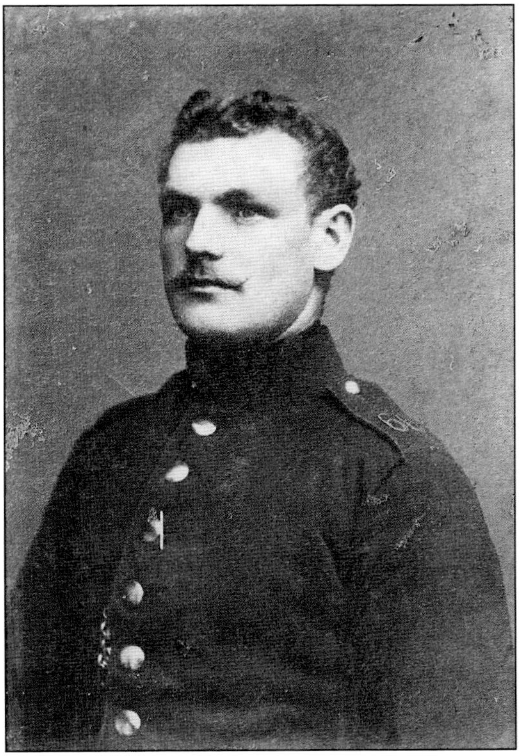

Heinrich Jacob Anton served in the Spanish-American War in 1898, which was between Spain and the United States. The war was fought primarily over the issue of the independence of Cuba, and the Treaty of Paris ended the war with the United States receiving temporary control of Cuba. In this portrait by C.L. Hickman Photographers, Heinrich is in uniform. (Courtesy of Ona Anton.)

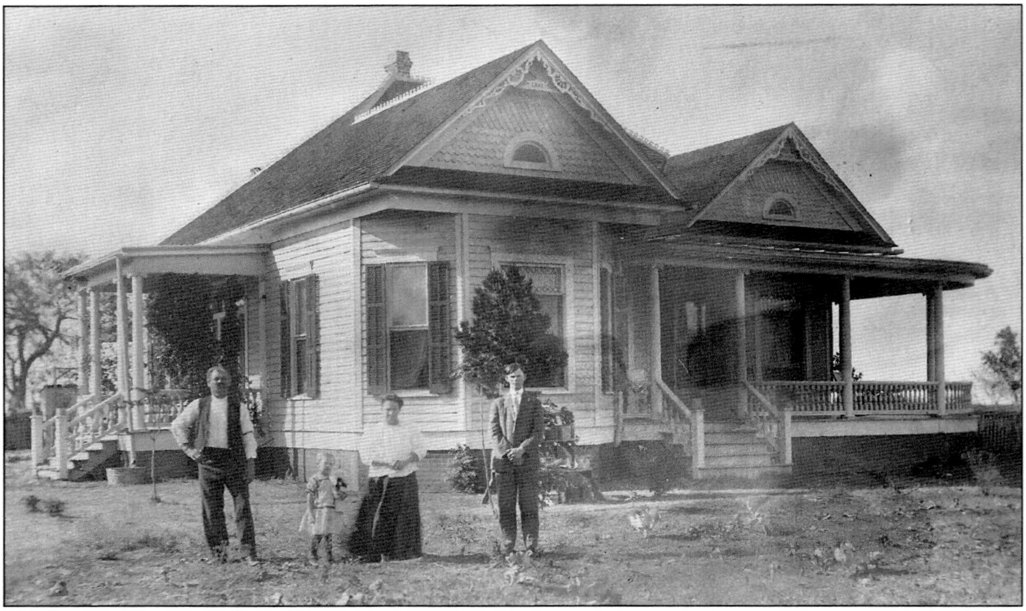

Standing in front of their "German-built" Victorian country home are, from left to right, Heinrich Jacob Anton, daughter Elsa Augusta Victoria, Augusta Maria Germer Anton, and son Hermann Jacob Anton. The home was located on 640 acres on what is today's Long Road (County Road 110). The area was named Black Ankle. They were cotton farmers. (Courtesy of Ona Anton.)

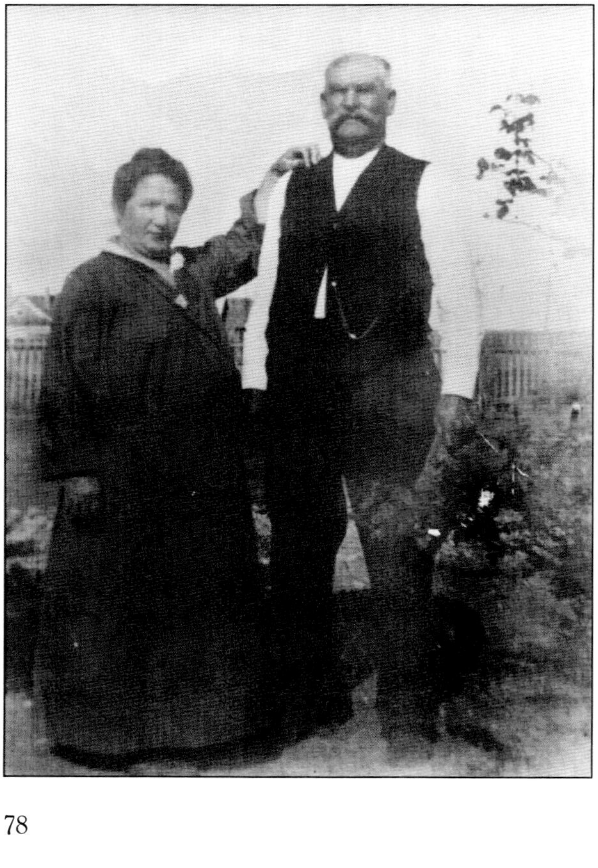

The Lockhart settlers brought German customs, recipes, and a good German work ethic with them. They were instrumental in forming the Ebenezer Lutheran Church in nearby Maxwell in Caldwell County, Texas. Heinrich Jacob Anton died on July 17, 1931, in New Braunfels, Texas, and his wife, Augusta, predeceased him on November 7, 1925. Both are buried in the Comal Cemetery in New Braunfels. (Courtesy of Ona Anton.)

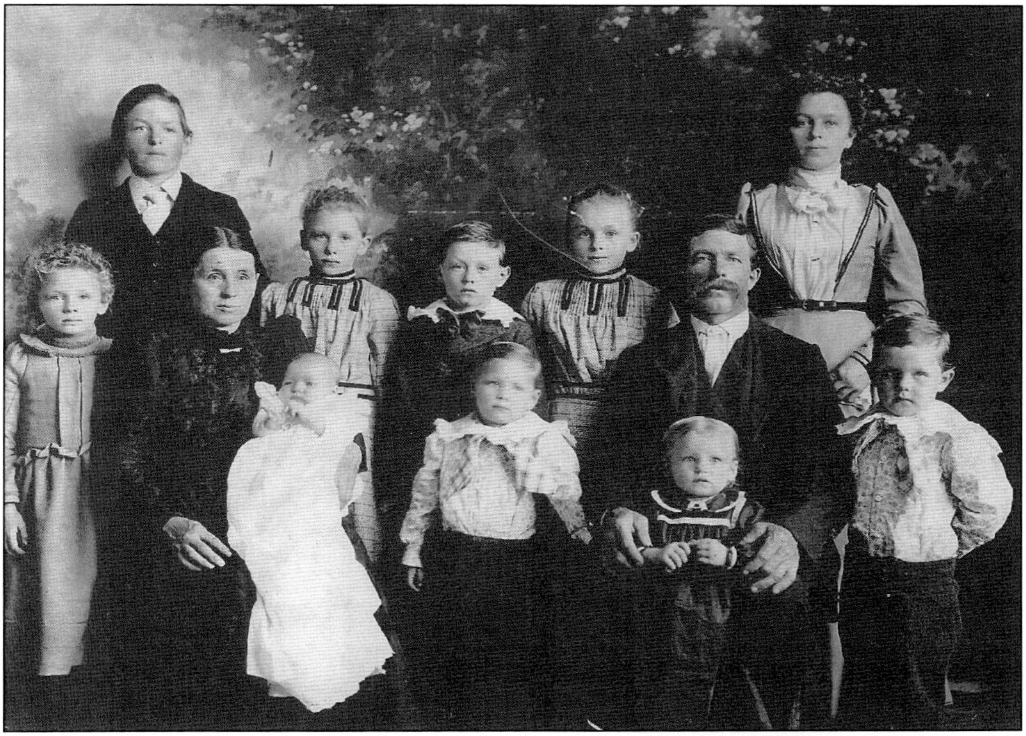

In the early 1900s, the German immigrant family of Frederick Wilhelm Andreas Germer and his wife, Minna Maria Traetzel, were living between Maxwell and Lockhart. Sitting for their family portrait are, from left to right, (first row) Hulda, Minna (mother) holding baby Alma, William Frederick, Andreas (father) holding Ella, and Gustav; (second row) Andreas Jr., Emma, Frederick Wilhelm "Fritz," Anna, and Minna. Four other children were born but did not survive. Andreas Sr., who emigrated from Laugenweddingen, Germany, received his naturalization papers on September 26, 1906, in San Marcos, Texas. (Courtesy of Ona Anton.)

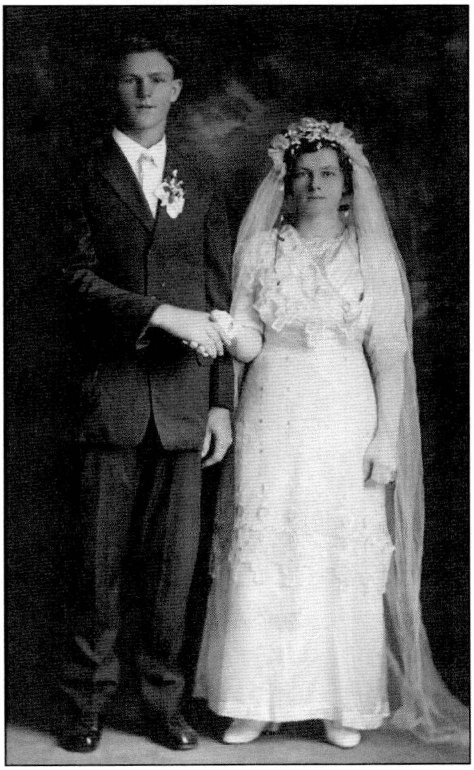

Roots intertwined when Hulda Germer (the curly-headed blonde shown above on the far left) married Hermann Jacob Anton (the blonde boy pictured on page 77), merging the Germer and Anton families. They were married on June 4, 1914, in Caldwell County. The couple moved to his birthplace home and farm in Black Ankle where they reared four daughters, Ella, Florene, Irene, and Hildegard, and one son, Herman William Anton. First-born Clara died at age two. (Courtesy of Ona Anton.)

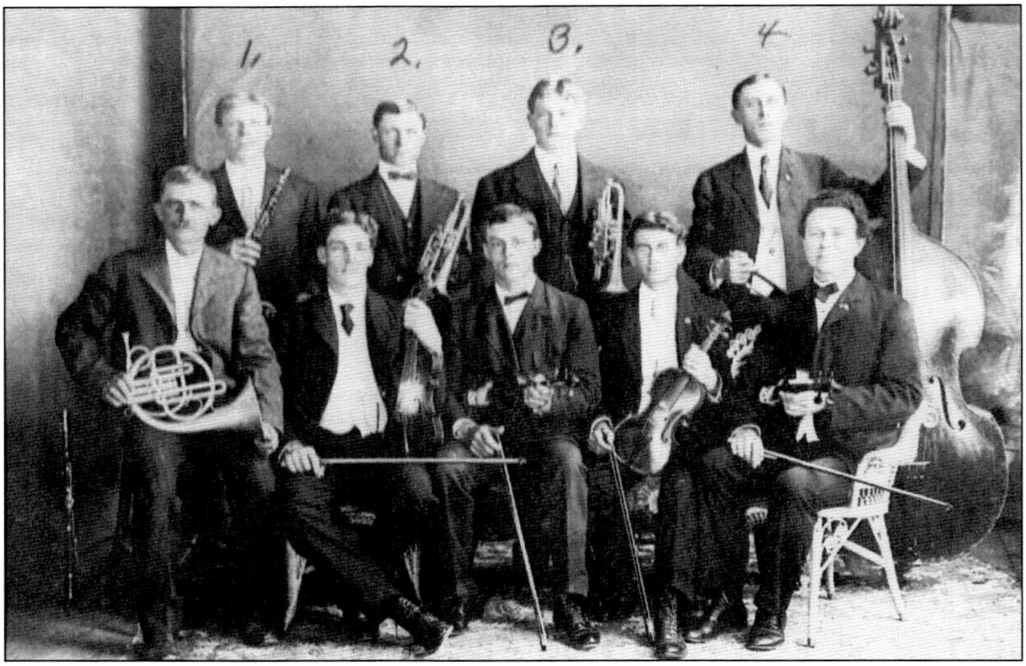

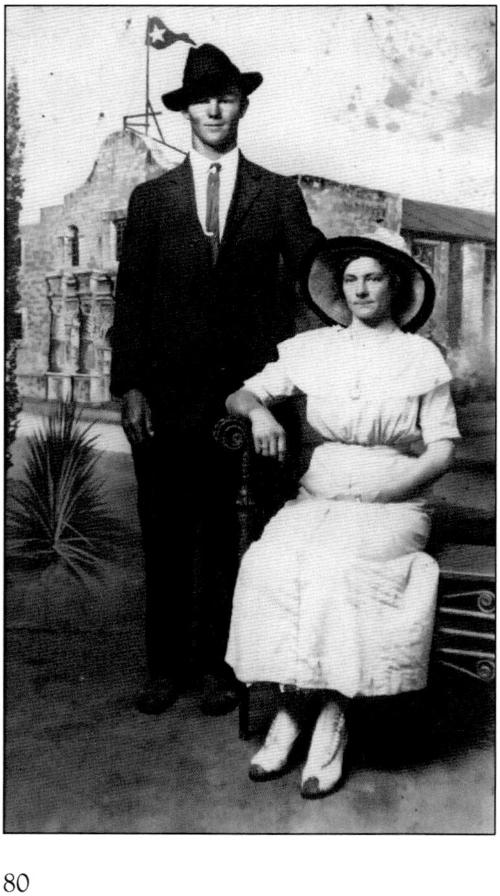

Maxwell is a small town on the Missouri-Kansas-Texas Railroad line, eight miles west of Lockhart. After the arrival of the Katy in 1887, the name was changed from New Martindale to Maxwell in honor of Thomas Maxwell for having obtained a land grant in 1845 for a league of land. The town is centered on that league. The first settlers here were from Alabama, but in the 1880s, groups from Germany began to arrive. They were farmers and ranchers. Their cultural influences and social activities remain today, including their music, dance, singing, shooting clubs, and churches. The Maxwell Band with strings or simply its "Brass Band" performed frequently. On Sunday afternoons, admission was $1 and included free beer. In this early 1900s image, members are, from left to right, (first row) Henry Richter Sr., Robert Schulze, Willie Wiede, Professor Ruebsam, and druggist Christian Shee; (second row) C.A. Kruse, Edwin Boenig, Andreas Germer Jr., and Albert Echkard. At the left, this early Texas tourism souvenir photograph is of Hermann Jacob Anton and Hulda Germer Anton posing in front of a backdrop of Texas's most iconic symbol, the Alamo. (Above, courtesy of Ebenezer Lutheran Church; left, courtesy of Ona Anton.)

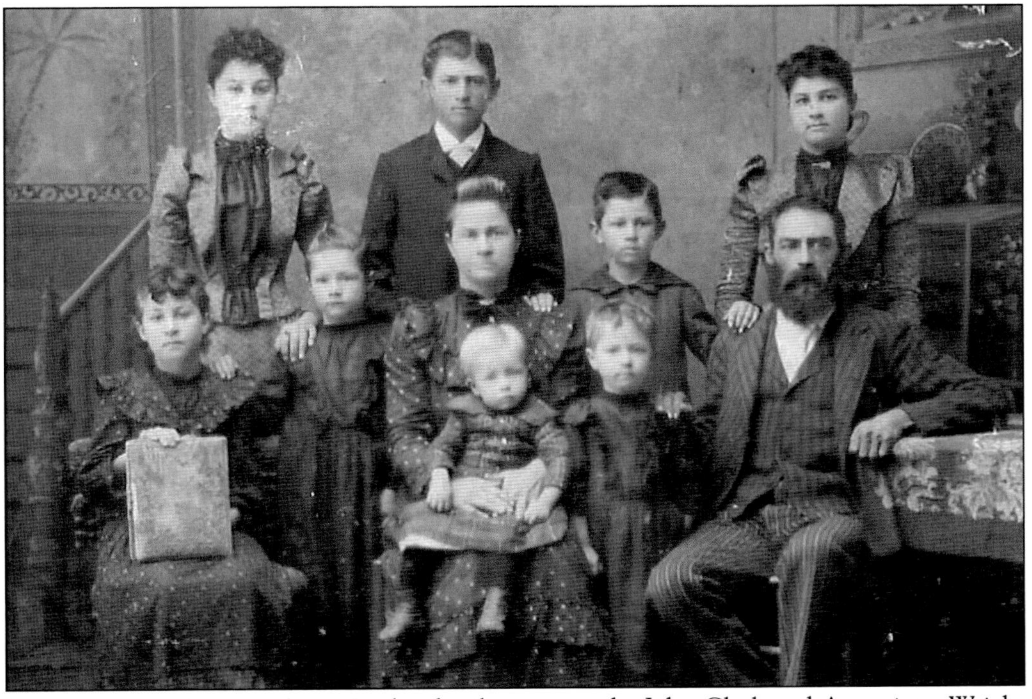

Early Texas families were large. In this family portrait, the John Clark and Antoniette Wright Clark family consists of 10 members. Clark (b. Aug.27, 1842) fought in the Civil War. Shown below is an example of another early Texas home in Lockhart. Standing on the porch at the far left are William and Lenora Clark Blanks. John Clark is next to the right porch column. Reminiscing in 1936 about life in the earlier days of Lockhart, Emma S. Lay, who arrived here in 1855, said, "The settlers were generally well-educated and in comfortable circumstances financially. They had brought their slaves, household goods. Their parlors, as they were called in that day, were well-furnished with carpets and draperies for the windows and furniture better than today, more substantial. Some of it is still in use, as I know. We brought our piano and used it many years. Of course we did not have the conveniences that we now have—electricity, gas, phones, radios," (Both, courtesy of Harry Hilgers Jr.)

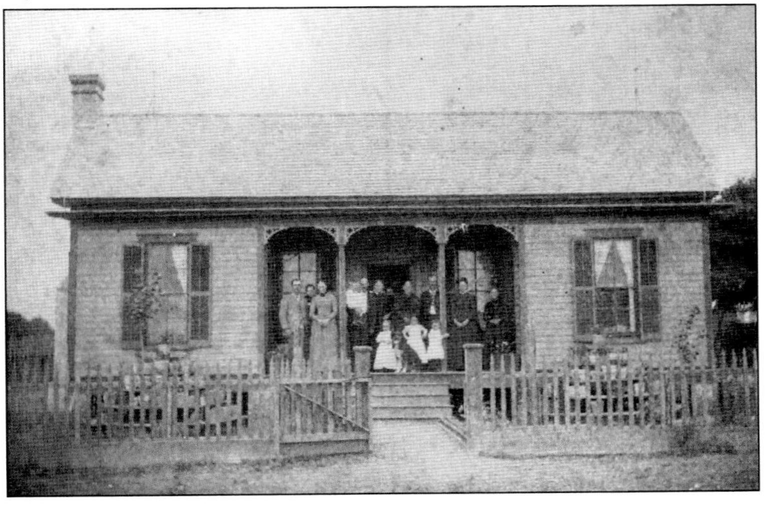

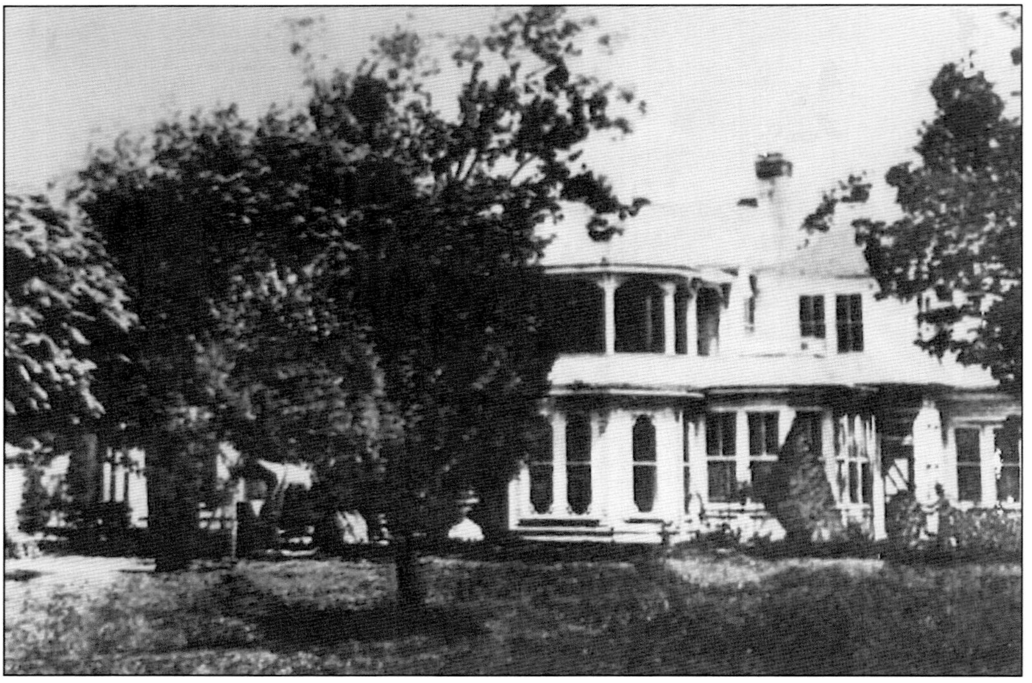

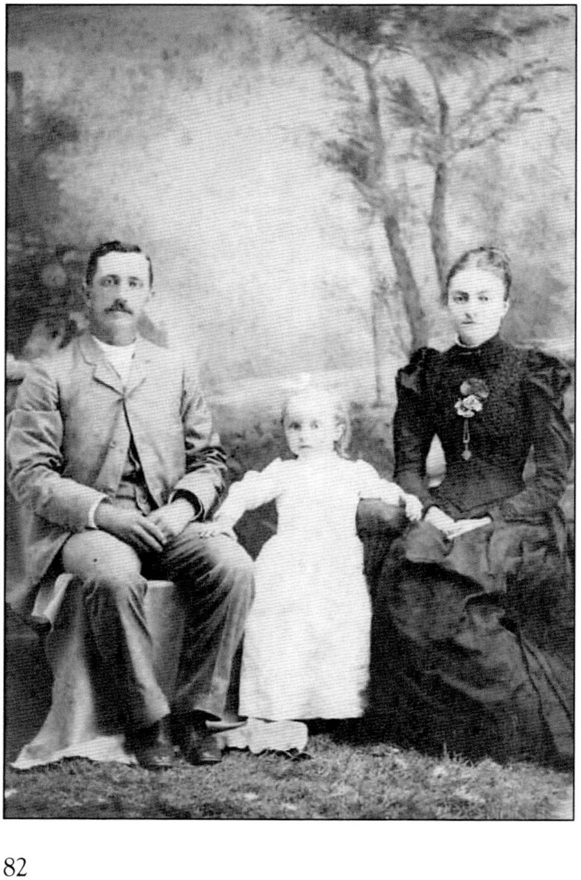

John G. Blanks was a physician from Missouri. He came to Lockhart and bought thousands of acres of land between Lockhart and Maxwell to Uhland for $5 per acre. He married Martha Montgomery, and they had four sons and two daughters together. They built this magnificent home near the Methodist church on West San Antonio Street. Three of the sons of this prominent family also built very stately homes, many of which still exist today, near their parents' home. When Doctor Blanks's sister became ill and he could not save her, he quit practicing medicine. The Blanks were the first land sub-dividers in Lockhart. After the doctor's death, Martha had the big house taken down and built five homes from the lumber. Son Joseph Blanks built the home at 412 West San Antonio Street, putting a second story on the "shotgun" home in 1899 and sold it to Dr. Benton Coupwood. Pictured at the left are William and Lenora Clark Blanks with their daughter Elizabeth in this early family portrait by Carter of Luling, Texas. (Both, courtesy of Harry Hilgers Jr.)

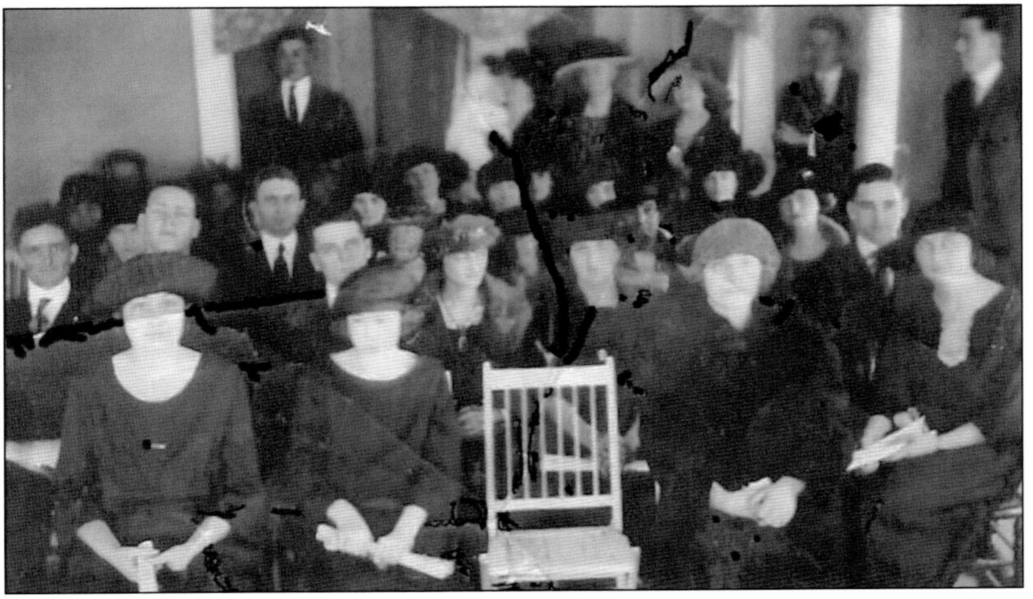

This interesting recorded image was taken at the funeral of William Blanks in 1930. The empty chair is symbolic of the family member "no longer with us." William Blanks owned Blanks's Corner Grocery (119 South Main Street) on the southwest corner of the square and a mule-and-horse business. The John Blanks family was one of the wealthiest families in Lockhart. In a true philanthropic spirit, Martha Montgomery Blanks built Blanks Memorial Hall, shown below, as a memorial to her deceased husband John, and gifted it to the city to be used for civic and cultural events. It was located at 313 West San Antonio Street. The city sold it to the Methodist church around 1950 for $6,000. The church was reportedly built around it, incorporating it into the design. One has to search hard to find any of the original details. Martha and John's six children were Martha, John, Elizabeth, James, William, and Joseph. (Both, courtesy of Harry Hilgers Jr.)

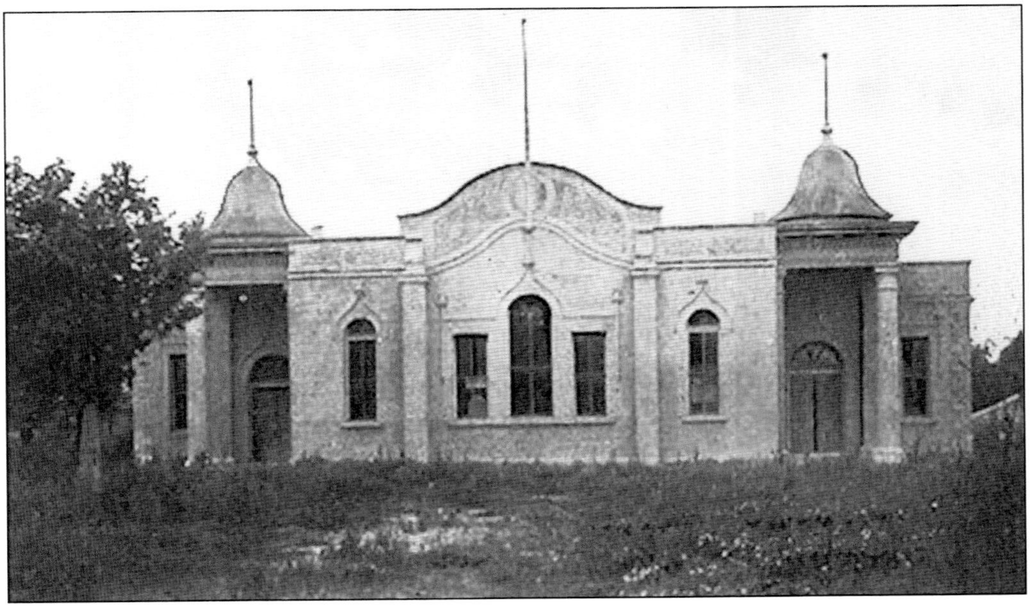

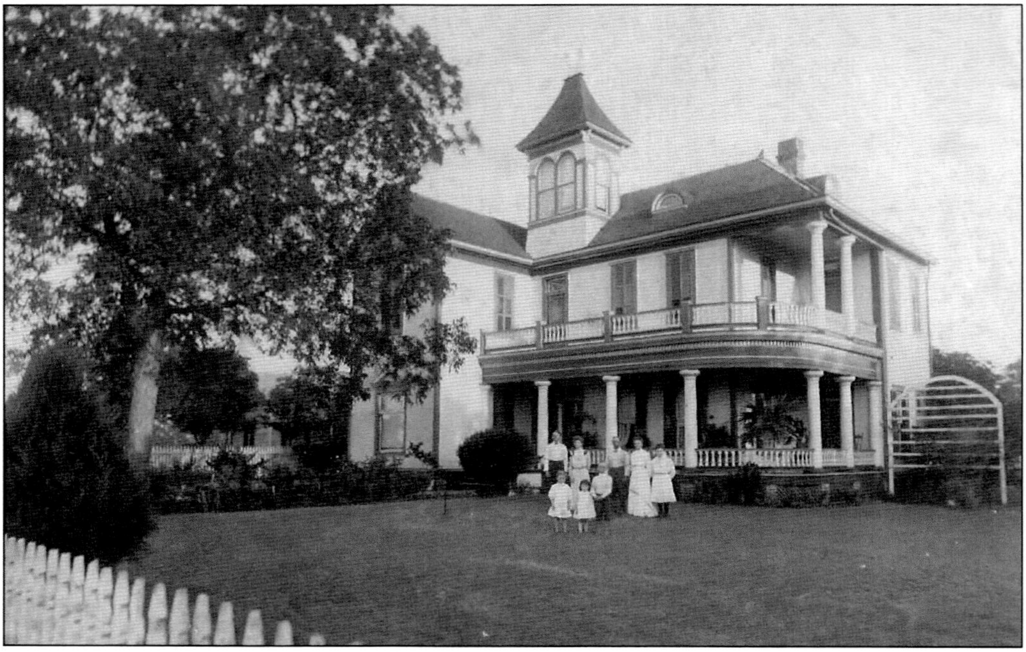

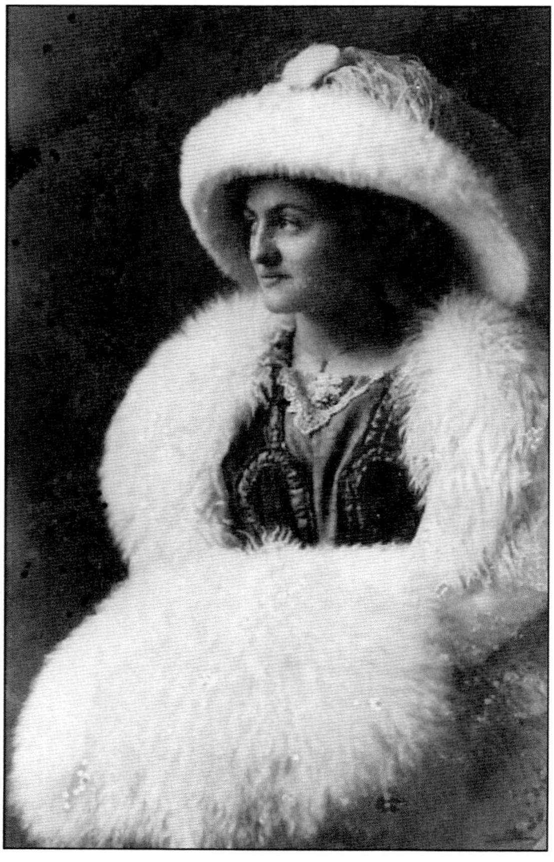

This grand Victorian was owned by William Montgomery Blanks and Lenora Clark Blanks. It still stands in Lockhart today at 617 West San Antonio. However, it is almost unrecognizable. It was remodeled in the 1920s and is now a redbrick home with a tile roof. The porch as shown was removed as well as the tower on the roof. The columns were used in building a house next door to the west for Florence Blanks Horne. Standing in the front yard of the home in this early image are, from left to right, (front) children Florence Blanks and Katherine Blanks, who died in childhood; (back) Walter Holmes, Elizabeth Blanks Holmes, Clark Blanks, William Blanks, Lenora "Nora" Blanks, and Minnie Jo Blanks. Pictured at the left, Minnie Jo Blanks is a striking beauty. In the early 1900s, her grandmother Martha Blanks took Minnie Jo to Chautauqua, New York. They carried as many as five steamer trunks—enough to carry their finest clothes, according to her son Harry Hilgers Jr. Their names appeared often in the *Chautauquan Daily* society pages. (Both, courtesy of Harry Hilgers Jr.)

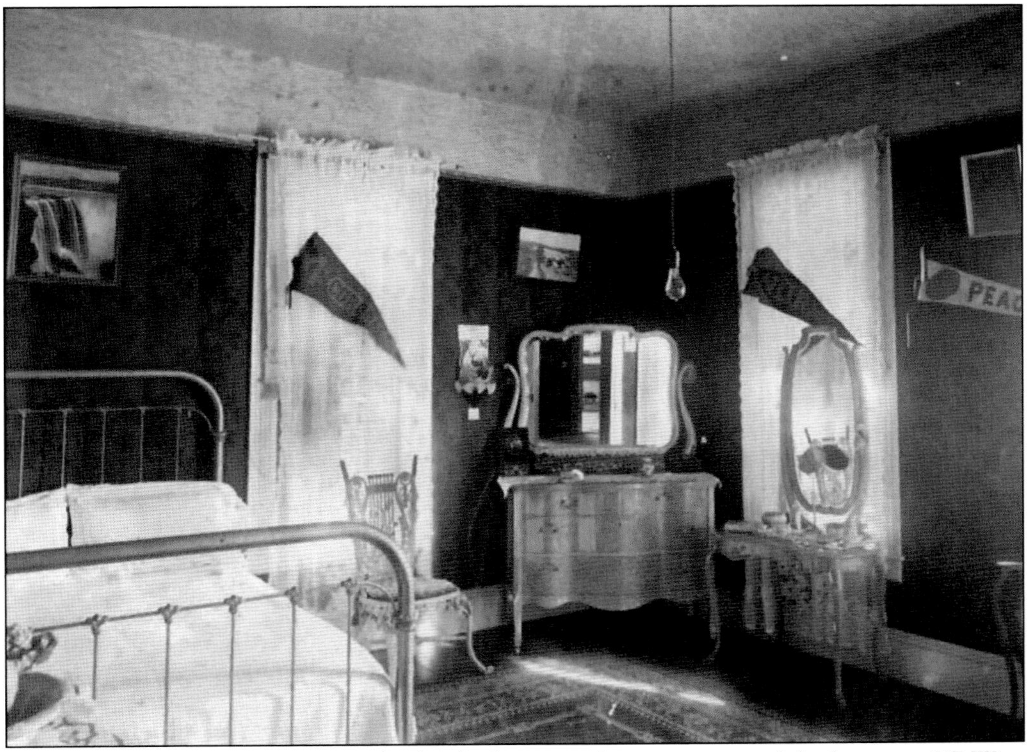

One gets to see inside Minnie Jo Blanks's bedroom in this rare image of the house at 617 West San Antonio Street. The dressing table and chest with a mirror are made of bird's–eye maple. The room is accented with a Persian rug, a wicker chair, and banners from the Coronal Institute in San Marcos, Texas; the San Marcos Normal School (Texas State University); and Peacock Military Academy in San Antonio. A single exposed light bulb hangs from the ceiling. Blanks, pictured below seated at the far right, sought a higher education at Texas Christian University (TCU), a private school founded in Fort Worth in 1873. From 1895 to 1910, TCU moved to Waco to be nearer a larger population and better transportation. The university moved back to downtown Fort Worth in 1910, where it developed into a 300-plus-acre campus of higher learning. (Both, courtesy of Harry Hilgers Jr.)

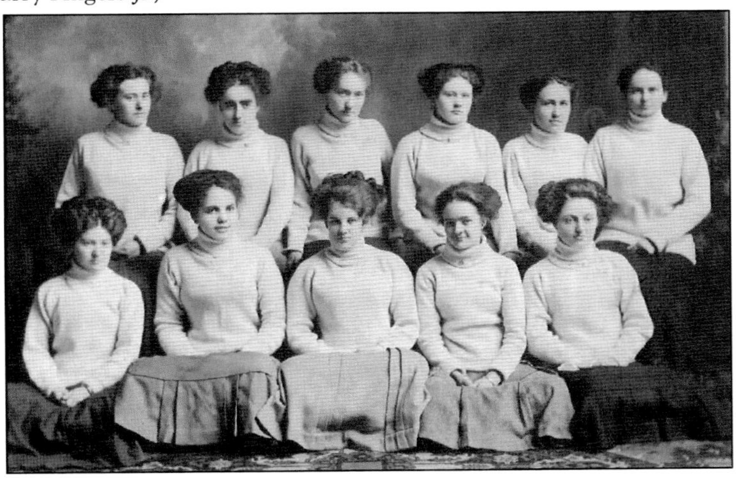

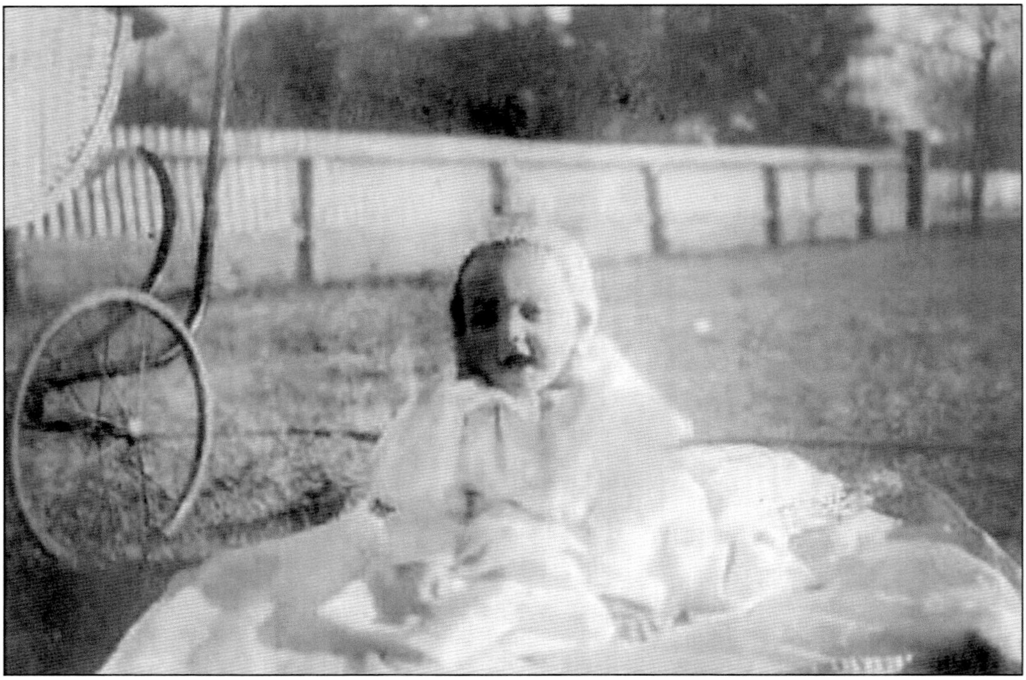

The baby pictured is Kathryn Hilgers, daughter of Minnie Jo and Harry Hilgers. Although very poor quality, it is a touching image. The below photograph is labeled "first home in Lockhart." Minnie Jo Hilgers with baby Kathryn are sitting on the porch of an example of Craftsman Bungalow architecture. It can still be seen at 409 West San Antonio Street. (Both, courtesy of Harry Hilgers Jr.)

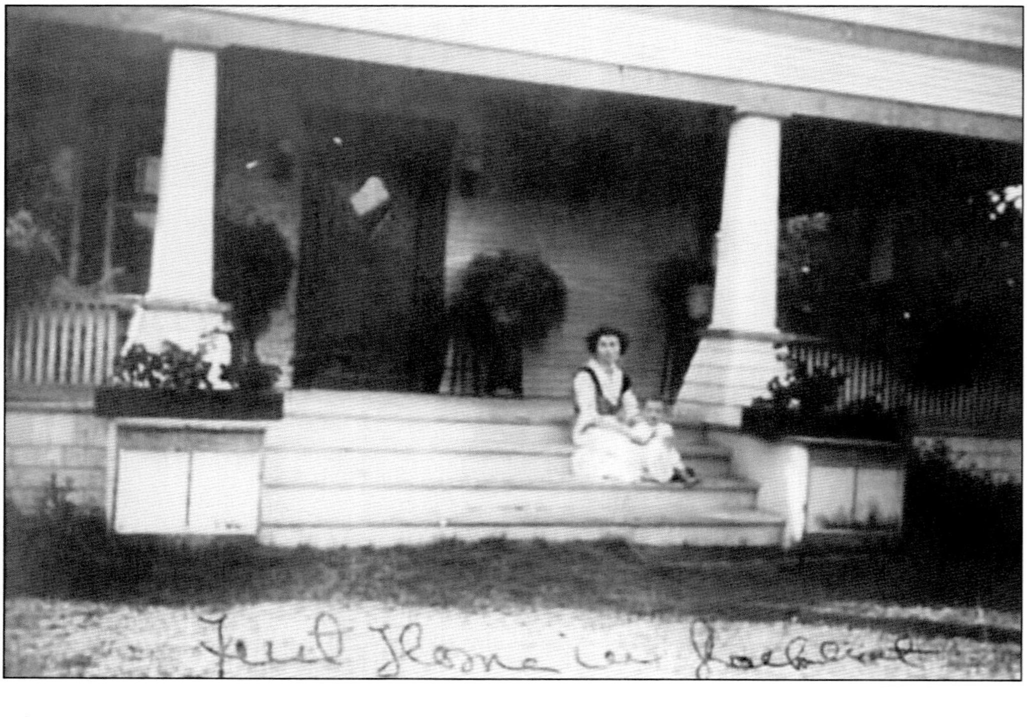

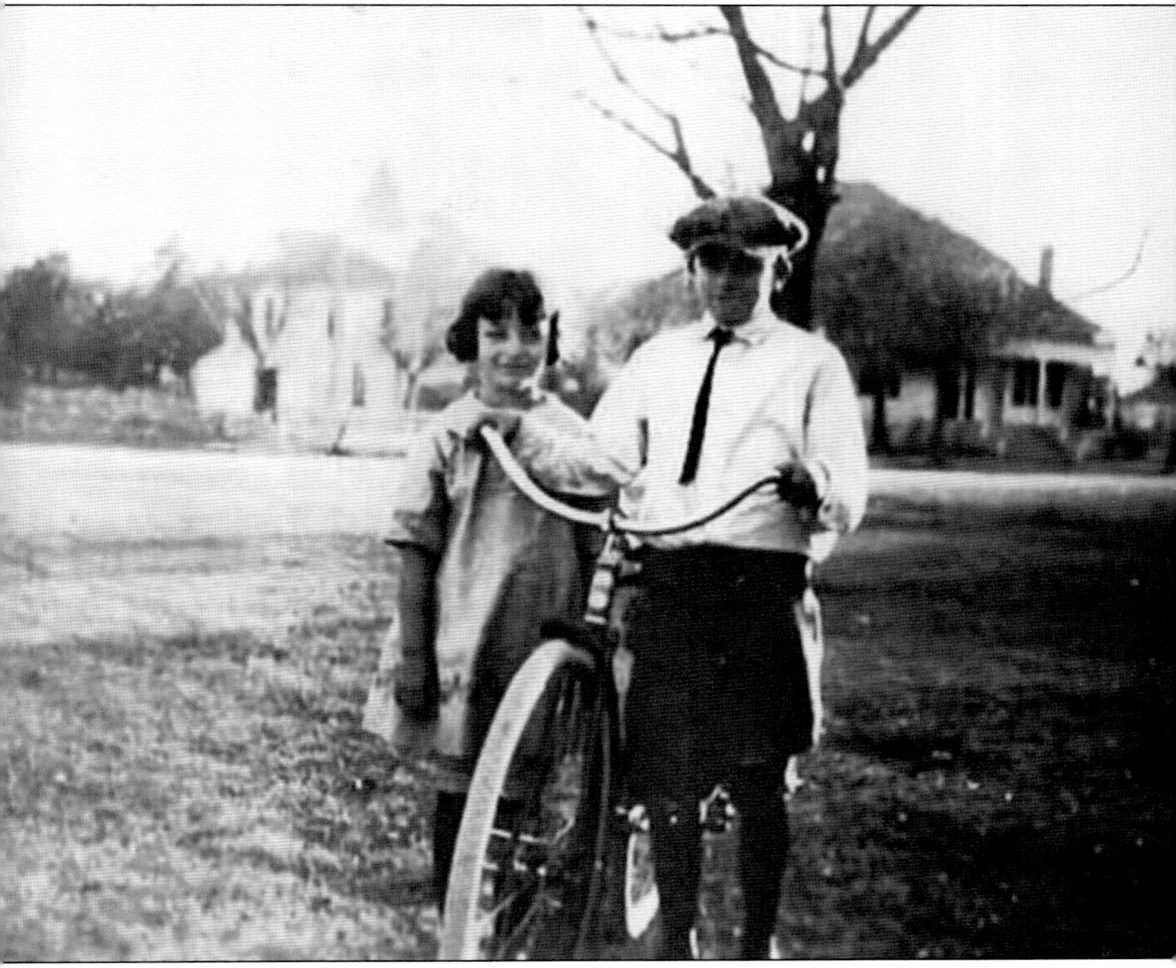

Kathryn Hilgers is pictured here with Joe Holmes of Lockhart. Joe went on to become the first hurdler for the University of Texas at Austin, according to Harry Hilgers Jr. They are standing in the front yard of Kathryn's home on the north side of West San Antonio Street. (Courtesy of Harry Hilgers Jr.)

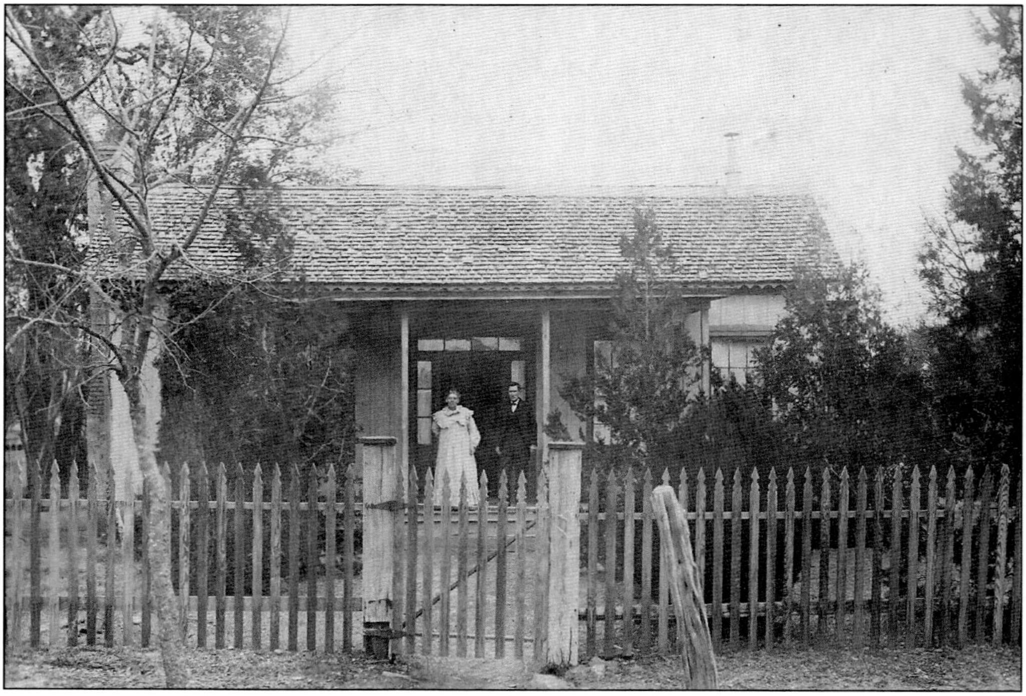

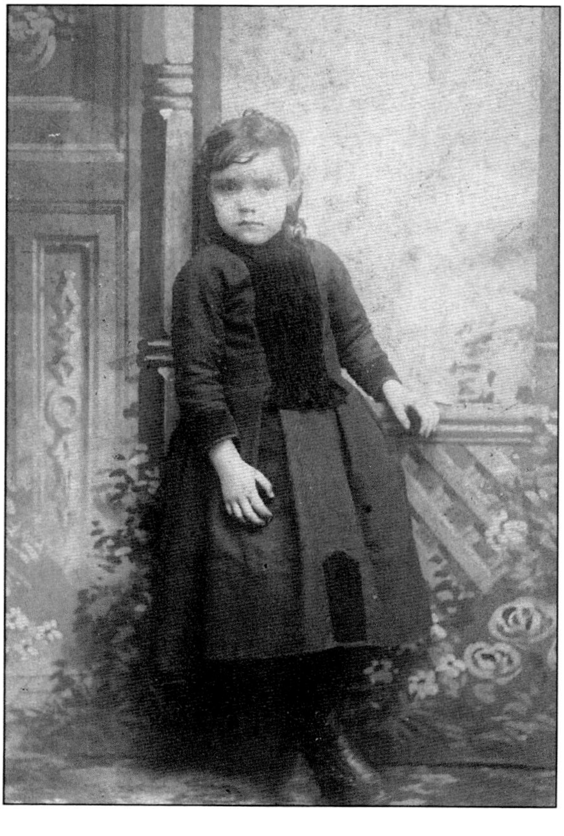

This home once stood on the north side of Prairie Lea Street, very near town. It was the home of Joseph and Jenever Magee, who are pictured standing on their front porch. They came first to the San Gabriel River above Austin in a covered wagon train, arriving in Lockhart in 1871. The home had a cedar shake roof with scalloped trim, a fireplace chimney on the left, an elegant front door flanked by side lights, and a transom light. A picket fence adorns the front yard and a hitching post stands out front for visitors. At the left, the Magees' young daughter who was born in this house, Nora Lee (1884–1979), poses for the Howell Photography Studio on the east side of the square. Nora Lee died in 1979 at 95 years of age. Shortly after her death, her house, shown above, was torn down for a duplex to be built. The address today is 413 and 417 Prairie Lea Street. (Both, Nora Lee Magee Collection, courtesy of Dianne Stevenson.)

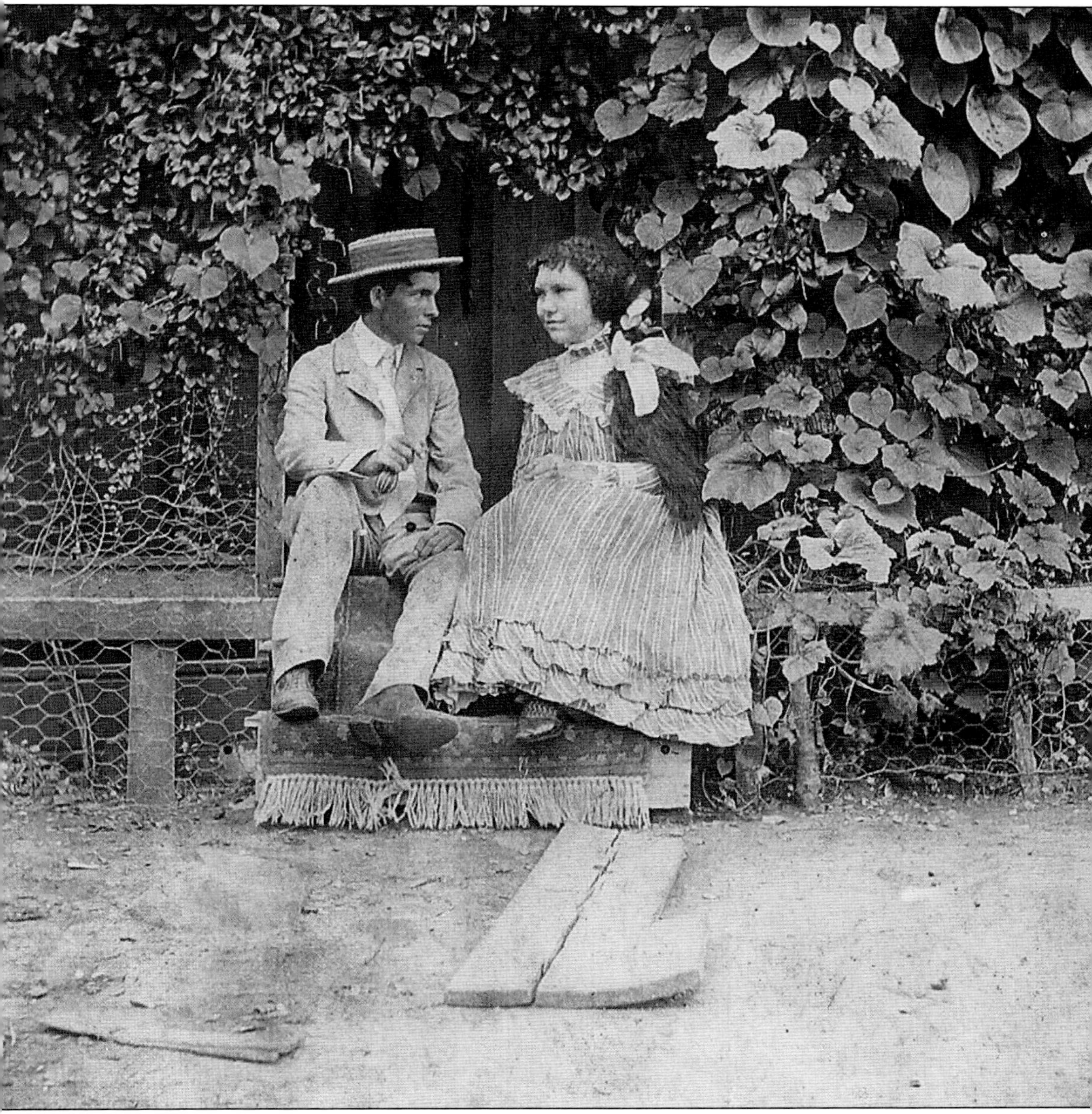

In a personal conversation with her neighbor Dianne Stevenson, Nora Lee Magee shared family stories, including the heartfelt story about this image. Nora Lee was engaged to Dr. Oran Holt (left), but sadly, they never married; the young doctor died after becoming ill. Nora Lee and her beau are shown here visiting as they sat on the back porch of her home. Notice the details such as the nice rug they are sitting on and the lack of grass. It was common to have dirt right up to the house in those days. Just in case it rained, there was a wooden board to step onto the porch, which was draped in gourd vines. Nora Lee lived in this house her entire life. (Nora Lee Magee Collection, courtesy of Dianne Stevenson.)

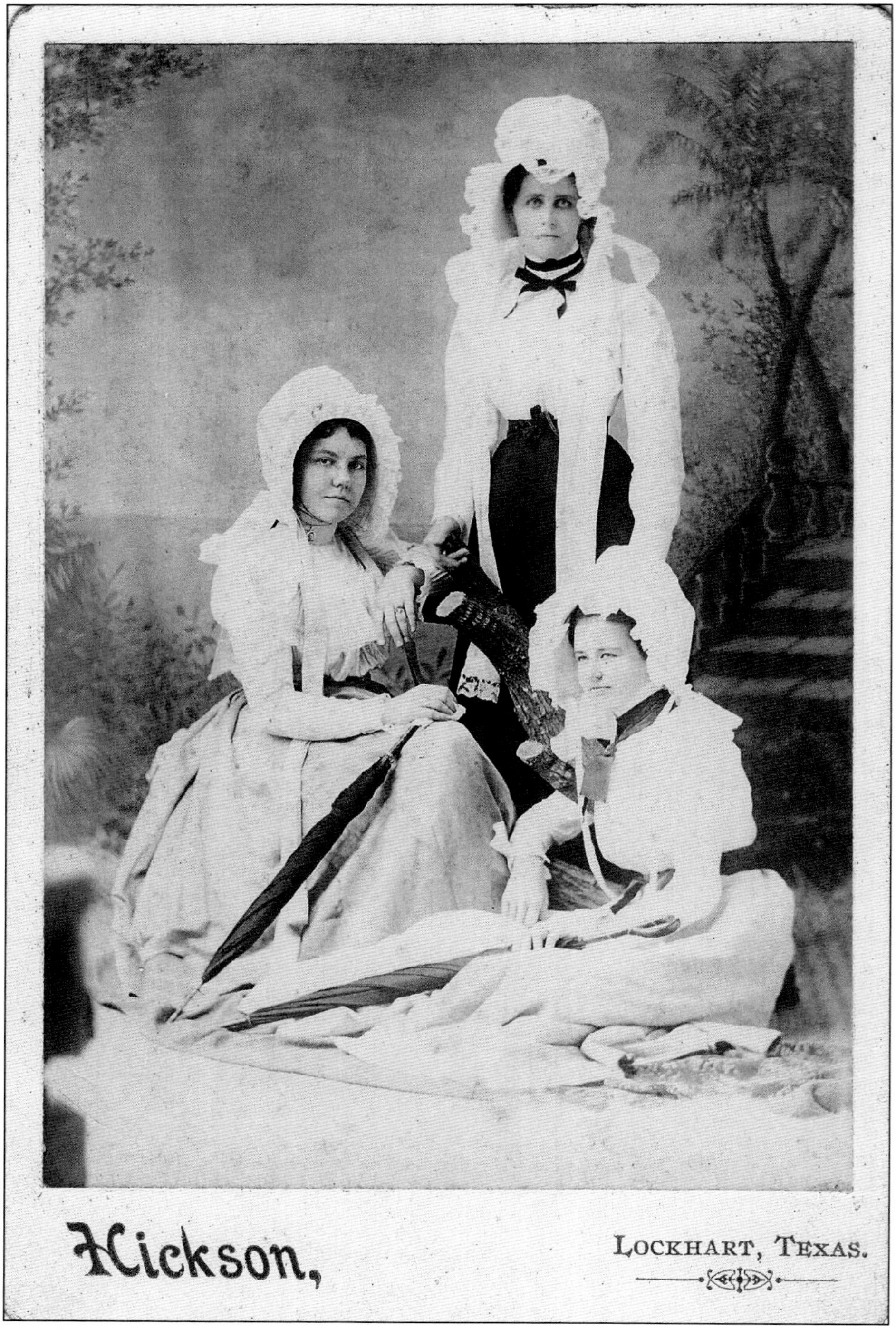

Wearing their finest dresses and bonnets, these three Lockhart ladies sat for their portrait in the 1900s. Nora Lee Magee (left) is pictured along with Mollie Bowden (standing) and Annie Bowden Lamb. This is the work of Hickson's photography studio in Lockhart. Props included a recently sawed-off tree branch and a parasol. (Nora Lee Magee Collection, courtesy of Dianne Stevenson.)

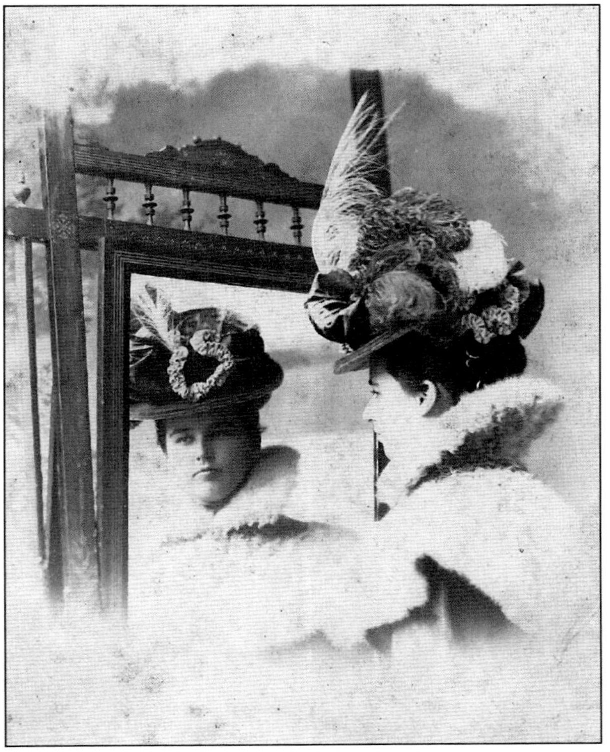

Shown in a very creative photograph of a reflection in a mirror is Annie Bowden Lamb (b. October 6, 1880; d. December 27, 1919). She was married to Robert S. Lamb, who ran Lamb's Gin. They had three sons, Merritt Lamb, Ray Lamb, and Robert Lamb. Annie, looking very serious, is wearing a fur cape and a fine hat adorned with feathers. Striking a pose below in a wonderful lace trimmed and ruffled dress is Jessie Lamb Vogel, who appears to be quiet a model for the photographer. (Right, Nora Lee Magee Collection, courtesy of Dianne Stevenson; below, courtesy of Ronda A. Reagan.)

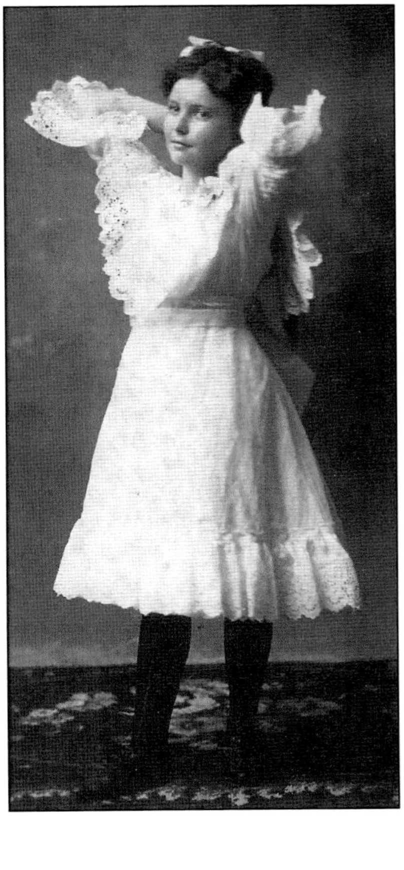

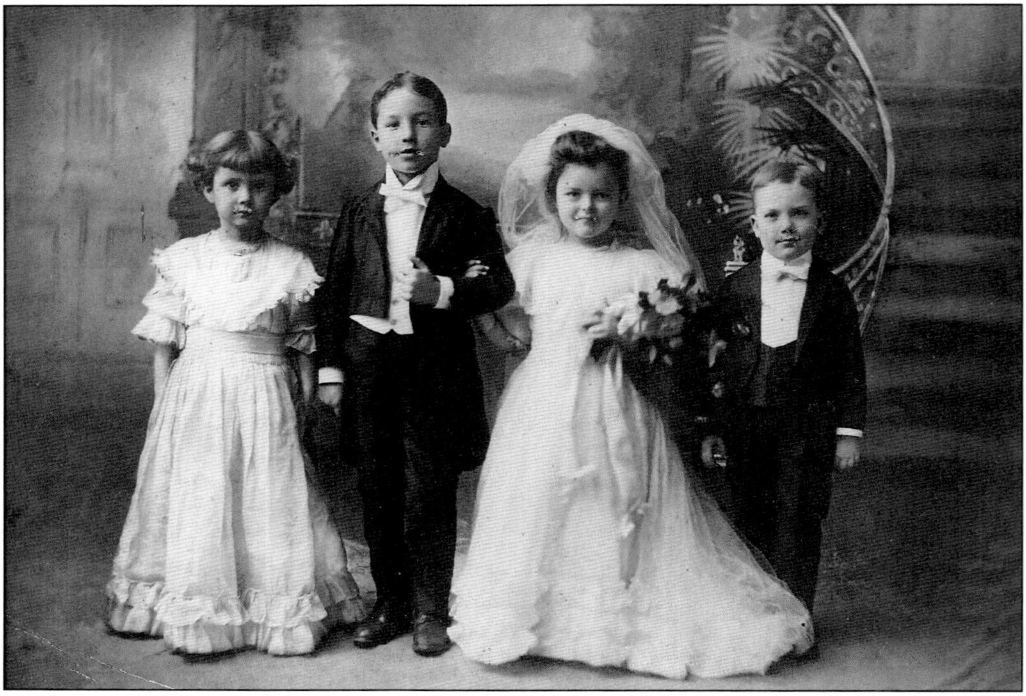

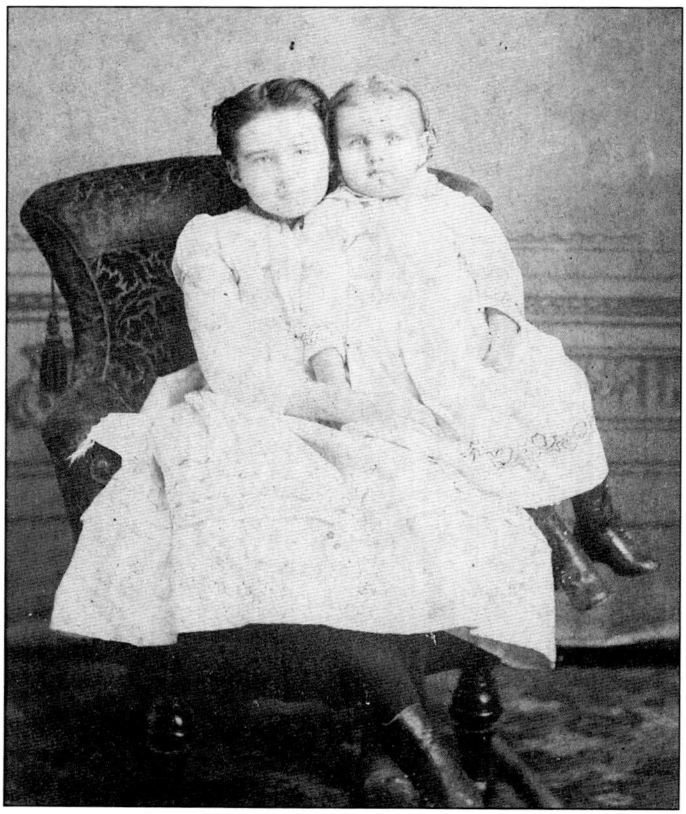

After little people Charles Stratton and Lavinia Warren were married on February 10, 1863, the world became fascinated with their wedding. In 1898, about 35 years after their wedding, the play *The Greatest Little Wedding* debuted, telling the story. Dr. Abner Ross (second from left) was the groom in the "Tom Thumb Wedding," and his best man was James Magee (far right). The photograph at the left is of Annie Bowden and Mary Bowden by Howell Artist, East Side Public Square, Lockhart, Texas. (Above, Nora Lee Magee Collection, courtesy of Dianne Stevenson; left, courtesy of Ronda A. Reagan.)

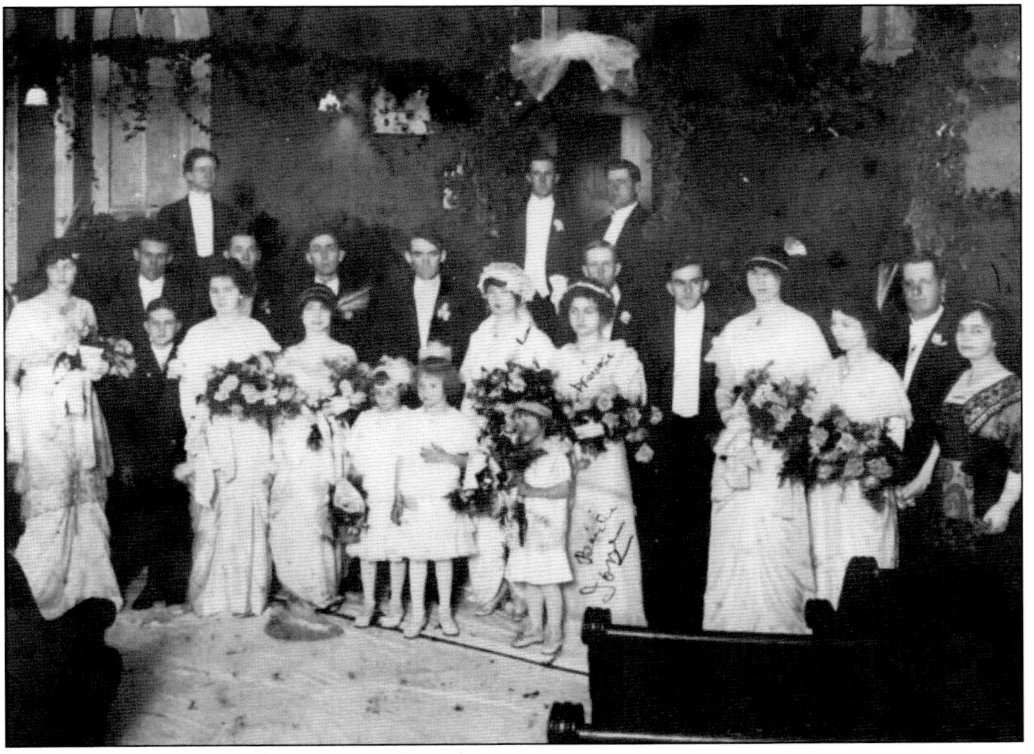

The wedding of Lee Mebane McCurdy and Ione Lay, on January 28, 1914, is pictured above. At the right is a photograph of the young couple. Ione is wearing a gingham frock. (Both, courtesy of Harry Hilgers Jr.)

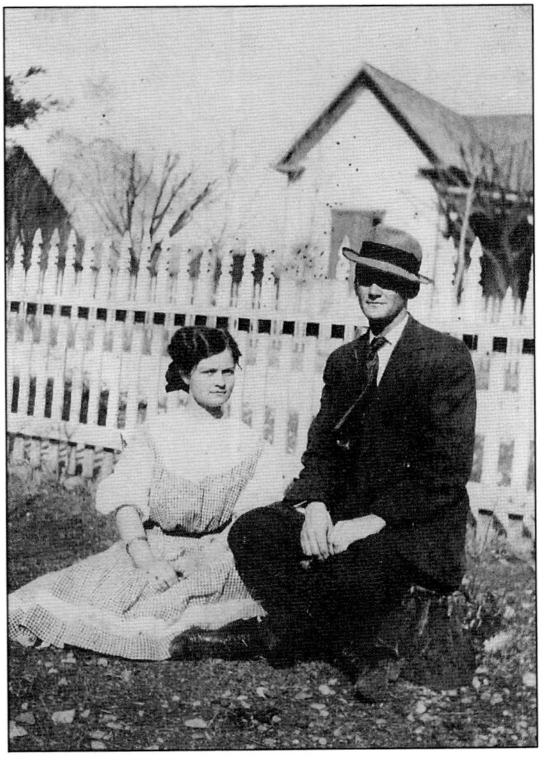

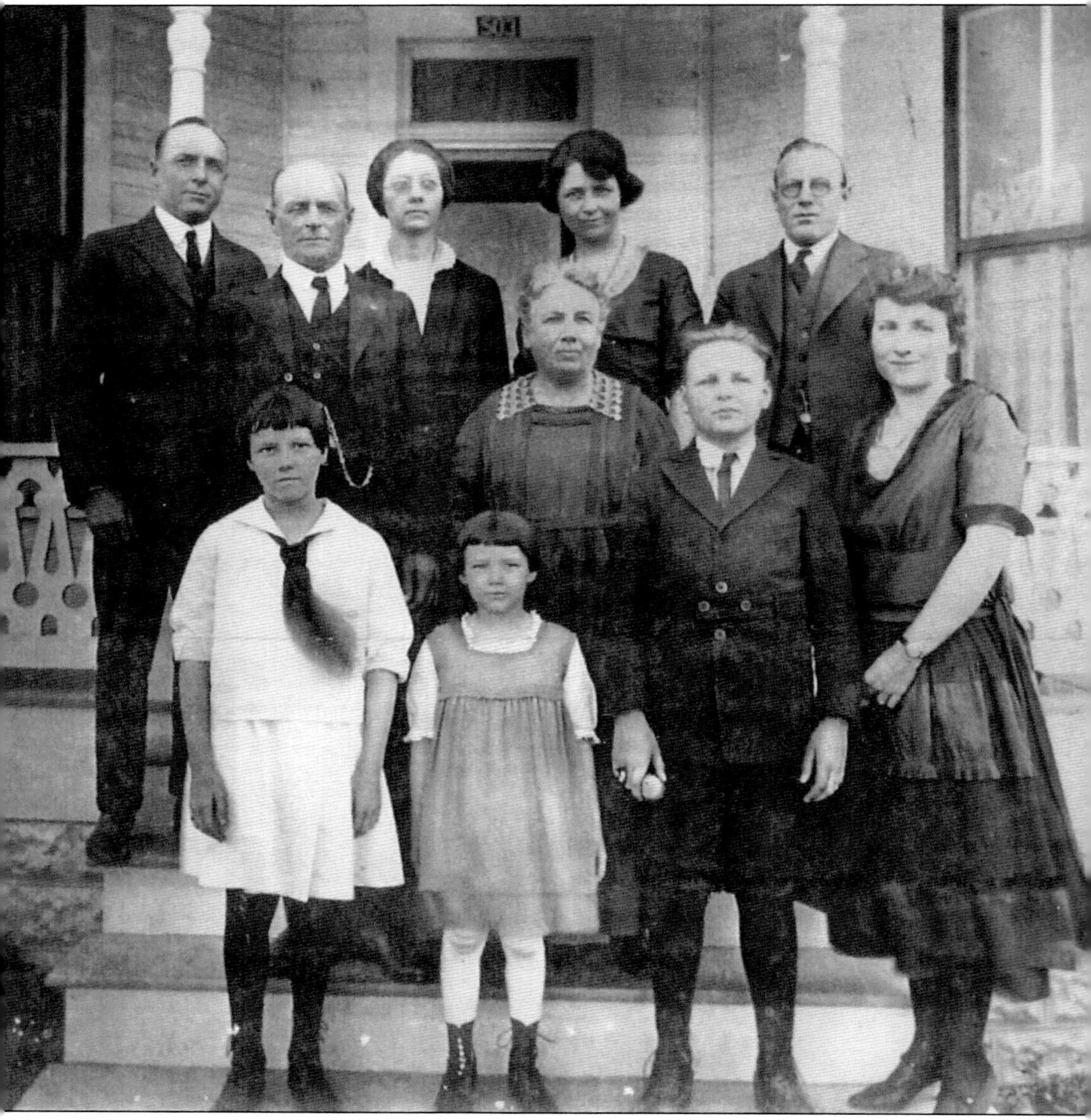

Descendants of A.L. and Rebecca Brock are pictured in this family photograph. (Courtesy of the CCHC.)

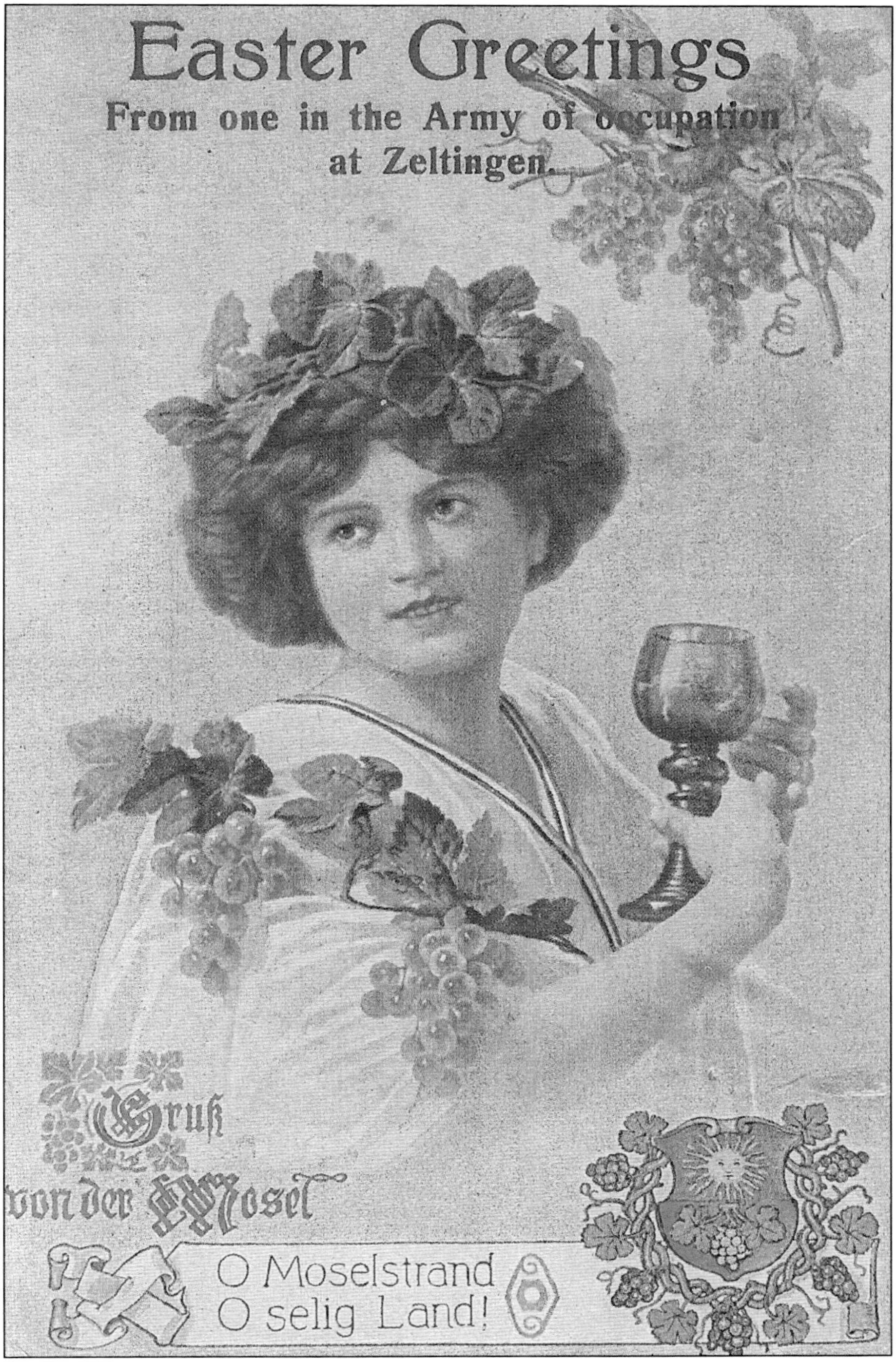

This Easter greeting postcard was mailed from oversees by one of Lockhart's own soldiers to Miss Ruby Ellis (author's grandmother) on March 8, 1919, a few months after the signing of the armistice on November 11, 1918. The young man said he was well and anxious to return home. (Courtesy of Ronda A. Reagan.)

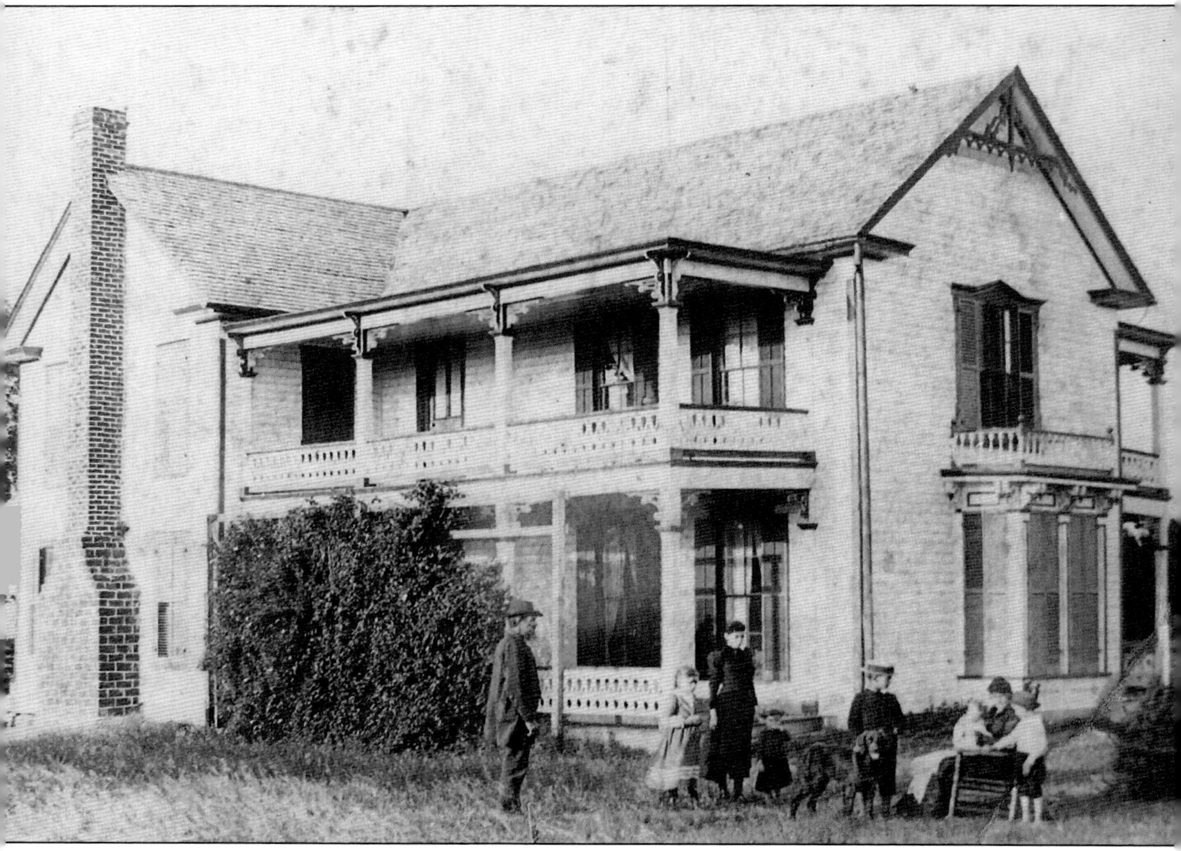

Pictured in 1892, this is the home of early Lockhart resident James Andrew McCurdy. McCurdy was born in May 1840 in Virginia. The spacious two-story home with a double veranda was located just outside the town on the north side of the Bastrop Highway (today's Highway 20 East). The family is standing and sitting in front of the home. Although officially undocumented, it is believed that James and his wife, Mary Elizabeth "Minnie" Mebane McCurdy, are present along with six of their nine children and the family dog. The McCurdys had three boys and six girls. The children were Elizabeth McCurdy Field, William David McCurdy, Lee Mebane McCurdy, James Leroy McCurdy, Margaret McCurdy Bell, Mary Kerr McCurdy Purcell, Carrie Lyle McCurdy Patton, Annie Steel McCurdy Cardwell, and Virginia Ruth McCurdy Chapman. The house was torn down in the 1960s. Today, only the chimney stands at the original homesite. (Nora Lee Magee Collection, courtesy of Dianne Stevenson.)

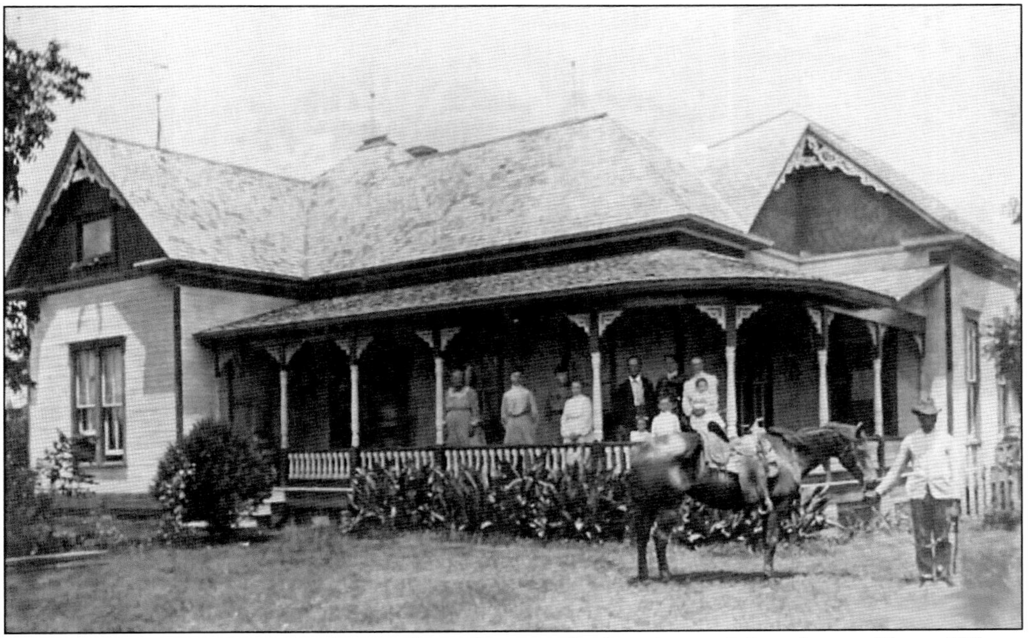

It was customary to have family members photographed in front of their home. Harry Hilgers Jr. provided this photograph, and it is believed to be of a Clark family home. His grandmother Lenora, who married William Blanks, was a Clark. Although Harry could not positively identify all the people standing on the front porch, he did know that the man on the far right holding the horse is Levi, who worked at William Blanks's mule barn in town (see page 36). (Courtesy of Harry Hilgers Jr.)

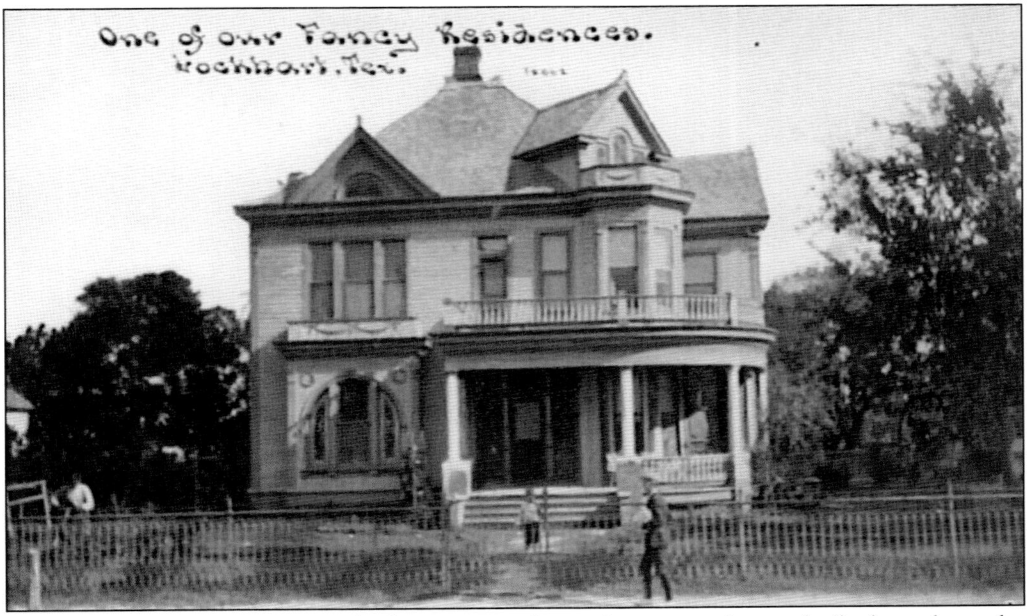

Beautiful homes like this one, which survives only on this postcard, were built throughout the heart of the county seat. Nothing is known about the address or the owner of this grand example of "one of our Fancy Residences" in Lockhart, Texas. (Courtesy of Harry Hilgers Jr.).

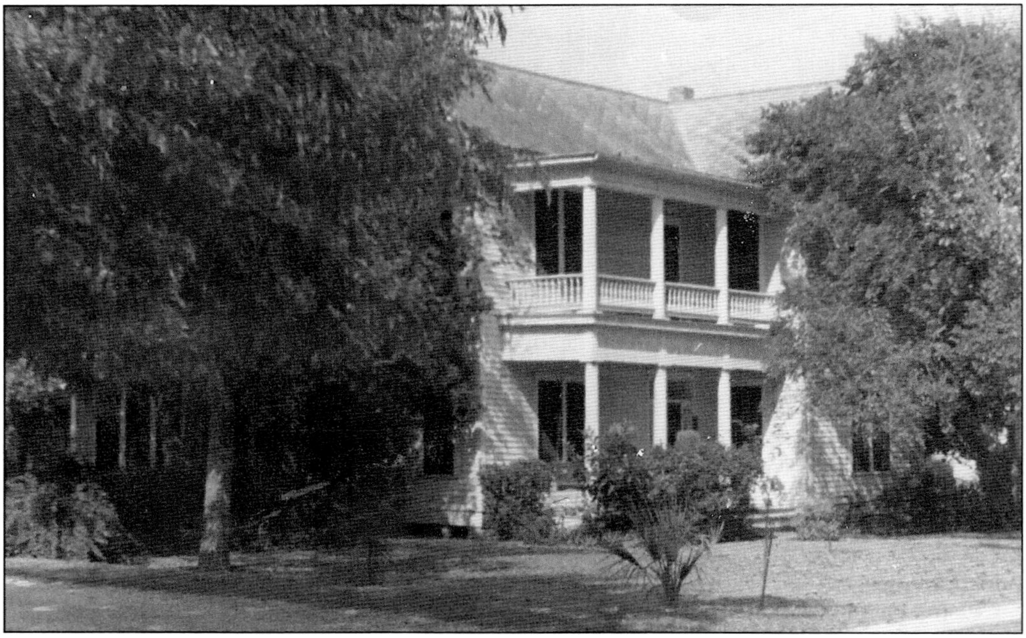

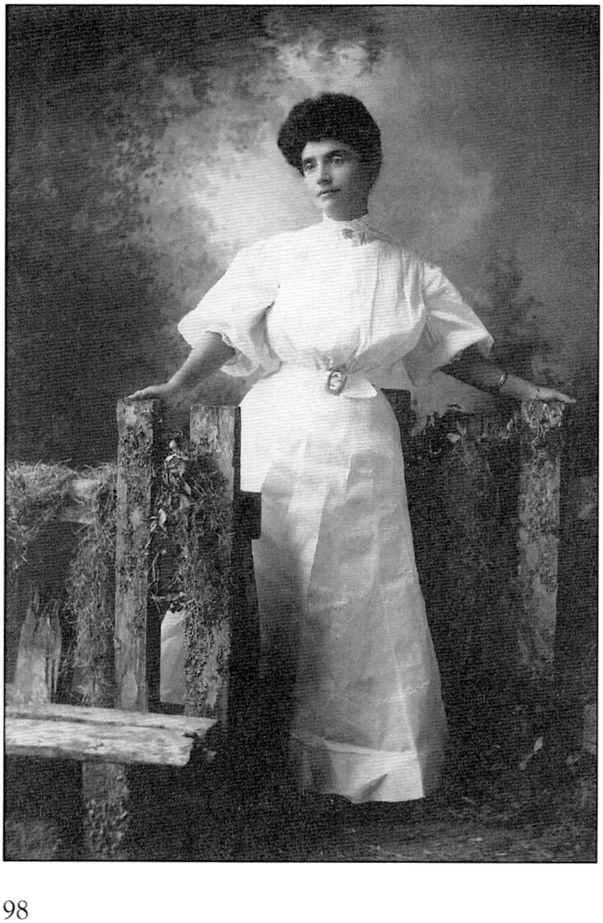

This is the J.E. Lay residence, which is located at 121 Nueces Street. Photography was a big business in Lockhart with many studios from which to choose. Professional photographs in this book are from works by Wranitzky Bros.; W.T. Wells, photographer, San Antonio Street; C.L. Hickman; Harry Annas; Cozby & Son Artists; Carter; Grueter & Tannenberger; and Howell. However, Sally L. Lay, wearing a crisply starched dress, had this photograph made in Alvin, Texas. (Above, courtesy of Ronda A. Reagan; left, Nora Lee Magee Collection, courtesy of Dianne Stevenson.)

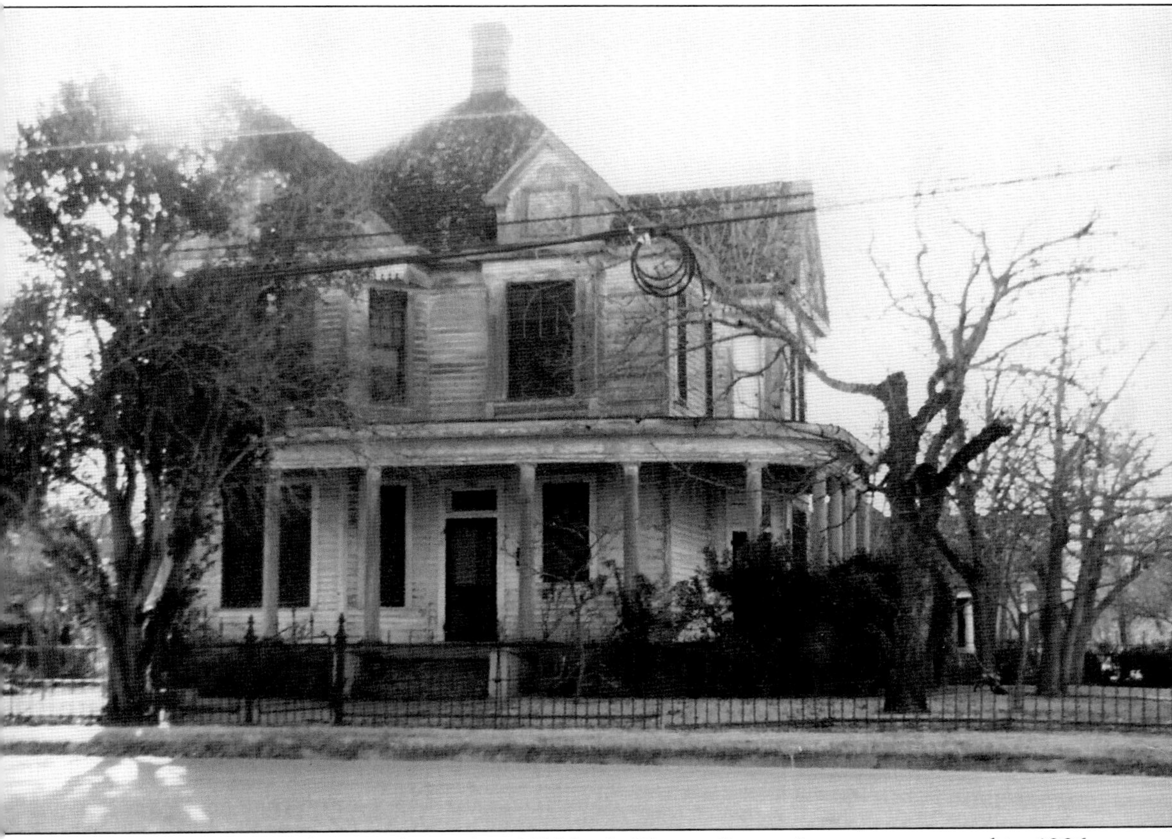

The Joseph Masur Jr. home is located at 217 North Blanco Street. It was constructed in 1906 and remained in the same family until 1987 when Ed and Anita Strayer purchased it. The Masur brothers—Joseph Jr., Henry, and Edward—all worked in their father Joseph's furniture and hardware store. Two later built and owned hardware stores of their own in Lockhart. Their uncle was Joseph Hannig, who married Susanna Dickinson, an Alamo survivor. This is a photograph of the home prior to restoration by the Strayers. The iron fence around the front yard was once around the Caldwell County Courthouse. The County judge ordered it taken down shortly after the hitching posts and rails were cut down by the city in the middle of the night. About 200 feet are here and it was recently discovered that the balance of the fence was given to A.L. Brock, who put it around his second home on Boggy Creek. (Courtesy of Ed and Anita Strayer.)

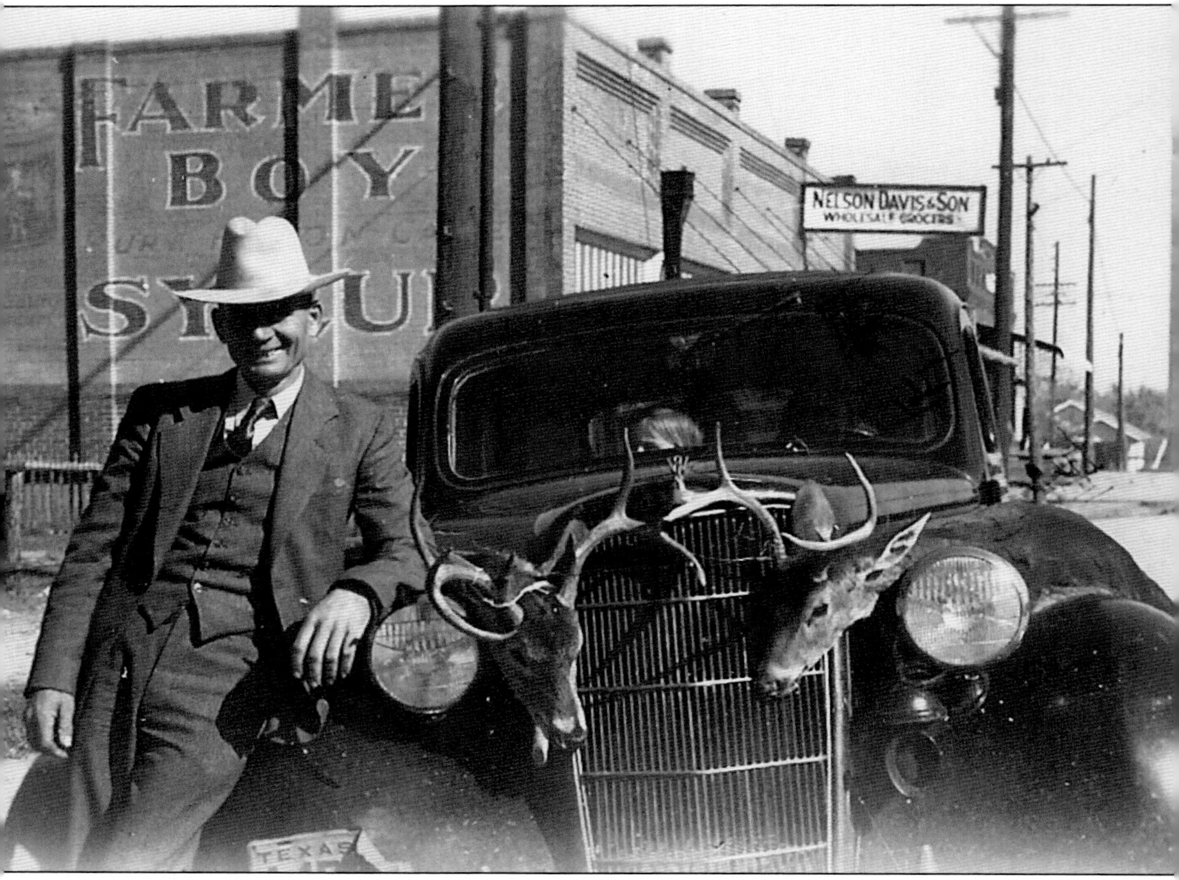

Dressed in a three-piece suit, Bart Hutchison McGee (the author's grandfather) brought his "trophy" bucks to town to take them to the butcher. It is difficult to make out, but the carcasses are thrown over the fenders of the car. This late-1930s image was taken next to Nelson Davis & Son Wholesale Grocers, east of what is today's State Highway 183. If one looks closely, the head of a little girl can be seen peeping out the front windshield. McGee (1893–1970) was a World War I veteran and Lockhart native. He married Ruby Ellis (1901–1984). He was a farmer and rancher. During his lifetime, he raised racehorses and Black Angus cattle, baled hay, and planted Coastal bermudagrass for others from sun-up to sundown. They had three daughters, Ona Lea Anton, Annie Ray Henry, and Oneta Joyce Maynard, the little girl behind the windshield. (Courtesy of Ona Anton.)

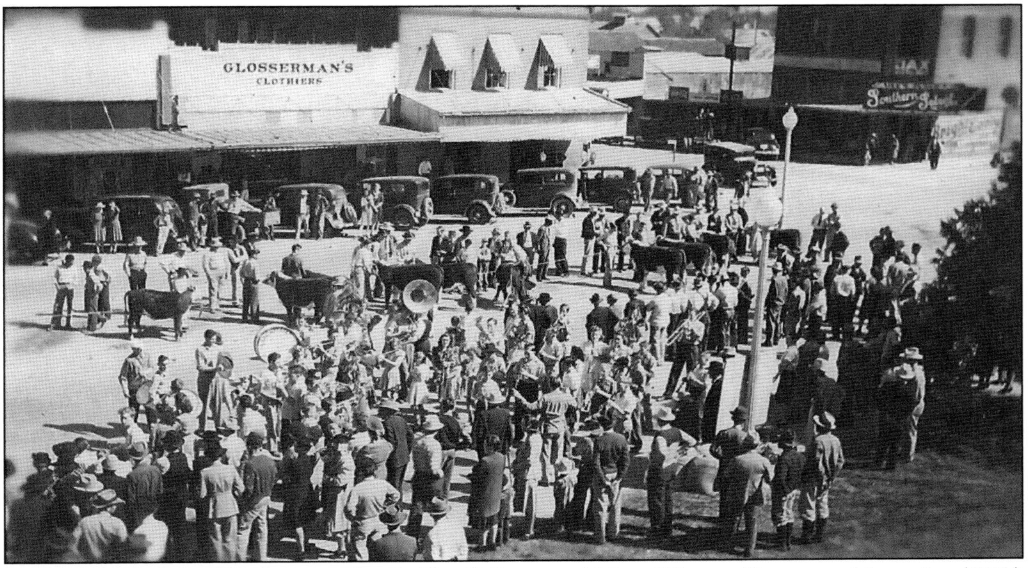

This is a scene of calf judging at the Caldwell County 4-H and Future Farmers of America (FFA) Fat Stock Show held on the east side of the town square on March 3, 1941. Some 41 calves were shown by the 4-Hers. The first female to ever show a calf in Caldwell County was Ona Lea McGee of McMahan (the author's mother). Her calf received fifth place. "When I picked it out at Scrutchin Ranch in Hays County [along with other youth from Lockhart], they all told me I got the worst one," said McGee. Caldwell County Judge Callihan purchased her calf for $11.10 per 100 pounds. J.E. Palm reported, "You do not have to be a man to raise cattle nor a boy to be a good 4-H club member. At least that's the way . . . Ona Lea McGee . . . feels about it." In the interview, she said she liked raising cattle better than making clothes and cooking. Harry Annas took most of these pictures. (Both, courtesy of Ona Anton.)

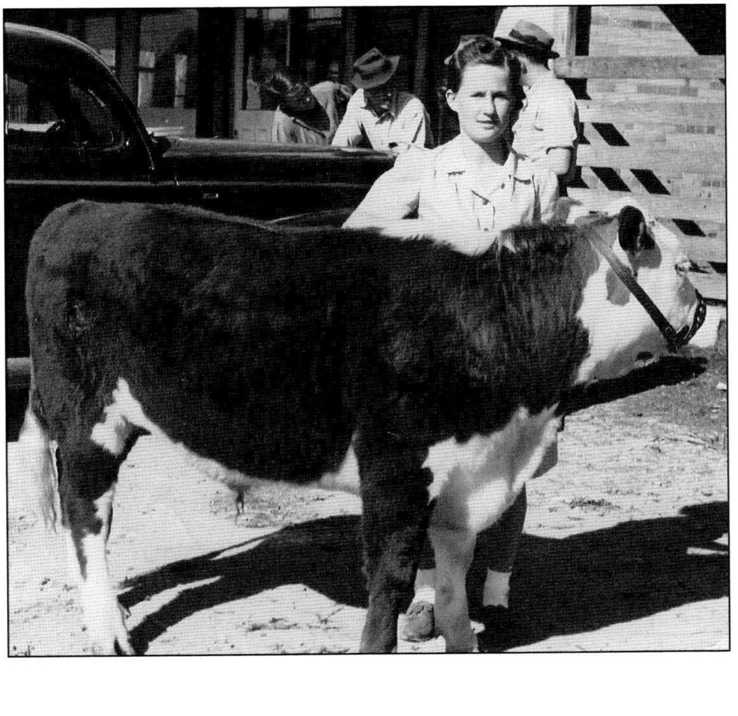

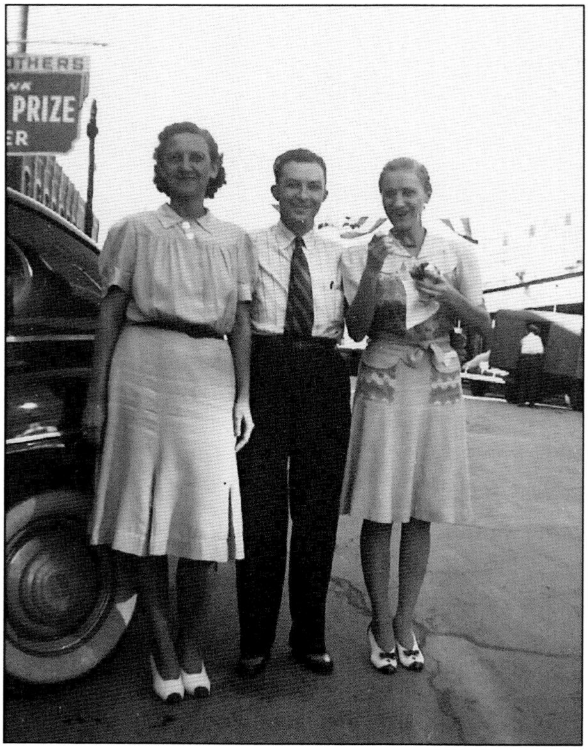

Having just left the Corner Drugstore, where they were served by soda jerk Joe Henry Bunch, are, from left to right, Mattie Ray Jolley, Foster Jolley, and Hazel Jolley with a dish of ice cream. The two women are sisters. To the left is a Two Brothers sign advertising Grand Prize Beer. (Courtesy of Joe Henry Bunch.)

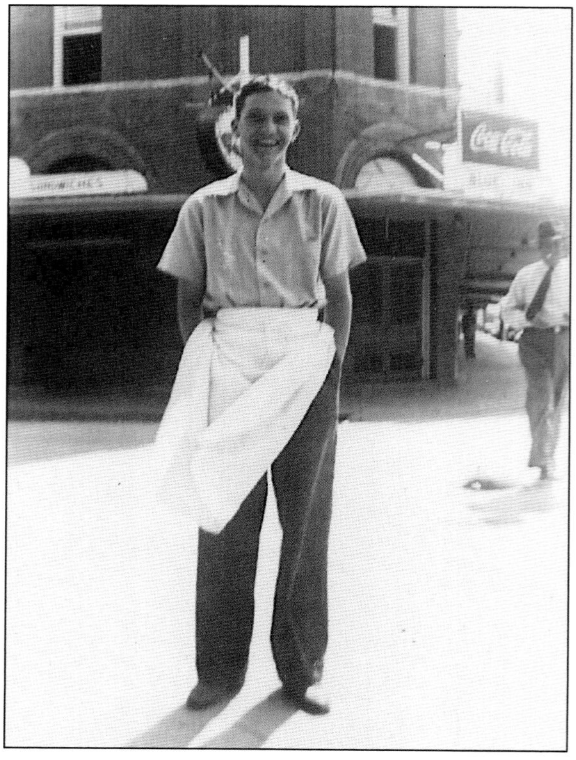

Lockhart-born resident Joe Henry Bunch enjoyed his first job as a teenager being a soda jerk at Ploeger Drugstore on the south side of the square. In this picture, Bunch is standing in front of the Corner Drugstore on the north side of the square, where he also worked. Bunch said "This was a large soda fountain with a double fountain, 20 stools and six booths to serve, plus curb service." (Courtesy of Joe Henry Bunch.)

Five

Schools and Churches

As the town developed and families moved into it, the first school classes were held in the Masonic lodge, and there were private schools that met in homes. Lockhart's first school was the Lockhart Academy, which was located in a two-story building across the street and west of the Episcopal church on Church Street. Other early schools included the Plum Creek School and the Catholic school. The first "little red schoolhouse" building was constructed in 1907, and the campus subsequently grew. Today, the Lockhart Independent School District has two high schools, a freshman campus, a junior high, four elementary schools, and a public kindergarten. There is also a private residential treatment center for boys called Pegasus.

Religion played a major role in the town's development. Clear Fork Baptist Church was organized in 1848 and is listed as the first church in the area. Other early churches included the Episcopal and the Tinney Creek churches, both started in 1852. Within two decades of the town's birth, 11 churches were in existence in the town and surrounding county. Many were serviced by itinerant preachers and ministers who traveled from town to town to preach the Word. Camp meetings on the ground also played an important role in the religious development of the county. One such meeting that takes place today just east of Lockhart is the Sacred Harp Singing in McMahan at Bethel Primitive Baptist Church. Two of Lockhart's early churches still operate in their original buildings from the 1800s.

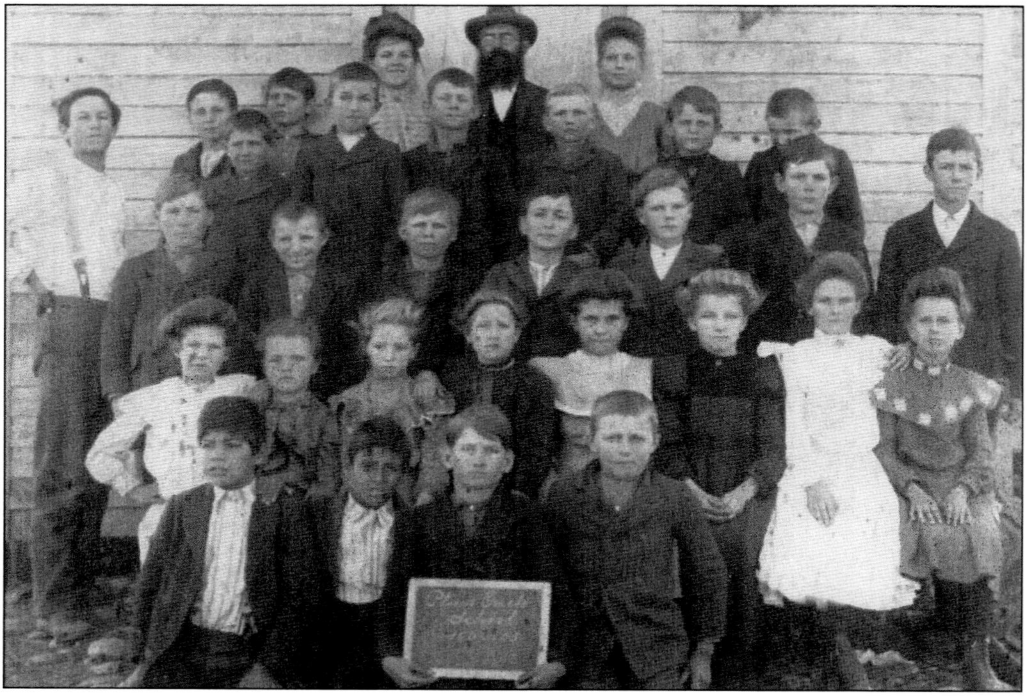

In this early class picture, some 37 young students pose outside the one-room schoolhouse known as Plum Creek School. The slate chalkboard reads 1904–1905. On the back row are two unidentified female teachers and perhaps the principal in the center. The young gentleman on the far left may also be a teacher. Today, there is a modern-day Plum Creek Elementary School in Lockhart. (Courtesy of the Caldwell County Genealogical and Historical Society.)

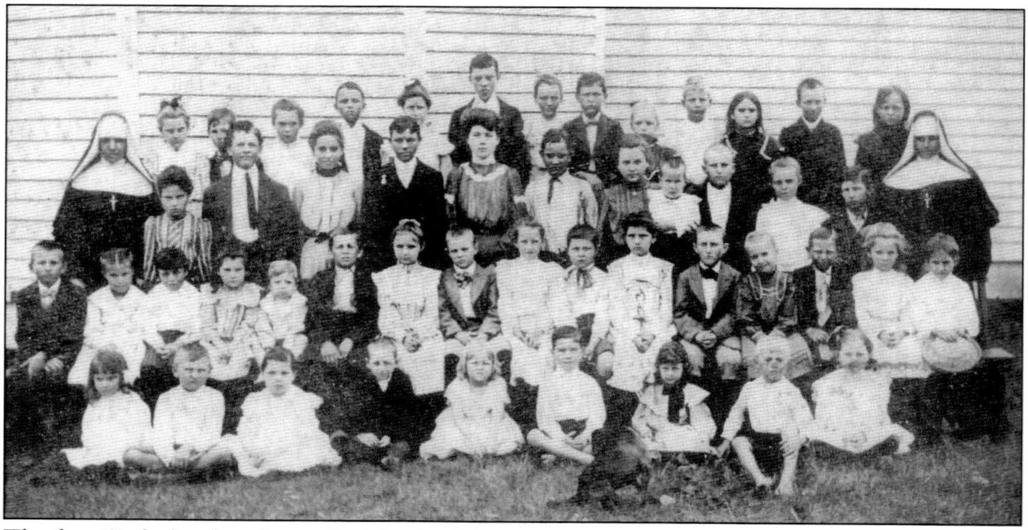

The first Catholic church was St. Mary's of the Visitation, built in the 1880s. It also ran a school in early Lockhart, which included the first through 11th grades. Back then, the 12th grade did not exist. There is a "class mascot" sitting in the front, a large dog. Two nuns were the teachers of all these pupils who appear to be dressed in their Sunday best. St. Mary's had its first baptism in 1882. It is located at 205 West Pecan Street. (Courtesy of Gerry and Conrad Ohlendorf.)

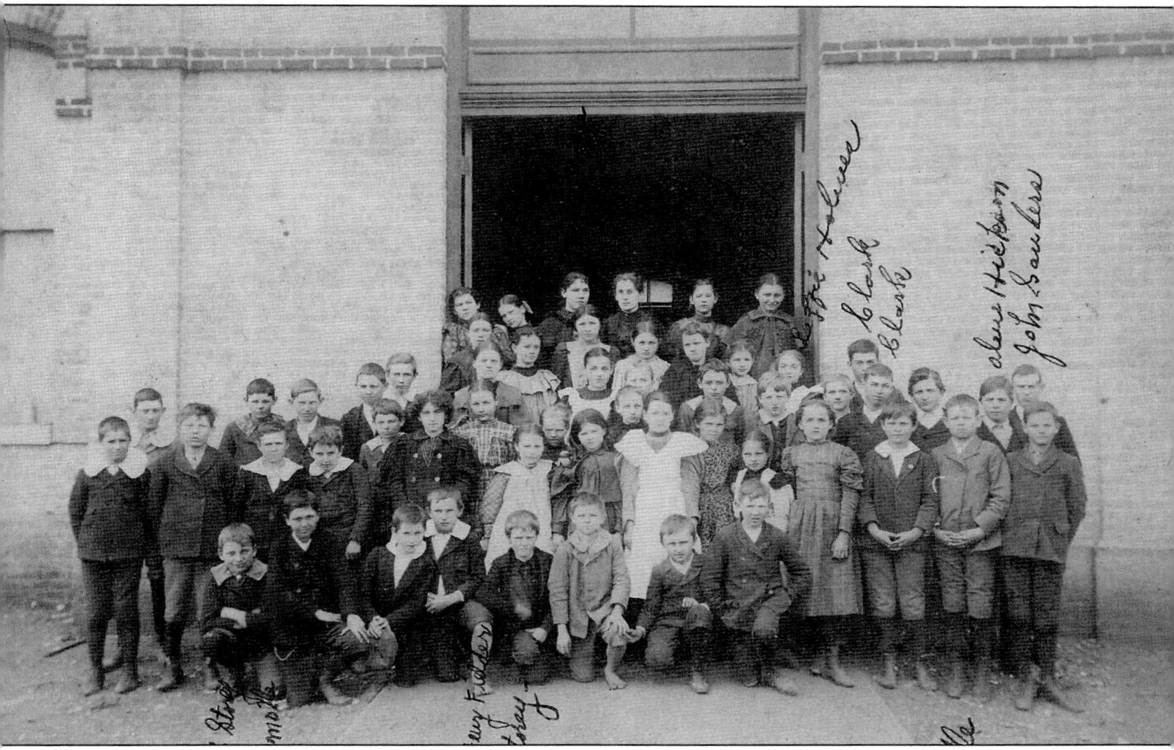

Here, with her classmates, teenager Nora Lee Magee is pictured third from the left in the last row. Her schoolteacher is to the right of her. The full and partial hand-written names of others include Vick, Lizzie Holmes, Clark, Clark, Claus Hickson, John Sanders, Dick Storey, Walter Mohle, Henry Fielder, Jeff Storey, and Mark Raudle. Many of the young boys have on high-top boots and large white collars draped outside their jackets. Despite the fact that it must be a fall or early-winter day, four young boys on the front row are barefoot, which is likely the more normal dress for everyday school during those times. (Nora Lee Magee Collection, courtesy of Dianne Stevenson.)

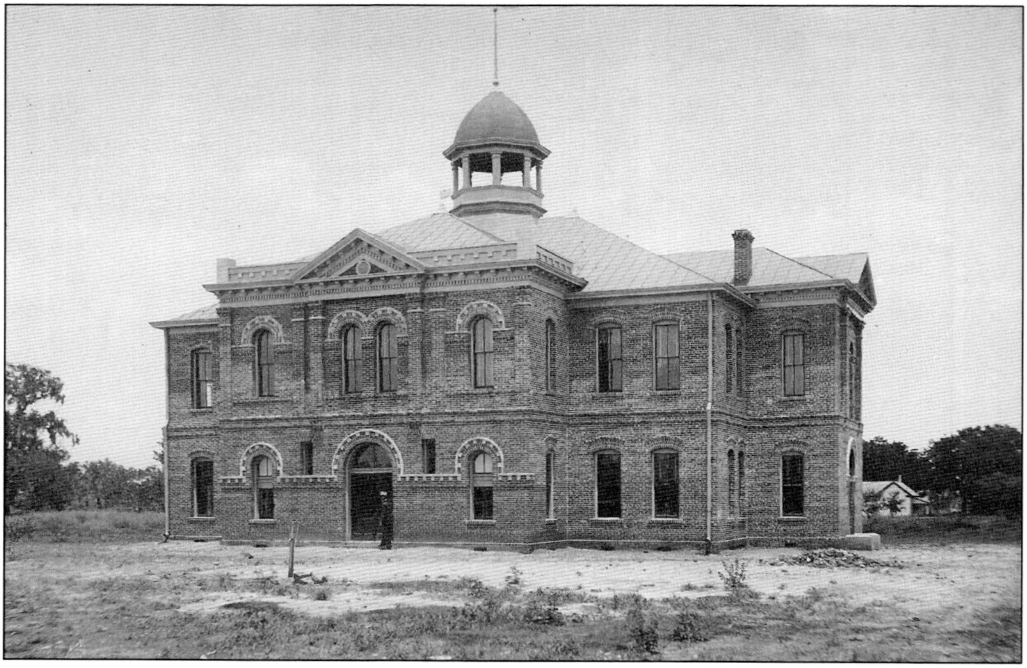

City council purchased the land known as Jordan Institute to build a high school worthy of the town. A $10,000 bond was voted in to erect a public free school building in 1907. Affectionately referred to as the little red schoolhouse (above), this 1908 image was taken just after completion. There is an unidentified man standing out front. Pupils recall starting first grade there in 1930 in the first room on the right on the first floor. The teacher was Bessie Coupland. The second floor served home economics, which was taught by Marie Hillard. A second, equally splendid building, the buff brick school pictured below, was built on the school's campus for upper-grade levels. (Above, courtesy of Joe Henry Bunch; below, courtesy of Ronda A. Reagan.)

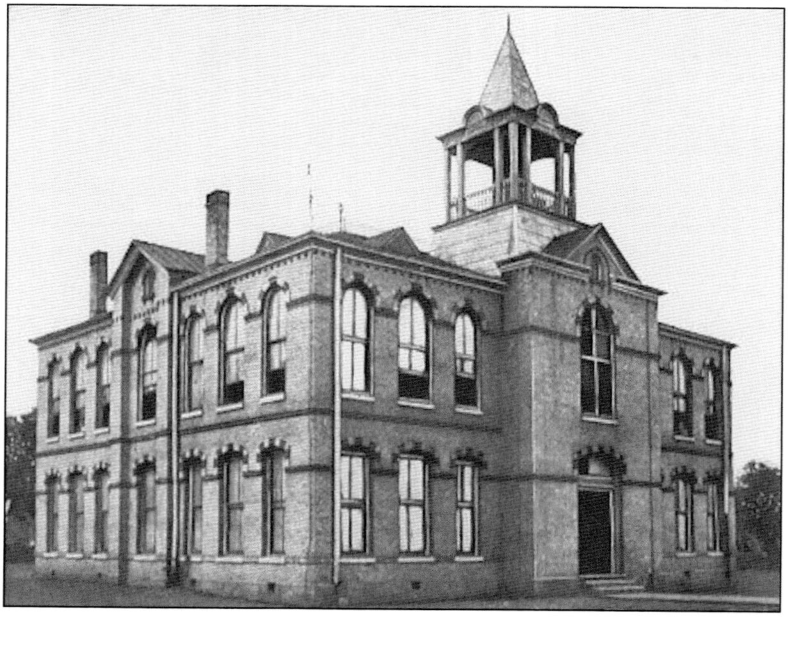

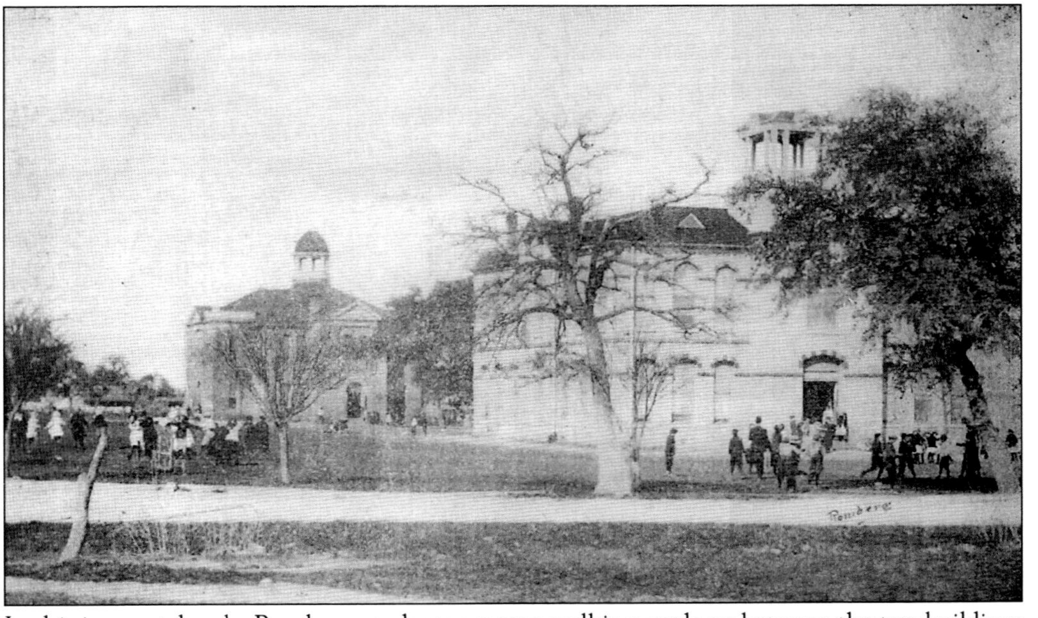

In this image, taken by Romberg, students are seen walking outdoors between the two buildings and perhaps playing Ring around the Rosie on the far left. It appears to be early spring, as one of the smaller trees shows flowering buds. Both of these magnificent buildings were demolished in light of progress to make way for a bigger and more up-to-date Lockhart school campus. The demolition is documented in the image below, showing the removal of the roof and most of the windows. A worker is standing in the front doorway. (Above, courtesy of Gerry and Conrad Ohlendorf; below, courtesy of the CCHC.)

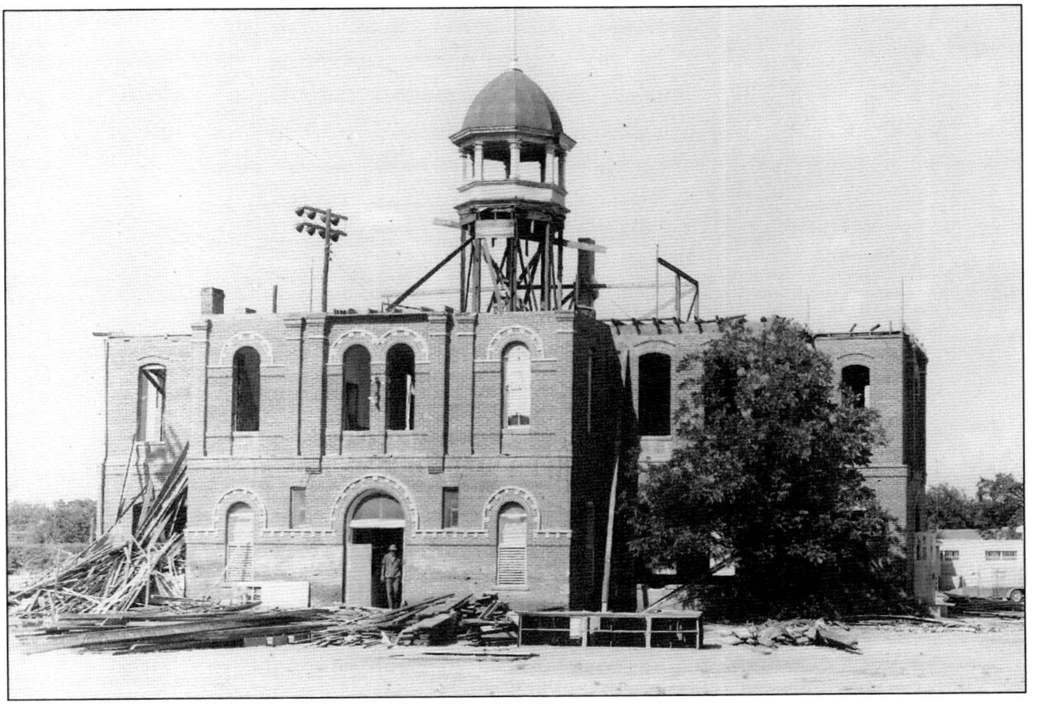

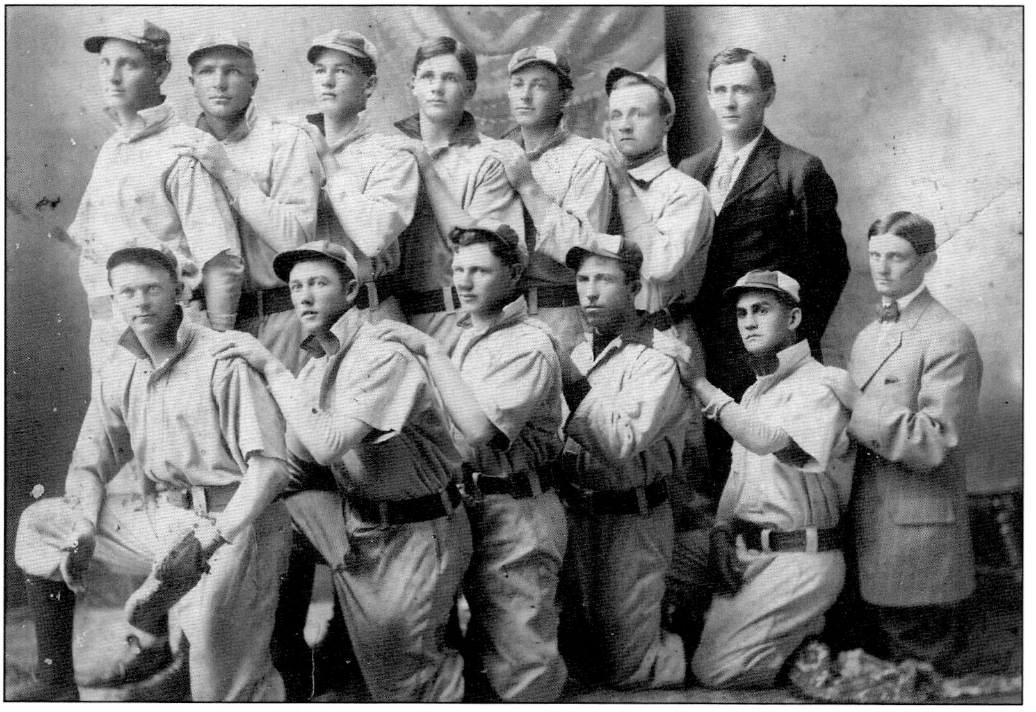

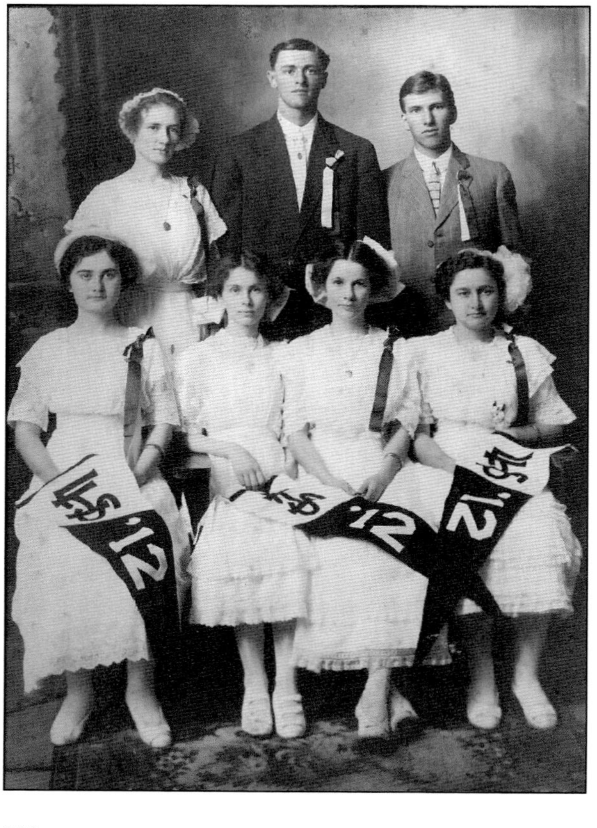

Members of the winning 1909 Lockhart Baseball Club, shown above, are, from left to right, (first row) Killough, Beaty, Blunt, Daily, Schusster, A.S. Carter, assistant manager; (second row) N. Trigg, Richardson, Tardy, Gambrell, R. Trigg, Cranland, Sam W. Smith, manager. The team record was 49 wins, 14 losses. Seen here are the seven graduates of the Lockhart senior class of 1912. Those pictured are, from left to right, (first row) Marie Swearingen, Marjorie Fields, Hattie Houston, and Bertha Withers; (second row) Georgia Elmstead, Holland Page, and Malcolm Purcell. Capping off a high school romance, Holland Page and Bertha Withers married. Sara Mebane, wife of school board president A.D. Mebane, hosted a graduation luncheon at their home on Park Road. (Above, courtesy of Joe Henry Bunch; left, courtesy of Gerry and Conrad Ohlendorf.)

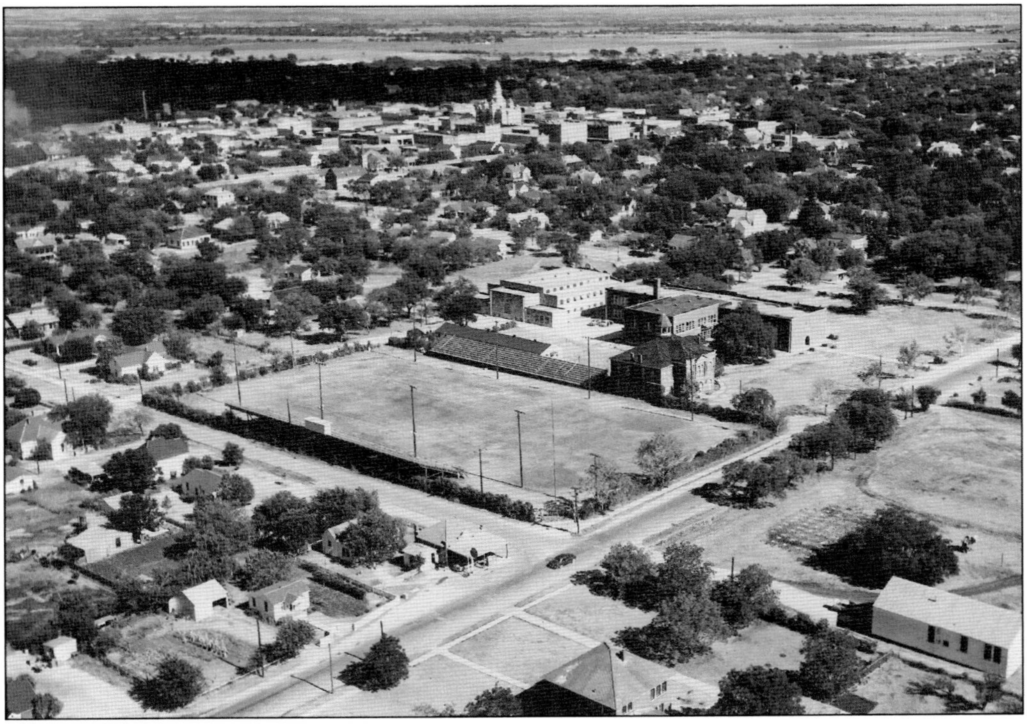

This aerial view of the school campus on Bois d'Arc and Pecos Streets was taken in the 1940s. The little red schoolhouse is in the right foreground. Visible on the lower right corner of the image is the agriculture building, and the Lockhart High School football field is in the center next to Pecos Street. In the far background is the Caldwell County Courthouse. Lockhart High had some notable years in football. Below is the Lockhart Lions team of 1935. The school song by Cliff Monroe goes as follows: "Lockhart High forever, firm together stand; comrades true and faithful, steadily we'll face the world and fearlessly. And through the days that follow, we'll pledge our loyalty for maroon and white. With all our might, we'll fight for victory!" (Both, courtesy of Gerry and Conrad Ohlendorf.)

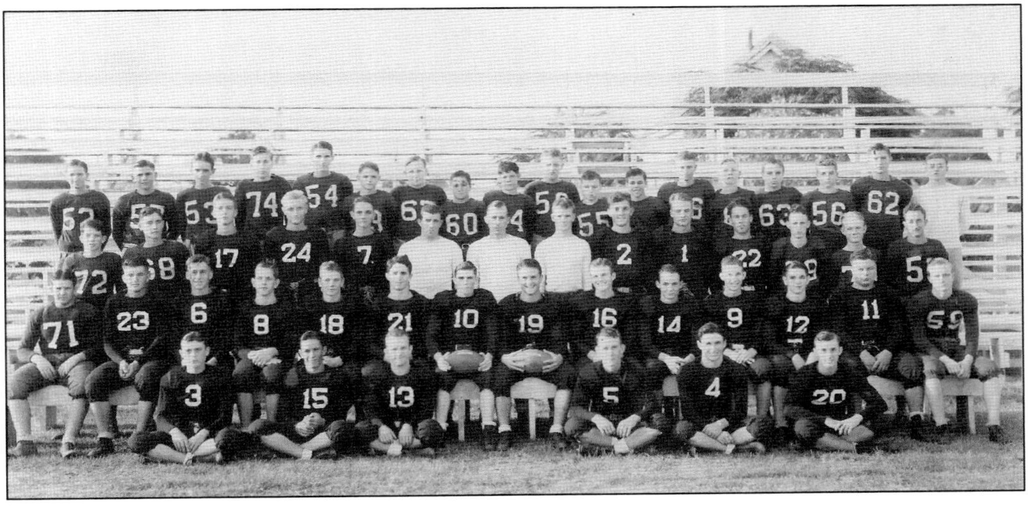

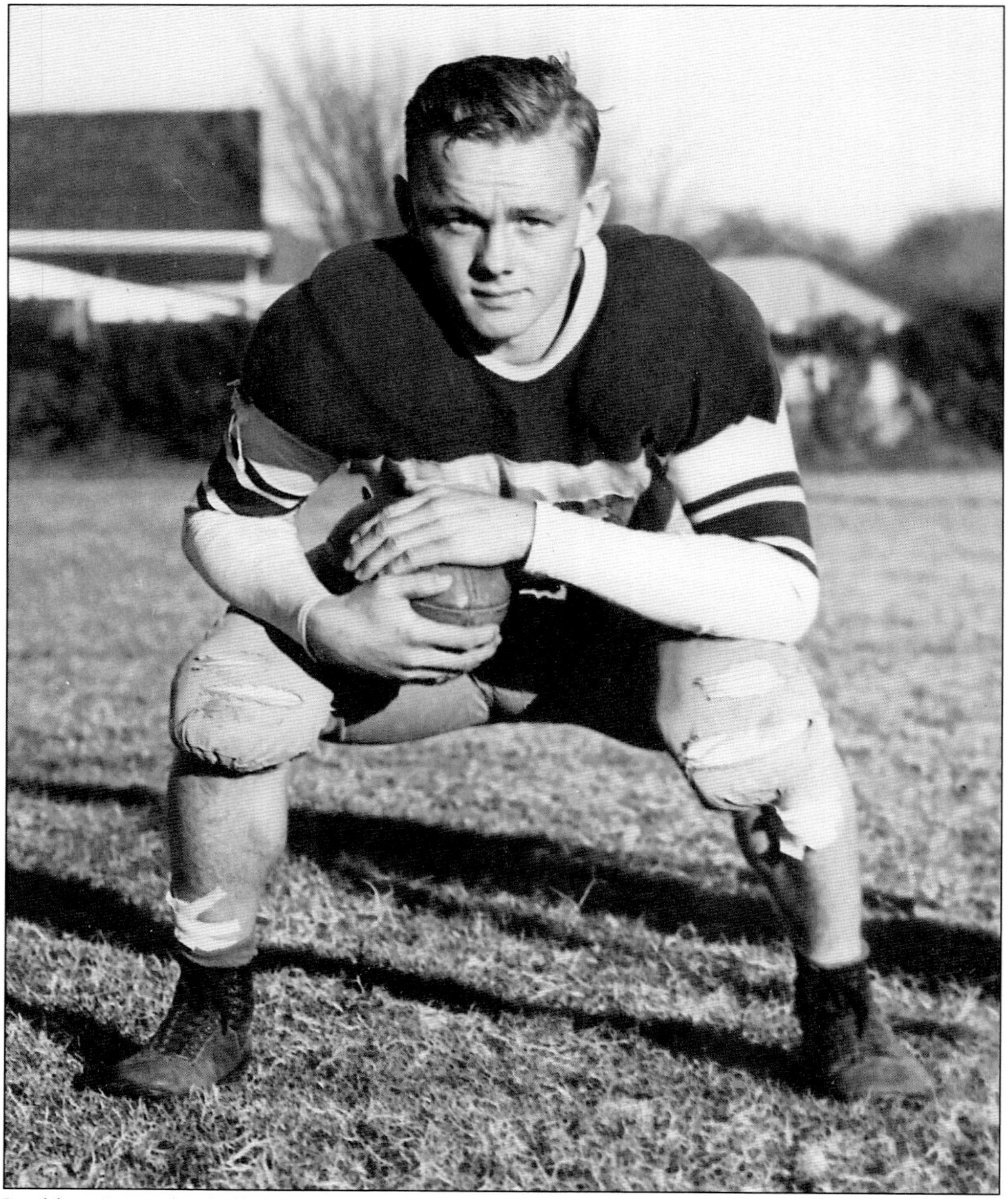

Lockhart Lions football player Herman William Anton (the father of the author) helped the team defeat the Gonzales Apaches, 26-12, in a District 35-A game in November 1942. "In the third period, H. Anton, by far the outstanding player on the field, took a Gonzales punt and carried it back 65 yards for a touchdown," reported the *Lockhart Post-Register.* According to classmate Harry Hilgers Jr., Lockhart High could not afford to outfit the Lions team, so lettermen back then wore hand-me-down equipment from the University of Texas at Austin. This included safety equipment, like leather helmets and knee and shoulder pads. The only exception was the jerseys, which were special ordered by coach Nick Frankovic. He told the team that he ordered "Chicago Red" shirts, but when they arrived, they were "maroon." (Courtesy of Ona Anton.)

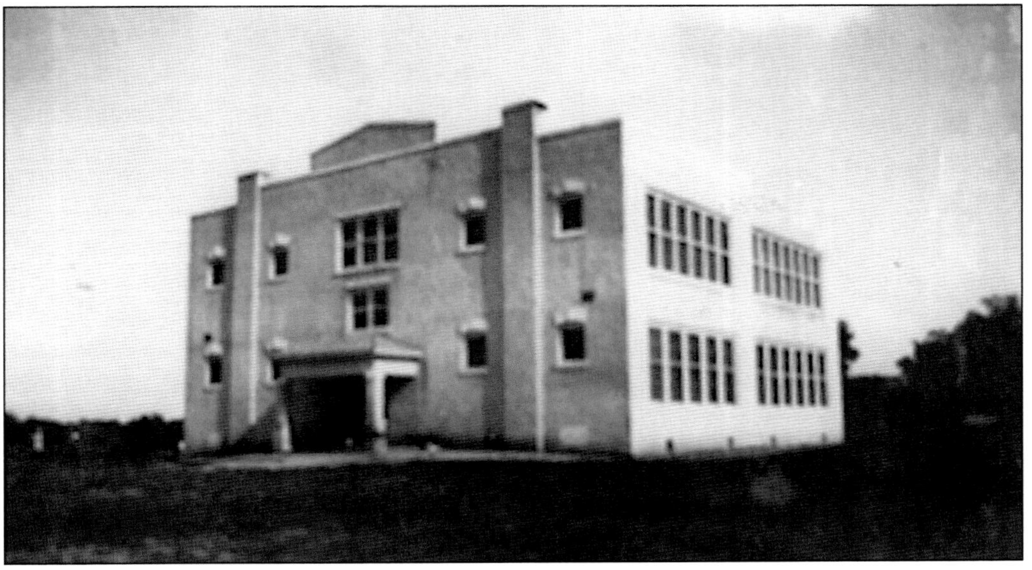

Lockhart Vocational High School or the Carver School was the first school in Lockhart for African American students. Located at 1104 East Market Street, it was built in 1924 with funding assistance. The school's design was from the Rosenwald Foundation of Chicago, and recycled lumber was used. Local African American citizens also raised the monies necessary to complete the school. In 1946, it was renamed the George Washington Carver High School. A Texas Historical Marker was unveiled at the site in 2009, in recognition of its historical importance in Lockhart's history. Carver's Green Hornet football team (below) went to the state championship in 1951 and 1952. The building stands vacant today awaiting restoration and reuse. (Above, courtesy of Homer and Shirley Williams; below, courtesy of Gerry and Conrad Ohlendorf.)

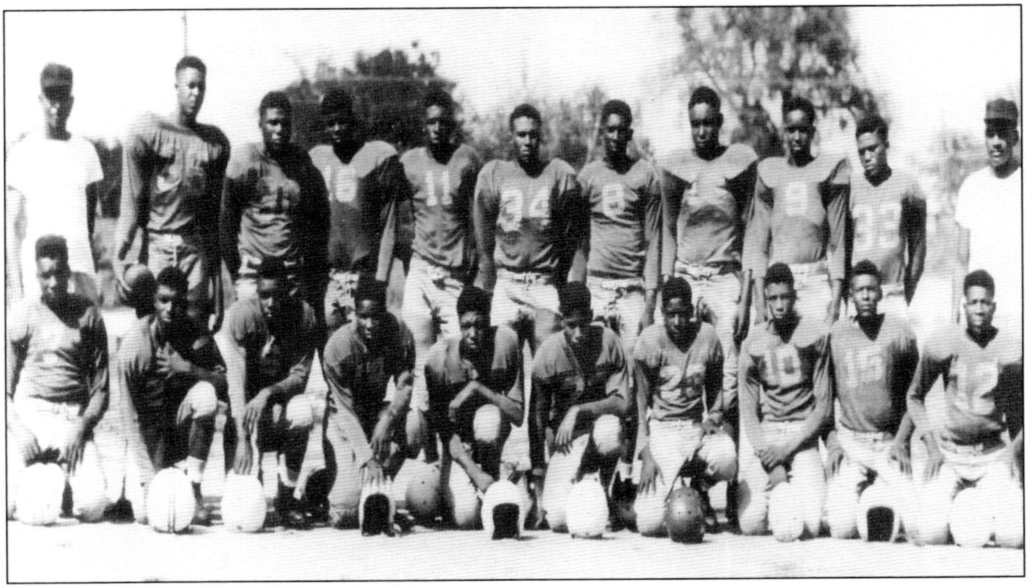

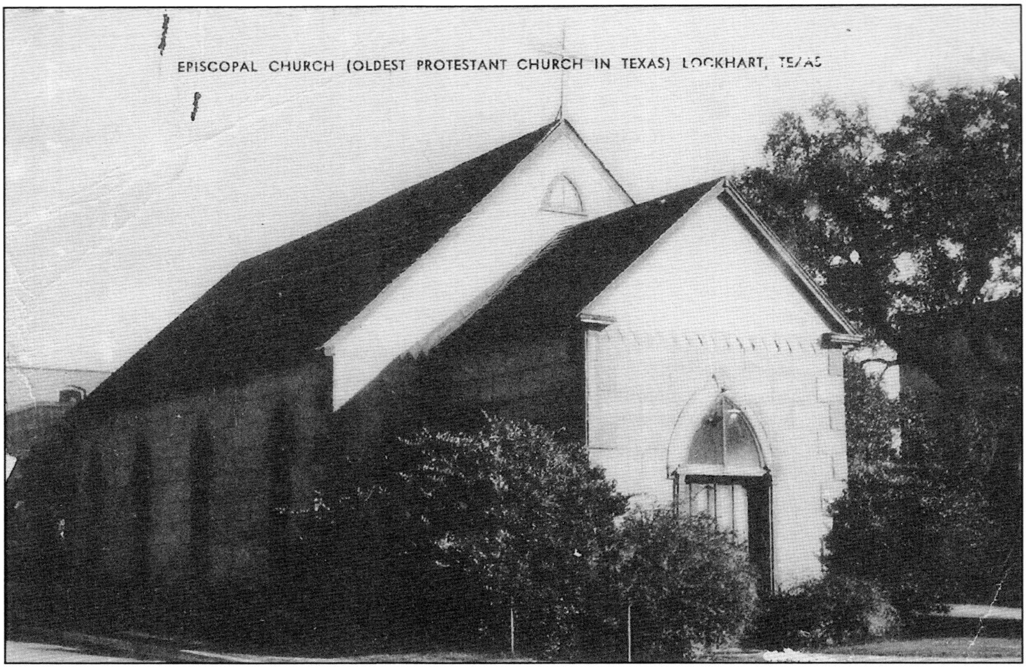

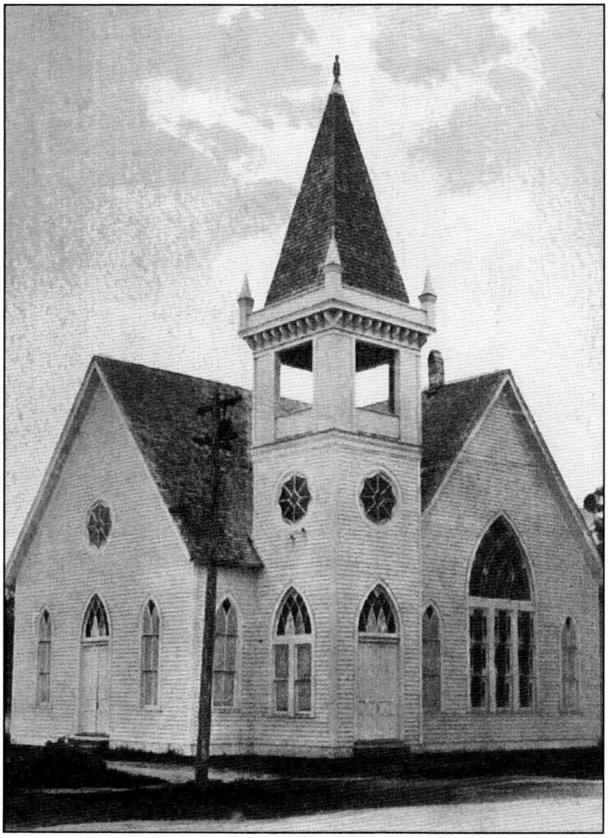

The Emmanuel Episcopal Church, a recorded Texas Historic Landmark, was built from 1855 to 1856 at the corner of 117 North Church Street at the cost of $4,800. The congregation was organized in Lockhart in 1853, just after the town was incorporated. The church is shown above in a c. 1910 postcard. In 1879, a tornado took its toll on the belfry, which was then removed. The little church, still in operation today, was entered in the National Register of Historic Places in 1974. The white frame First Baptist Church, pictured at the left, was built in 1903 and used until 1935, when it merged with another Baptist congregation to form what is today the First Lockhart Baptist Church on West Prairie Lea Street. (Above, courtesy of Gerry and Conrad Ohlendorf; left, courtesy of the Eugene Clark Library.)

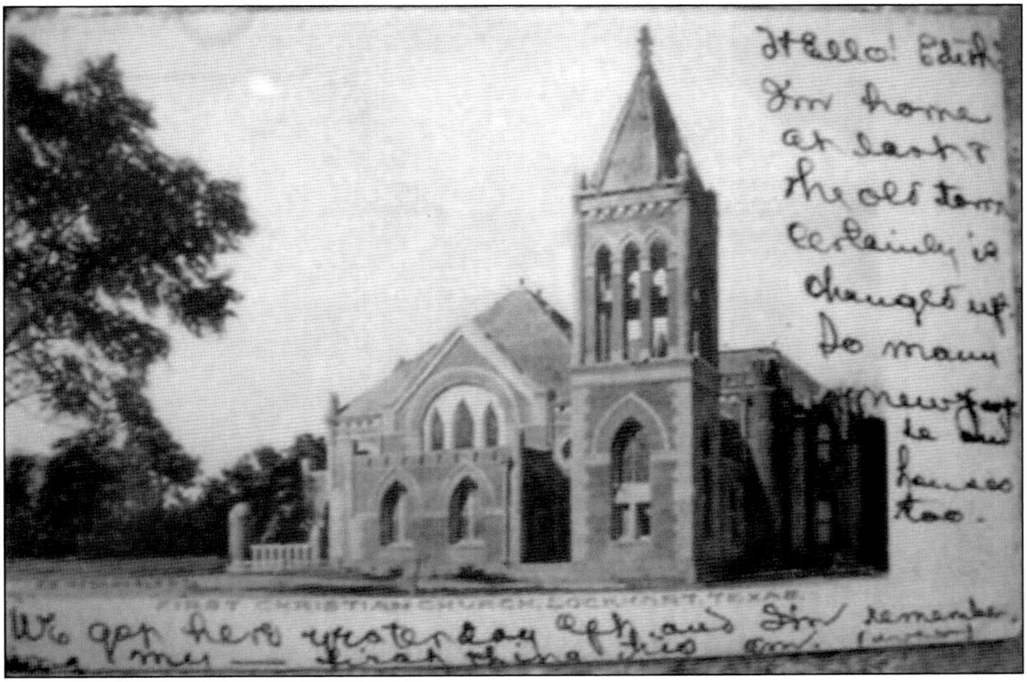

One of the oldest churches in Lockhart is the First Christian Church, which was founded in 1852 by seven members. The first sanctuary was located across the street from the current building. The congregation outgrew it, and in 1898, well-known architect Tom Hodges was commissioned to design this "new" Gothic Revival building, as seen in this early postcard. It features lancet window, decorative brickwork, and corner turrets. It is open and operating at the corner of West San Antonio Street and Church Street. The church is a recorded Texas Historic Landmark. Shown below, the First Christian Church Sunday school classes pose for a group photograph during a church picnic on the grounds. Little boys wore hats, and the girls work bonnets. The date is not given nor the photographer's name. Also, the identities of the people in the image are not available. (Above, courtesy of Ronda A. Reagan; below, courtesy of Harry Hilgers Jr.)

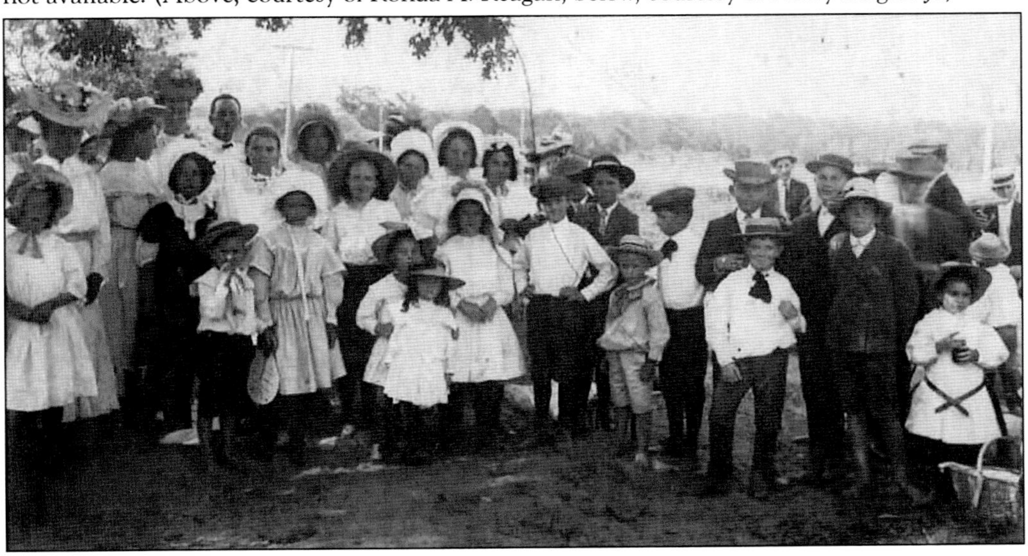

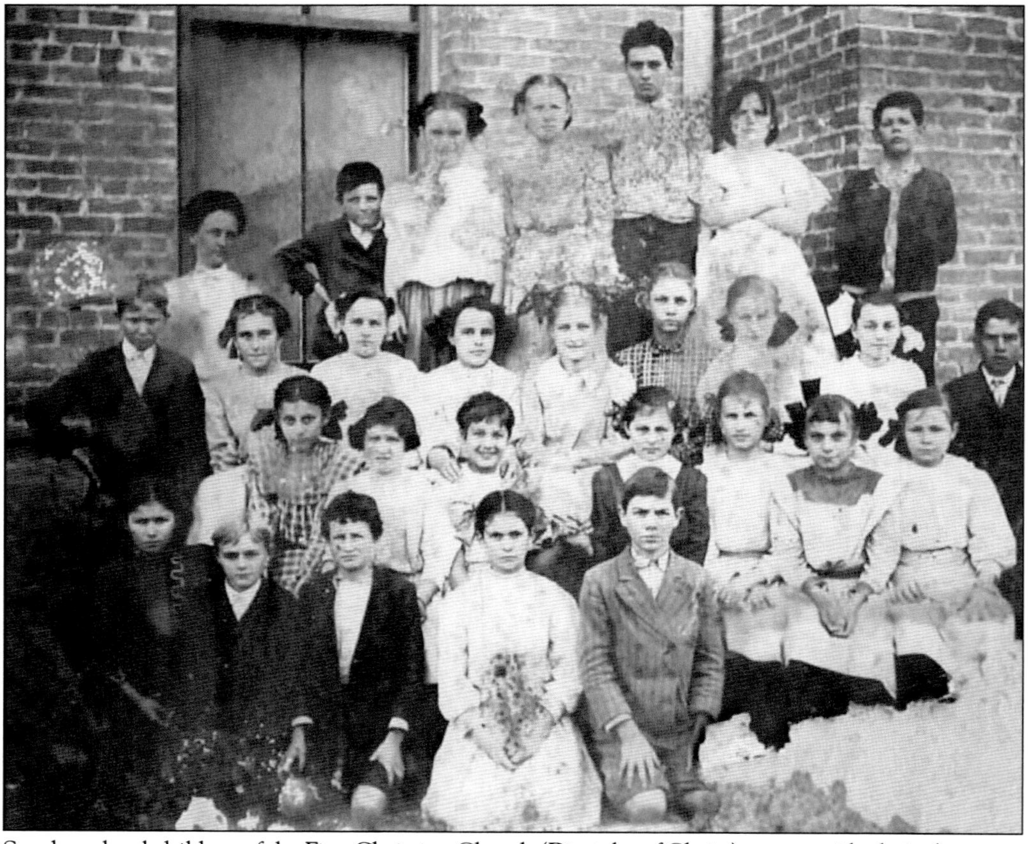

Sunday school children of the First Christian Church (Disciples of Christ) pose outside their classroom in this image, which is more than 100 years old. The names have not been recorded. Photographers in the early days most likely did not used the command "say cheese" to get their subjects to smile. The one child in the middle of the second row stands out with a large smile. The first Lutheran church in Lockhart, pictured below, was a traditional white frame structure at 762 South Main Street. It was torn down in 1960 to build St. Paul's United Church as seen on page 116. The new Grace Evangelical Lutheran Church was built in 1956 at the corner of 108 North Medina and West San Antonio Streets. (Above, courtesy of Harry Hilgers Jr.; below, courtesy of Ronda A. Reagan.)

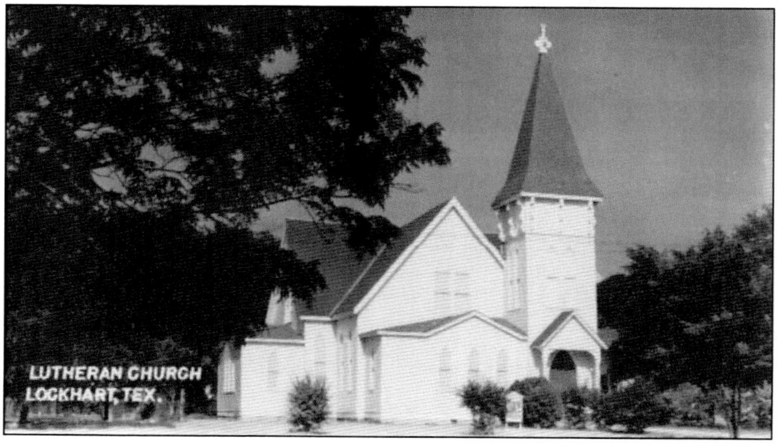

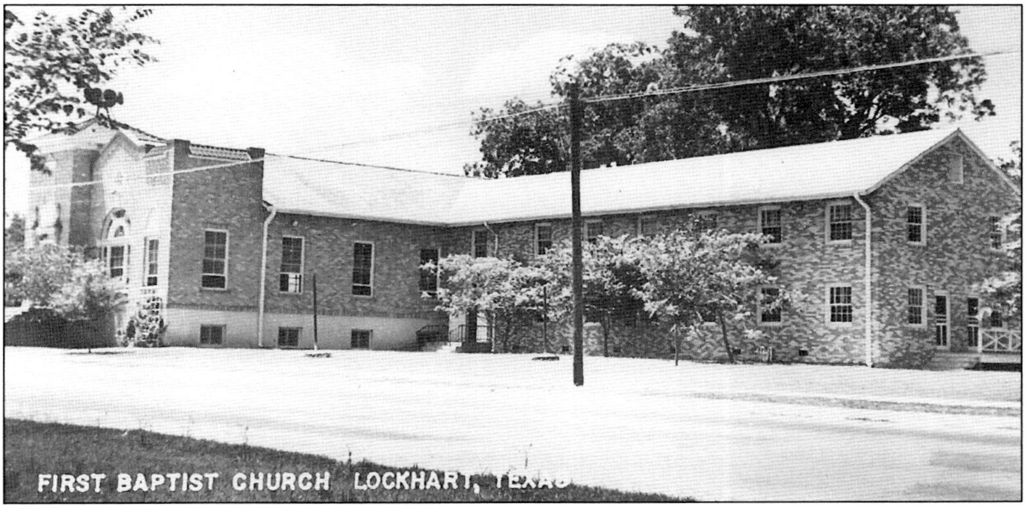

Baptists first organized in Lockhart around 1848, as the county was created. By the 1880s, two groups—the Southern Baptists and the Baptist Missionary Society—coexisted. The First Baptist Church was at the corner of West Prairie Lea and Church Streets (see page 112) and Lockhart Baptist at South Commerce and East Prairie Lea Street. In 1935, the two congregations merged and formed First Lockhart Baptist Church. They operated out of the brown brick church building at 315 West Prairie Lea Street, shown in the postcard above, until they outgrew it and built a new, modern sanctuary on the same location. Below, First United Methodist Church is located at 313 West San Antonio Street. It was built on the site of Blanks Memorial Hall in 1951–1952. The architect designed the new church building to utilize part of Blanks Memorial Hall as described and pictured on page 83. (Both, courtesy of Gerry and Conrad Ohlendorf.)

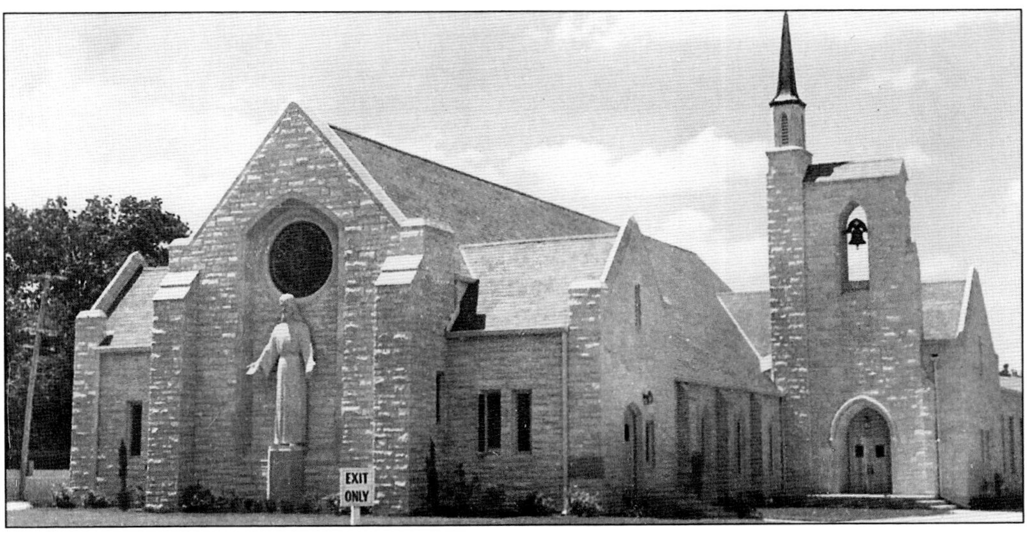

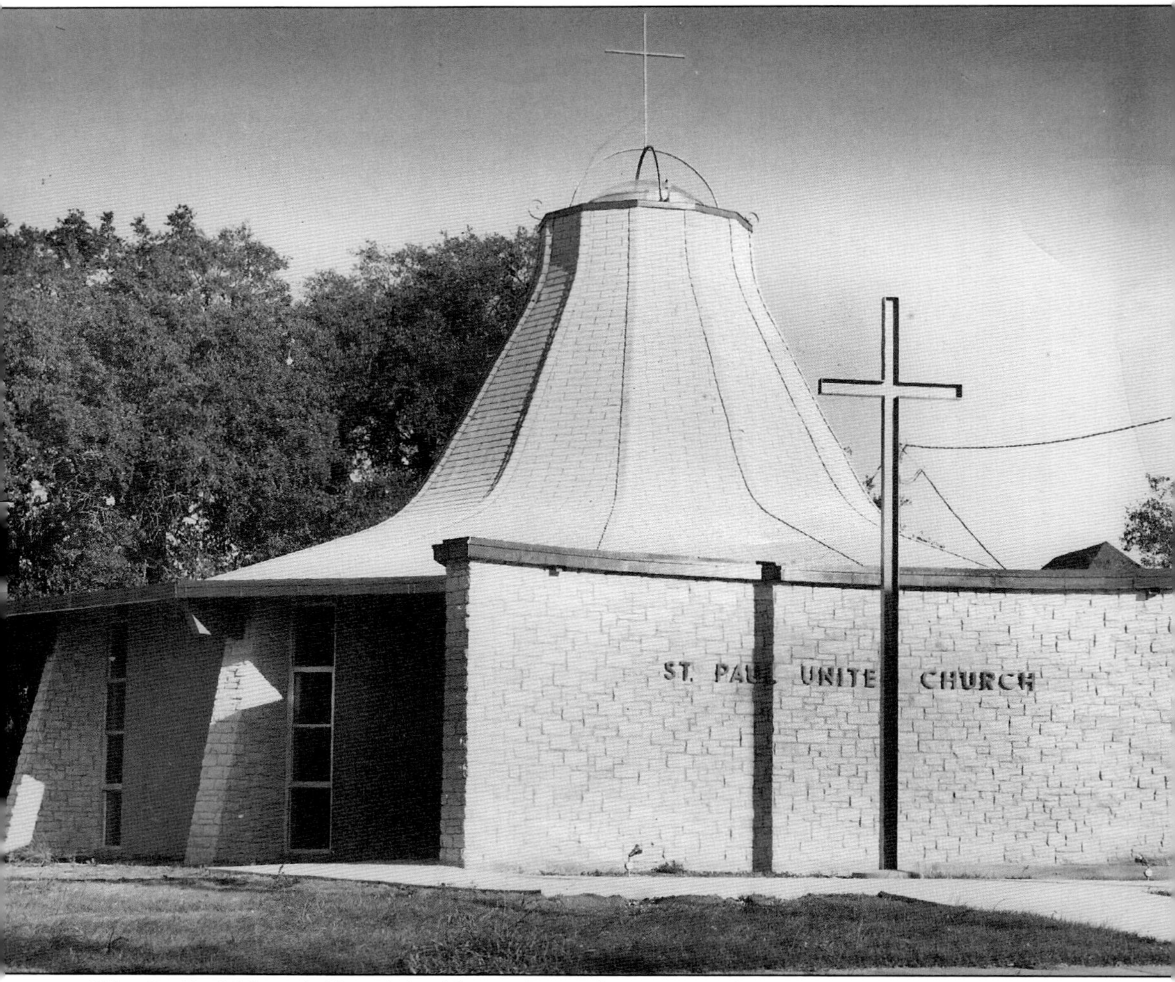

The St. Paul United Church building is located at 762 South Main Street on the site of the old Lutheran church as shown on page 114. This modern building was completed in 1962. Congregants said they were never really a Lutheran Church but had the name Evangelical Reform Lutheran Church. In the 1950s, they changed to United Church of Christ and go by the name St. Paul United Church. (Courtesy of Eugene Clark Library.)

Six

Fairs, Celebrations, and Parades

There is nothing like a parade! Lockhart has had a long history of fairs, trade days, parades, and celebrations. Once a year, Lockhart celebrated Trades Days, which booked special events, like a tightrope walker, who walked a high wire stretched over Main Street from the Corner Drugstore to Lockhart National Bank (affectionately known as John Storey's bank). Parades in Lockhart have heralded the end of World War I and the return of the soldiers in 1919, the 100th birthday of Caldwell County in 1948, Diez y Seis, and much more.

Today, Lockhart hosts an annual Chisholm Trail Roundup Parade in June as part of a five-day celebration of the famous cattle drives. It is Lockhart's largest parade, featuring an average of 150 entries, including elaborate floats from cities all over Texas with their queens and court, Shiners, horses, bands, cars, and children. There is a contest for the best floats. The parade takes two hours to complete its run. During the first weekend in December, Lockhart puts on a lighted Christmas Parade to kick-off a Dickens Christmas Festival, the lighting of the yule log, and the welcoming of Santa's arrival. Lockhart loves celebrating!

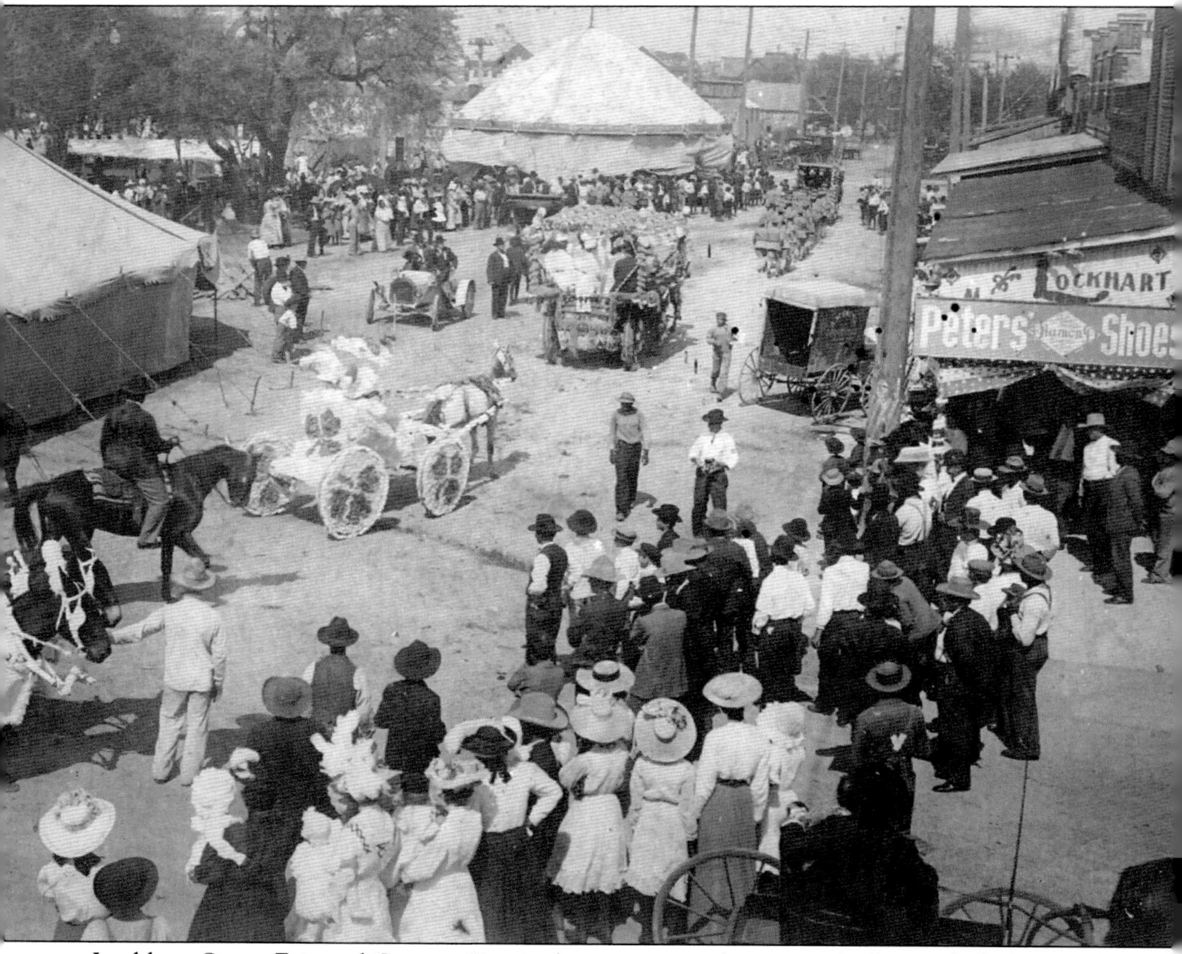

Lockhart Street Fair and County Carnival was an annual event and often included a parade through town. This image is easy to date to around 1893 as it shows the square prior to the 1894 courthouse being built. In the lead of the parade, on the upper right, is a troop of soldiers marching in formation, followed by horse-drawn decorated wagons and carriages. Parked on the right is the A.W. Smith Grocery covered delivery wagon. The storefront canopy sign on the right advertises Peters' Shoes. Looks like the whole town came out to watch the parade, and the ladies are dressed in their finest attire with hats. Locals competed in the fair for everything from best livestock entry to best or biggest vegetable with prizes ranging from 50¢ to $10. There was best jam, best butter, best molasses, and even prettiest baby with a $5 prize. Judges included J.M. Cardwell for livestock, A.D. Mebane for crops, and August Walter and R. Wilson were in charge of the poultry division. This event evolved into the county fair. (Courtesy of the Eugene Clark Library.)

This rare original Lockhart Street Fair and County Carnival Premium List brochure is well over 100 years old. It lists all the contest categories, including best bale of cotton with a $5 prize; best 10 ears of corn earned 25 pounds of flour, donated by W.E. Field & Company; and the best trio of turkeys won $2 with second prize being a buggy whip from August Walter. There was also best mule, best jack, best stallion, best pair of buggy horses, best cow, largest hog, and biggest litter of pigs, just to name a few. The spirit of the grand Easter parade in Lockhart is captured in the image below. Nora Lee Magee wrote on the back of the image that this buggy is "decorated with red paper poppies. We made them." They won first place and a prize of $10. Nora Lee Magee is at the reins with Jessie Lamb Vogel next to her. Julia Kyser and Lois Jolley are on the back seat. The church in the background was the Baptist church, "where Mrs. C.E. Jones lives on the lot now," wrote Nora Lee Magee. The home she refers to was built in 1903 and still exists today at 208 West Prairie Lea Street. The Baptist church (also shown on page 112) was taken down in 1935 when two congregations merged for financial reasons. This image was taken in the early 1900s. (Right, courtesy of Gerry and Conrad Ohlendorf; below, courtesy of Dianne Stevenson.)

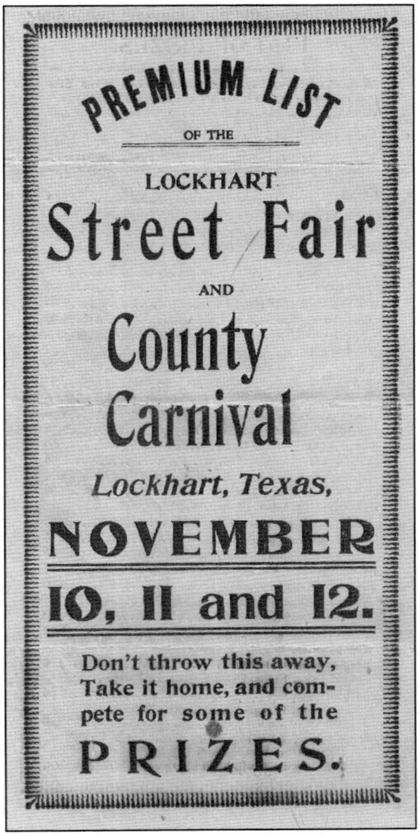
PREMIUM LIST
OF THE
LOCKHART
Street Fair
AND
County
Carnival
Lockhart, Texas,
NOVEMBER
10, 11 and 12.
Don't throw this away,
Take it home, and compete for some of the
PRIZES.

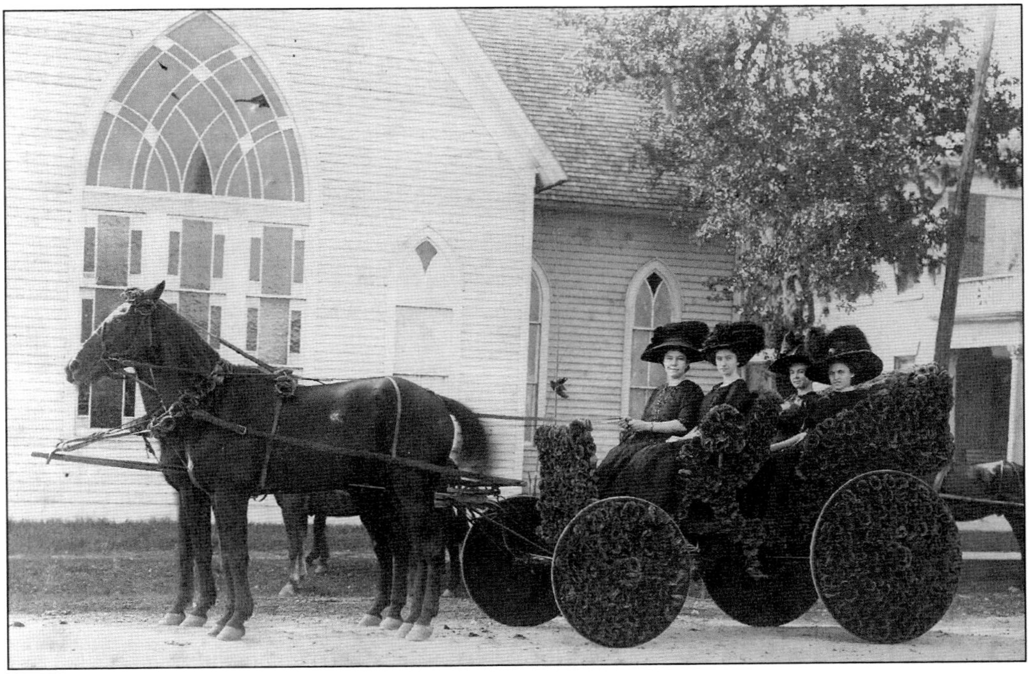

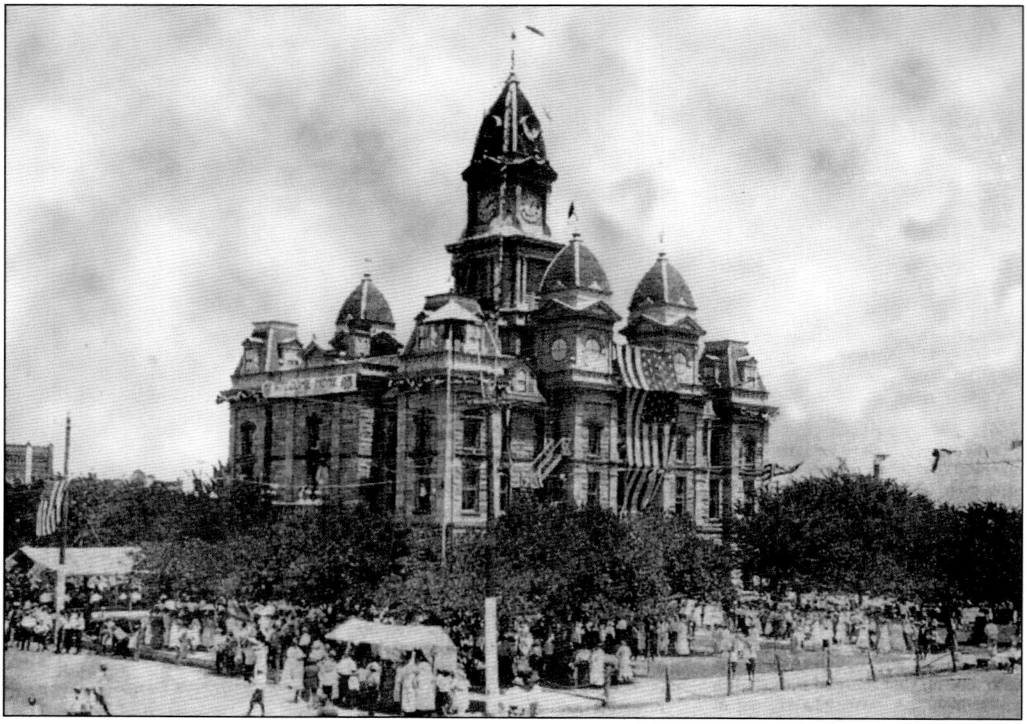

A "Welcome Home" banner and a huge American Flag adorn the Caldwell County Courthouse for a celebration welcoming home Lockhart soldiers from World War I. The event was held several months after the armistice signing on November 11, 1918. The image is of the southeast corner of the square. The old fire bell tower, which was moved to the rooftop of the fire hall, is visible. The clock reads 1:13 p.m. Winning first place and a $10 prize in another parade was the decorated automobile, shown below. Joe Vogel and his wife, Jesse Lamb Vogel, are in the front seat, and in the back seat are Nora Magee (left) and Nora Lamb. The First Christian Church can be seen to the right. The Vogel building (1908) in the background was built on a vacant lot where the original, wooded First Christian Church stood, before it burned in a blazing fire. Today a drive-through bank exists in its place. (Above, from the Centennial Celebration collection of Gerry and Conrad Ohlendorf as donated by Bill and Betty Parrish; below, Nora Lee Magee Collection, courtesy of Dianne Stevenson.)

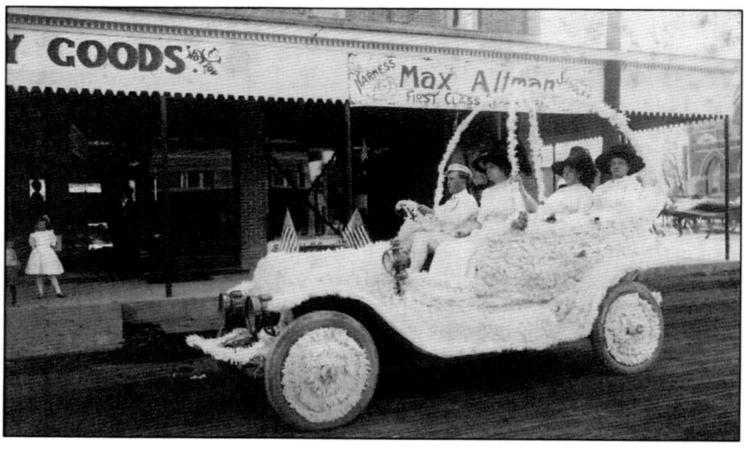

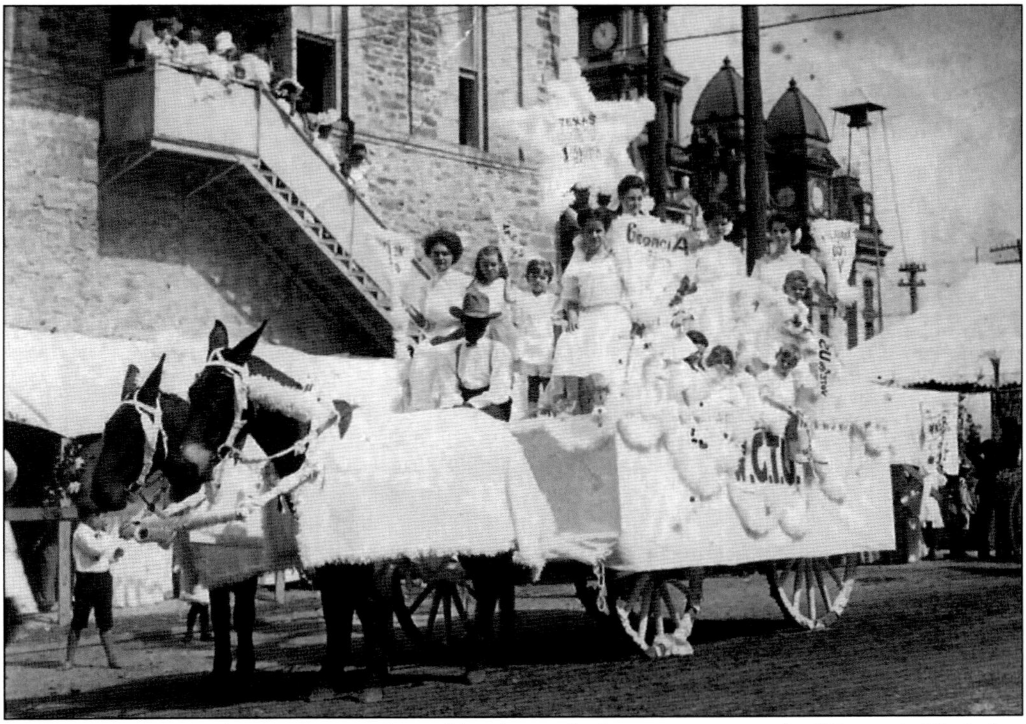

This very early parade entry, as evidenced by the mule-drawn wagon, is the Women's Christian Temperance Union (WCTU). The state pennants represent the various states that were participants in the WCTU cause. The women, accompanied by little girls, would go into the saloons with axes and literally chop up the bars in an effort to promote tolerance. In the immediate background is Blanks's Corner Grocery Store on Main and Market Streets. The courthouse and bell tower are visible in the right background. Paper lanterns, shown below, hang off a wooden trellis positioned over this parade entry covered in fringe and flowers. The car is from Lockhart Durant Company, which sold Flint, Durant, and Star Cars. The signage says the cars were "constantly improved but no yearly models." The four ladies and the young girl in the car are unidentified. (Above, courtesy of Harry Hilgers Jr.; below, courtesy of the CCHC.)

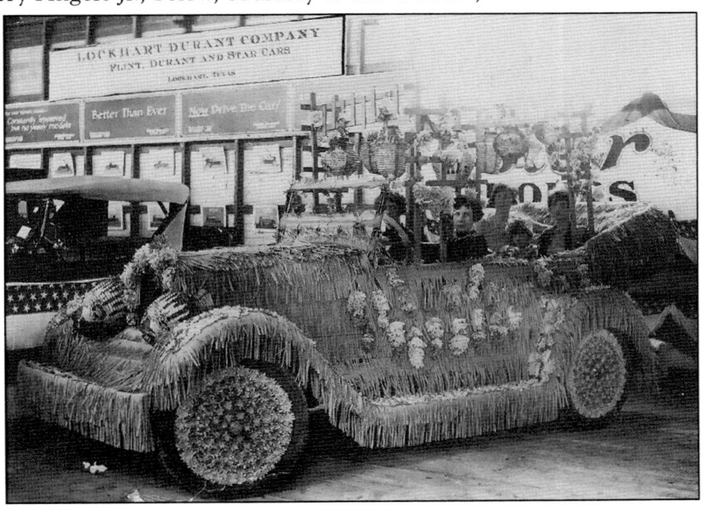

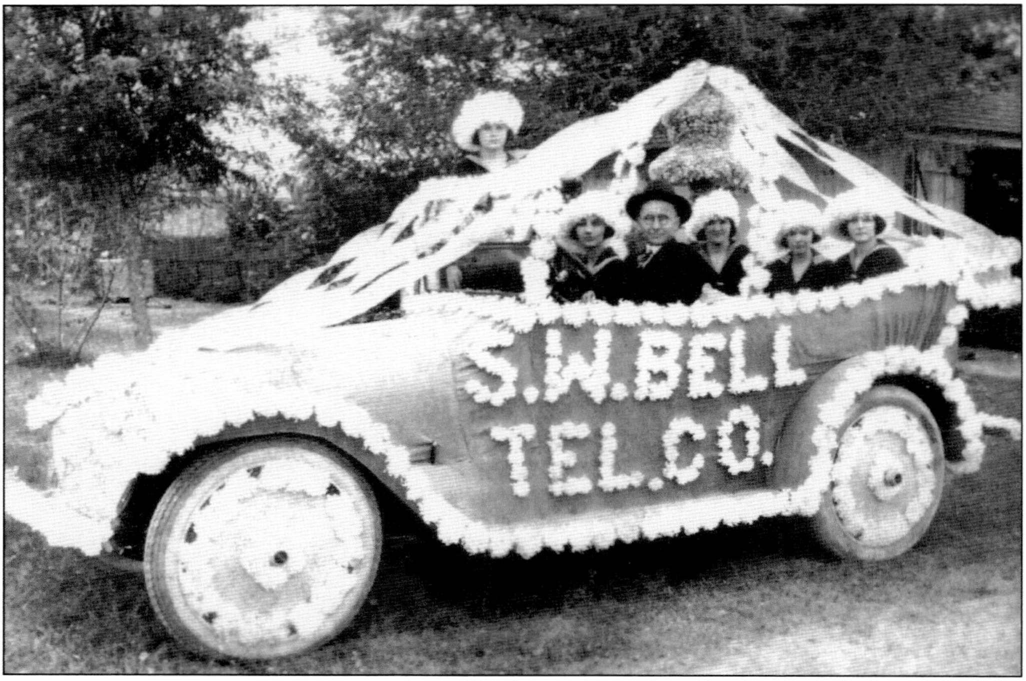

Completely covered in fabric and flowers is this early 1900s S.W. Bell Telephone Company float. Max Schulz is driving the car and his sister Lonie Schulz is sitting in the passenger seat. Unidentified ladies are seated in the back. Riding in style are "Miss Chevrolet" Annie Lee Bunch (Joe Henry Bunch's sister) and Harold Page, pictured below. This photograph was taken in 1923 in front of the Alhambra Hotel across the street from the fire hall. Holland Page, Harold's father, built the Alhambra Hotel on this site, which is where the First Methodist Church originally stood. He also purchased the Chevrolet car dealership, located on the first floor of the building, from C.E. Jones. There was a drive-in basement for servicing cars. This building stands today with the corner drive-through for gasoline removed and closed in. The hotel is vacant. (Above, courtesy of Gerry and Conrad Ohlendorf; below, courtesy of Joe Henry Bunch.)

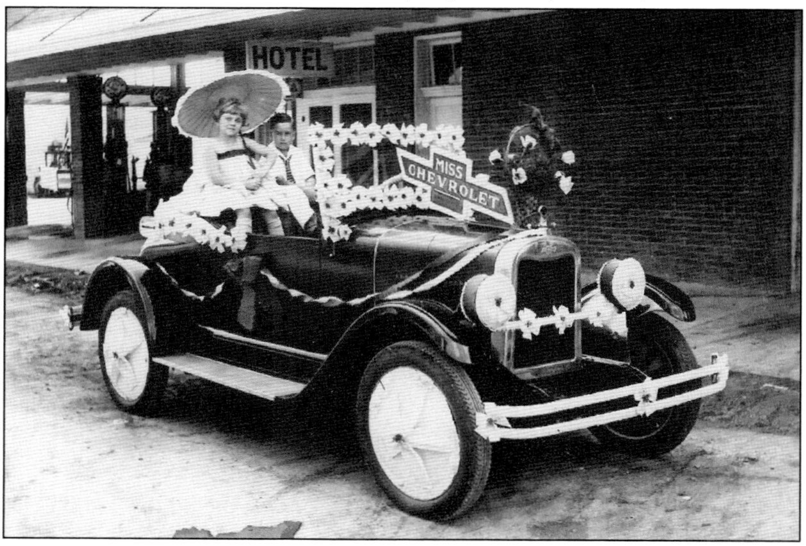

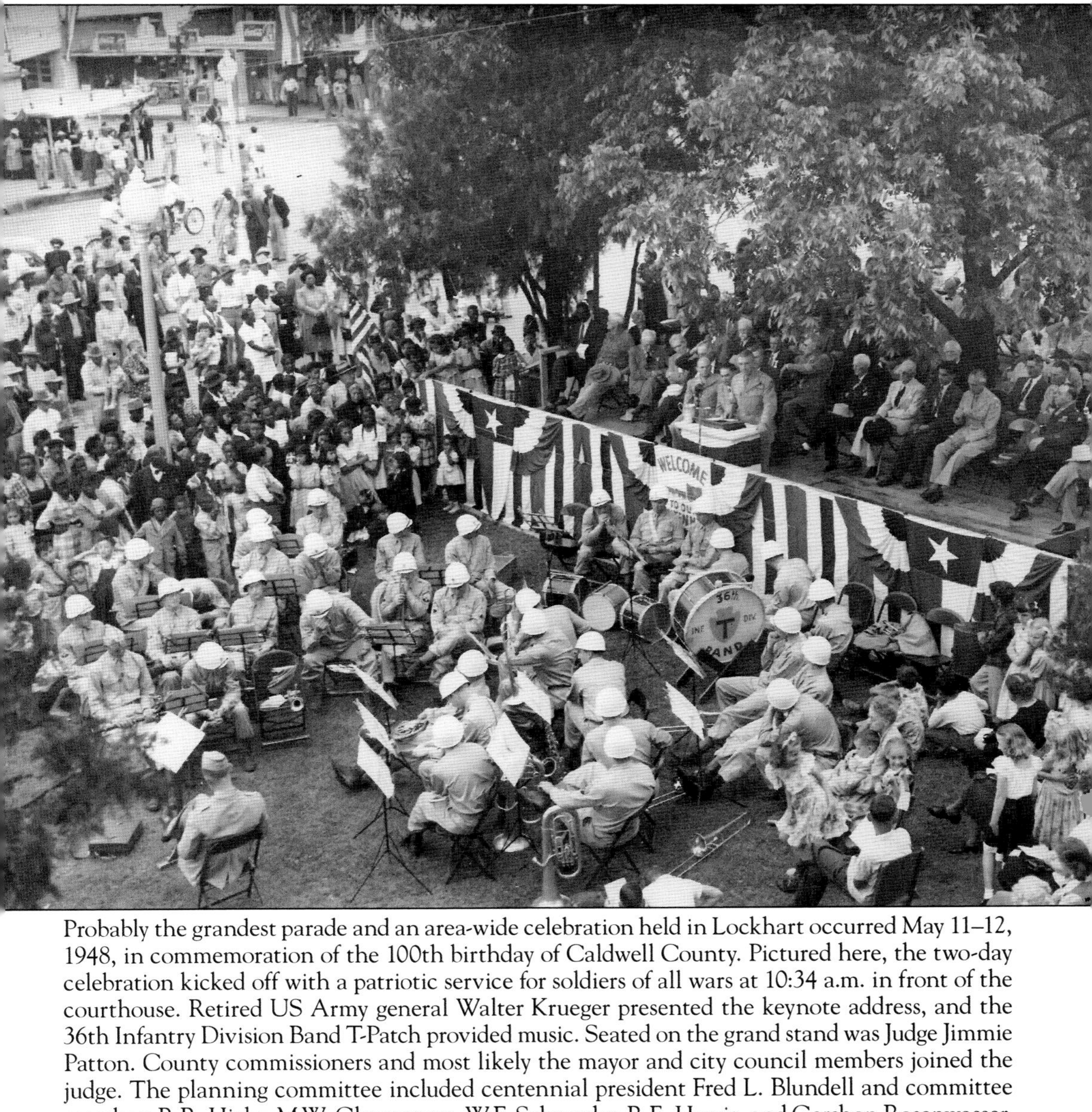

Probably the grandest parade and an area-wide celebration held in Lockhart occurred May 11–12, 1948, in commemoration of the 100th birthday of Caldwell County. Pictured here, the two-day celebration kicked off with a patriotic service for soldiers of all wars at 10:34 a.m. in front of the courthouse. Retired US Army general Walter Krueger presented the keynote address, and the 36th Infantry Division Band T-Patch provided music. Seated on the grand stand was Judge Jimmie Patton. County commissioners and most likely the mayor and city council members joined the judge. The planning committee included centennial president Fred L. Blundell and committee members R.R. Hicks, M.W. Glosserman, W.F. Schroeder, R.E. Harris, and Gershon Rosenwasser. The schools of Caldwell County put on a historical pageant depicting the independence of Texas; the Battle of Plum Creek; the swearing in of the first county officials in a log cabin; the area's first settlers and their homes, churches, and schools; and the cattle drives and cotton industry. After the coronation of the queen and her court pageant, there was a grand ball. The following day, the "Great Historical and Colorful Parade" was led by Gov. Beauford H. Jester. (Courtesy of Gerry and Conrad Ohlendorf.)

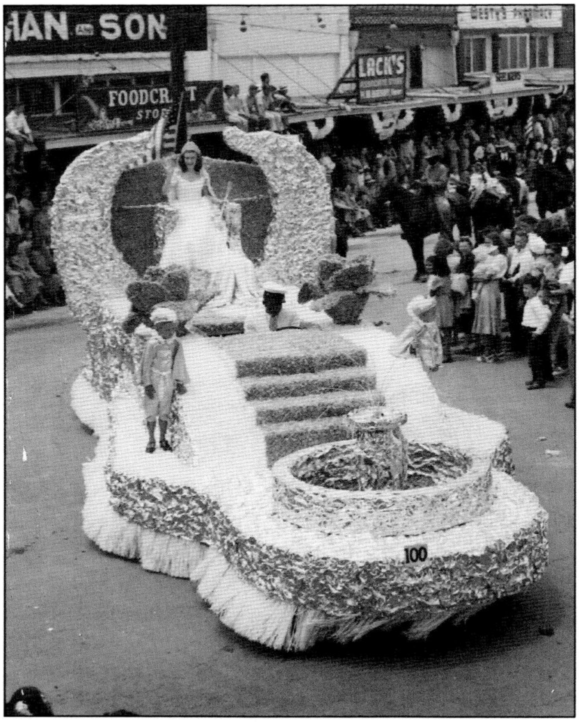

Riding on her throne is "her most gracious majesty queen Nancy of the House of Patton," also known as Nancy Patton. Nancy was escorted by David Wilson. It would not be a birthday without a birthday cake, and Texas Pioneer White Wings Flour provided this one with 100 candles, pictured below. Several thousand area residents and neighbors lined the town square to watch the Centennial parade, as this Main Street image depicts. Onlookers even sat on the awnings and perched themselves on the rooftops for a higher vantage point. After the parade, other events included a mass band concert on the courthouse lawn, a program honoring pioneers of Caldwell County, a calf roping, a concert by Brackenridge High School band of San Antonio, and a performance of the Sheriffs Mounted Posse of Bexar County. (Both, courtesy of the Eugene Clark Library.)

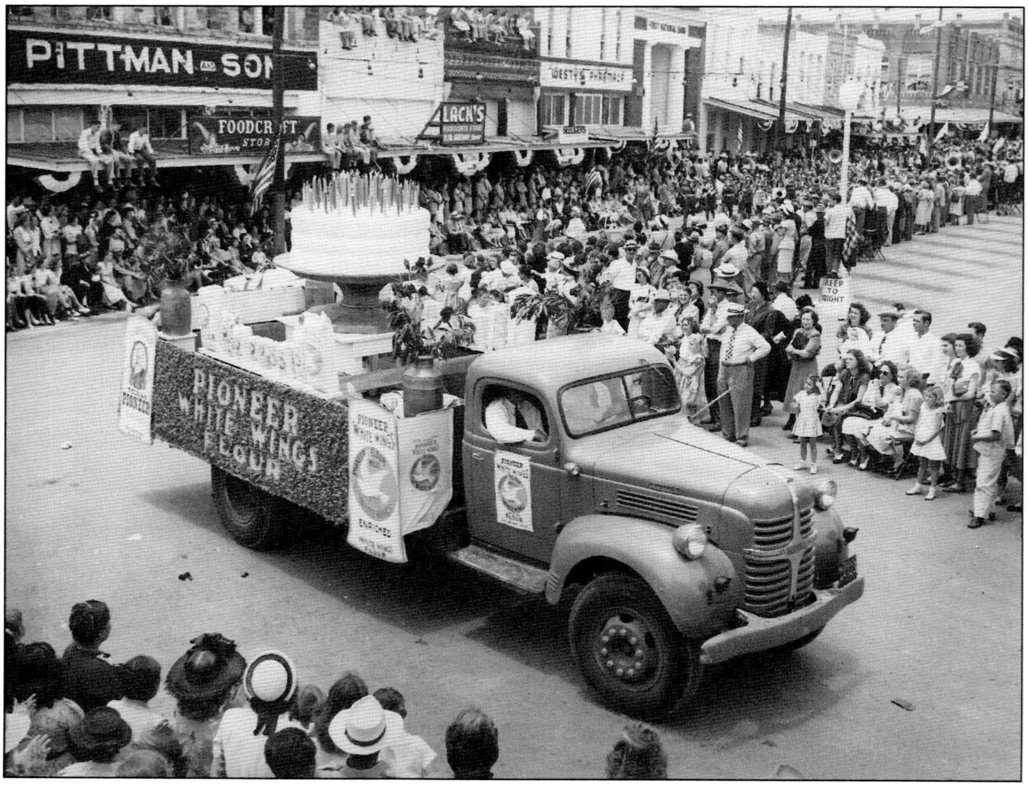

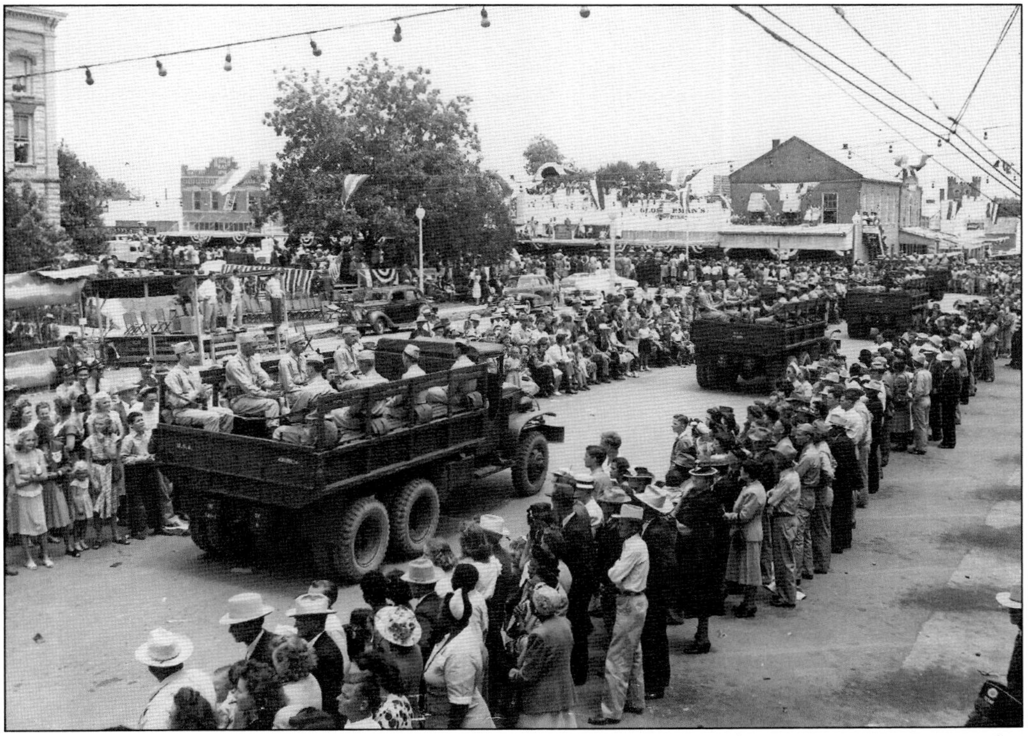

US Army troops helped to celebrate the first 100 years. In this Market Street, one can see the many open trucks carrying soldiers as thousands of onlookers watch. Parade-watchers are sitting on the rooftops and awnings of the buildings on the east side of the square. This photograph provides valuable historical documentation of how the buildings looked on the square, which is a National Register Historic District. (Courtesy of Gerry and Conrad Ohlendorf.)

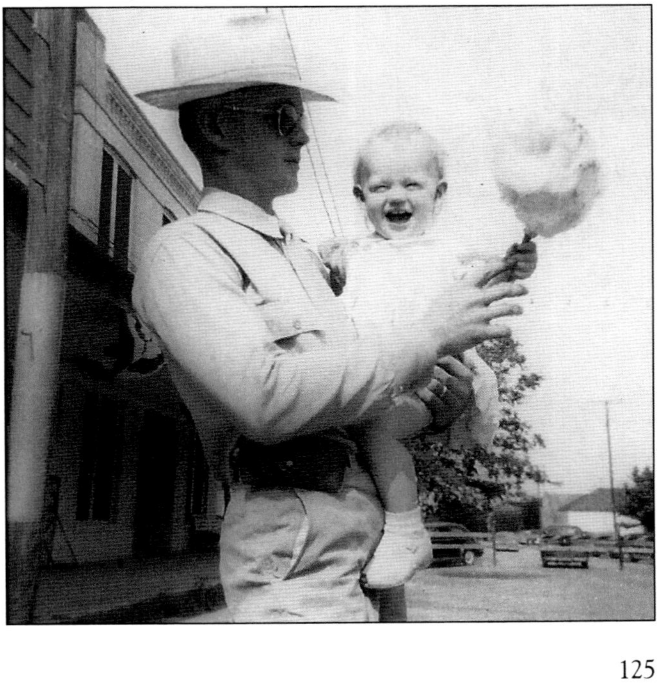

Returned home from World War II just three years earlier, parade watcher and native son Herman William Anton holds his happy toddler Sheila Diane. Herman's wife and Sheila's mother, Ona Lea McGee Anton, snapped this photograph. A spectacular fireworks display at Lockhart State Park culminated the county's two-day birthday celebration. (Courtesy of Ona Anton.)

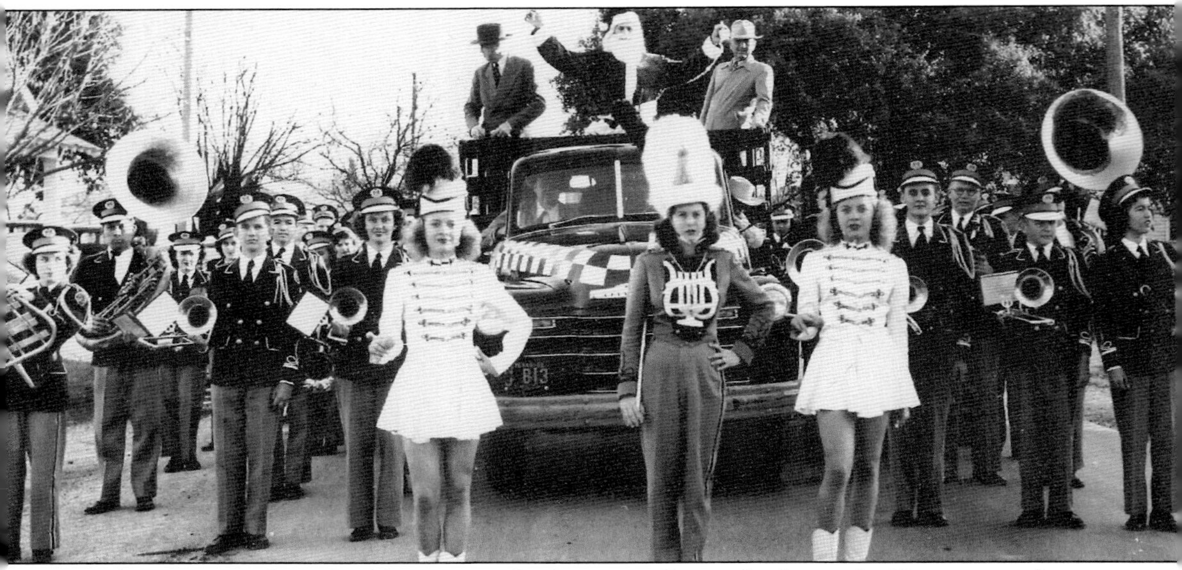

Christmas parades in Lockhart cannot be forgotten. Currently, the yearly Christmas tradition is held at night as a lighted parade on the first weekend in December, in conjunction with an annual festival, "A Dickens Christmas." As with most other Christmas parades, it is here that Santa Claus appears for the first time each season. Bringing in Santa in the 1948 Christmas Parade was the Lockhart High School Lion band, led by drum major Gerry Retherford (center) and twin drum majorettes, Connie and Bonnie Stein, on her left and right. "Don't let the parade pass you by." (Courtesy of the Eugene Clark Library.)

Bibliography

Brice, Donaly E. *The Great Comanche Raid Boldest Indian Attack of the Republic*. Eakin Press, 1987.

Cummings, Joe. *Texas Handbook*. Chico, CA: Moon Publications, Inc., 1990.

Dallas Morning News. *Texas Almanac and State Industrial Guide 1847–1958*. Dallas, TX: A.H. Belo Corporation, 1947.

Gard, Wayne. *The Chisholm Trail*. Norman, OK: University of Oklahoma Press, 1954.

Hunter, J. Marvin. *The Trail Drivers of Texas*. San Antonio, TX: Jackson Printing, 1920.

Interview with Harry Hilgers Jr. Interview by Ronda A. Reagan. May 2011.

Interview with Joe Henry Bunch. Interview by Ronda A. Reagan. April 2011.

Kelly, Martin. "A Cradle on Wheels: Stagecoach Travel in the Wild West." americanhistory about.com/library/weekly/aa120501a.htm

Kelsey Sr, Mavis P. and Donald H. Dyal. *The Courthouses of Texas*. College Station, TX: Texas A&M University Press, 2007.

Mark Withers Trail Drivers Museum. *Historical Caldwell County Where Roots Intertwine*. Dallas, TX: Taylor Publishing Company, 1984.

Sanborn Map Company Fire Insurance Map 1888. Lockhart, TX: Dolph Briscoe Center for American History, The University of Texas at Austin.

Save the Brock Cabin Committee. *Brock Cabin Cooking*. Lockhart, TX: 2010.

Steen, Ralph W. *The Texas Story Revised Edition*. Austin, TX: The Steck Company, 1960.

Twain, Mark. *Roughing It*. Scituate, MA: Digital Scanning, Inc., as published in 1886.

Rex H. Stever. "Stagecoach Lines: Handbook of Texas Online." www.tshaonline.org

Westmoreland, Peck. *Remembering Lockhart's First 150 Years: A Pictorial History 1852–2002*. Lockhart, TX. *Lockhart Post Register*, 2002.

Wilbarger, J.W. *Indian Depredations in Texas*. Austin, TX: Hutchings Printing House, 1889.

Withers, Zona Adams. *Historical Lockhart Then and Now*, Volume I and II. Lockhart, TX: Zona Adams Withers, 1981.

www.lockhartchamber.com

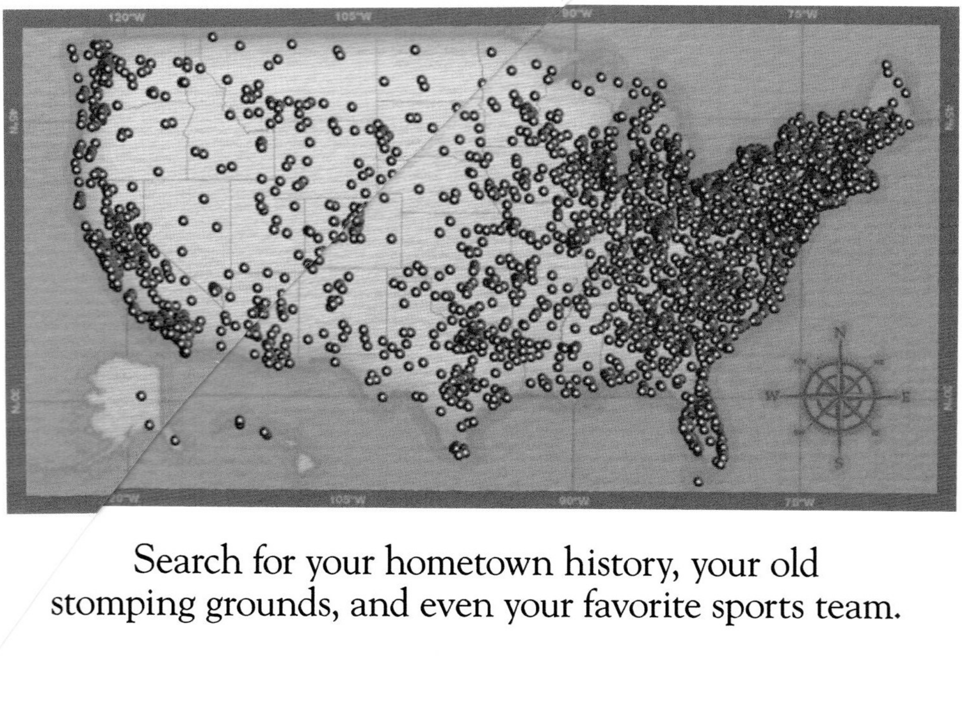